ACTA UNIVERSITATIS UPSALIENSIS
Studia Sociologica Upsaliensia
45

CAROLINE SUTTON

Swedish Alcohol Discourse

Contructions of a Social Problem

UPPSALA 1998

Dissertation for the Degree of Doctor of Philosophy in Sociology presented at Uppsala University in 1998

ABSTRACT

Sutton, C., 1998. Swedish Alcohol Discourse. Constructions of a Social Problem. Acta Universitatis Upsaliensis. *Studia Sociologica Upsaliensia* 45. 184 pp. Uppsala ISBN 91 554-4210-2.

In this dissertation it is argued that alcohol problems in Sweden are not strictly an objective phenomenon, but are largely discursive constructions that have been reconfigured in substantial ways since at least 1910. The empirical work aims to identify and discuss these reconfigurations. Additionally, a number of consistent features in the ways in which alcohol problems are defined is presented. Among other things, the Swedish case shows that definitions of the problem and models adopted to describe it, integrate a broad range of social actors, and encourage consensus. Moreover, these models do not strictly focus on the problematic drinker; they offer scientific support for state intervention into the lives of all members of society. Together these characteristics construct alcohol problems as truly a "social" phenomeonon.

Analysis follows a social constructivst approach, recognizing the potential for multiple interpretations of the problem, which are located in formal collective statements. Six major concepts for investigating and analyzing alcohol as a "social problem" are developed: discourse, discursive formation, stories of causality and threat, the dispersion of the problem, the distribution of authority, and the solution complex. These are applied in three related studies. The first study examines medical discourse on alcoholism viewed as disease. A second study considers the application and adoption of the "total consumption model" and public health approach to alcohol in Sweden within official and scientific discourse. Finally, the author investigates current shifts in these formations within the context of negotiations with the European Union on Sweden's membership; the study explores the impact of a new discourse, originating externally, upon the legitimacy of Swedish approaches. The dissertation ends with several considerations of the implications of the research both for future developments of the public alcohol discourse in Sweden and for further development of the theoretical framework presented in the dissertation.

Key Words: Alcohol, Social problems, Social construction, Sweden, Medicalization, Total consumption, Public Health, Discourse.

Caroline Sutton, Department of Sociology, Uppsala University, Box 821, SE-751 08 Uppsala, Sweden

ISSN 0585-5551
ISBN 91-554-4210-2

Cover design: Förenade Ord, Catarina Magnusson
Typesetting: Editorial Office, Uppsala University
Printed in Sweden by Gotab, Stockholm 1998
Distributor: Uppsala University Library, Box 510, SE-751 20 Uppsala, Sweden

Contents

List of Tables and Figures 8

Foreword 9

Preface 11
- From California's Wine Country to Sweden's Monopoly 11
- Overview of the Dissertation 12

Introduction 15
- The Alcohol Problem in Sweden 15
- Swedish Alcohol History 17
- The 'Social-ness' of a Swedish Social Problem 19
- Social Problems and Social Research 20
- Policy Variations and the Social History of Alcohol in Sweden 23
- Towards an Alternative Set of Questions 24

CHAPTER 1:A Conceptual Framework 27
- The Social History of Alcohol Issues 27
- Working Terms and Concepts 32
- Conceptual Framework and Method for Detecting Formations 35
  - Causal Stories 36
  - Stories of Threat 37
  - Dispersion of the Problem 38
  - Distribution of Authority 41
  - Solution Complexes 42
- Studies in the Swedish Discourse 42
  - Studying the Medical Discourse 43
  - Studying the Total Consumption and Public Health Formation 45
  - Swedish Discourse and the European Union 47

CHAPTER 2: Formations in the Swedish Alcohol Discourse 48
- Early Alcohol Discourse 48
  - An Open Field 48
  - The Threat and Causes of Intoxicated Behavior 49
- Formation 1: Poison or Person? 50
  - The Poison of Alcohol 50

Emergence of an Official Discourse on Temperance 52
Medical Discourse on Alcoholism 54
Further Institutionalization of an Official Discourse on Alcohol . . . 57
Formation 2: From Individual Control to Individual Responsibility . . . 58
Questioning the Solution 58
Towards a 'New' Surveillance System 59
Towards Individual Illness 60
Formation 3: Alcoholism as Symptom 61
Questioning the Cause 61
Questioning the Solution 63

CHAPTER 3: The Alcohol Problem in Medical Discourse.
From Alcoholism to Public Health 65
Medical Expertise and the Swedish Alcohol Discourse 65
The Alcoholism Formation 69
A Brief Context 69
Basic Propositions 70
Locating the Disease 71
Symptoms and Signs of Disease 73
Phases of Illness 75
The Role of the Physician 76
The Disease Model in Official Discourse 79
The Public Health Formation 81
Transformation of Discourse 83
The Public Health Formation and Strategies 85
Public Health and Official Discourse 90
Medical Discourse and the Social Problem of Alcohol 92

CHAPTER 4: Total Consumption, Public Health and the Official
Discourse 94
Transformation of Discourse 94
The Social Context 94
Emergence of the Total Consumption/Public Health Formation 96
Major Tenets of the Total Consumption/ Public Health Formation 100
Basic Parameters of the Formation 101
The Total Consumption Model 101
Introducing Public Health 103
The Definition of the Problem 104
The Cause of Alcohol-related Problems 104
The Threat Posed by the Alcohol Problem 106
The Dispersion of Alcohol-related Problems 109
The Distribution of Authority 112
The Solution Complex 113
The Alcohol Problem as a Social Problem 119

CHAPTER 5: Swedish Public Health and the European Free Market.... 121
Paving the way towards 'liberalism'.......... 121
Is There a European Alcohol Discourse?.......... 123
EU Discourse on Swedish Alcohol Policy.......... 127
The Road to EU Membership.......... 127
The EU Challenge.......... 128
Defending Swedish Solutions Outside Sweden.......... 131
Swedish Alcohol Discourse in Motion: Challenges and Confrontations 132
Defending the Swedish Solution Inside Sweden.......... 132
Challenges to the Solution Inside Sweden.......... 138
Epilogue Swedish Alcohol Policy in the European Union.......... 142

CHAPTER 6: Current Challenges and Future Directions.......... 146
Taking Stock.......... 146
The More Things Change, the More They Stay the Same.......... 149
Discursive Transformation Today.......... 151
Future Investigations and Applications.......... 152
Future Sociological Studies of Alcohol in Sweden.......... 153
Alcohol in a Future Europe.......... 154
Implications for Policy Analysis in General.......... 155

References.......... 157

Appendices

APPENDIX I: Data Sources.......... 170

APPENDIX II: Working with Texts.......... 173

APPENDIX III: Time Line of Events in the Official History of Alcohol . 180

List of Tables and Figures

Tables

Table 1: Events related to the disease formation 82
Table 2: Symptoms: Alcohol Dependence Syndrome 85
Table 3: Public health formation in official discourse 91
Table 4: Disease formation vs. public health formation. 92
Table 5: Discursive objects—alcohol harm 110
Table 6: Damage effects from alcohol consumption 112
Table 7: To limit demand and availability 117
Table 8: Definitions of the alcohol problem in Sweden. 148

Figures

Fig. 1: Benjamin Rush, Thermometer 39
Fig. 2: Jellinek, the Progression of Disease 40
Fig. 3: The Total Consumption Model 102
Fig. 4: The Dispersion of Prevention 115

Foreword

My analysis of the Swedish alcohol discourse, like any other discourse, is truly a social accomplishment. As such, there are a number persons whom I would like to recognize and thank for their support. First and foremost, Tom Burns has acted as my advisor for the last four years. I have benefited not only from his sharp and insightful comments, but have also appreciated his ceaseless encouragement and enthusiasm for my work. Thank you also to Jim Kemeny for acting as a second reader, and providing support and helpful comments during recent months.

Several people have provided comments and critique of my work. I am endebted to Börje Olsson, Stockholm University, who generously read several drafts of my work and provided constructive comments that have helped to sharpen my writing and analysis; unfortunately I have not been able to incorporate all of his good advice and suggestions. Thanks also go to Sven Hort, my masters thesis advisor, for his continued support. Håkan Johansson and Lars Båtefalk acted as opponents at a final seminar, providing useful comments. Fredrik Spaak provided an important introduction to medical interest in alcohol.

Colleagues at the department of sociology have provided comments on my work as well as other forms of support. Special thanks to: Sandra, Gloria, Fredrik, Nora, Kerstin, Johan, Stina, Dan; a big thank you to the Network Group—Marianne Ildiko and Margaret. Jorge Calbucura helped me think through my work and formulate ideas (as well as having made the train trip between Stockholm and Uppsala more enjoyable).

I would also like to thank the Nordic Council for Drug and Alcohol Research (NAD), particularly former Secretary Christoffer Tigerstedt, for encouraging and supporting young researchers. My work has benefited from the NAD summer school in 1997, and from NAD research meetings. During the last year I have had the pleasure of taking part in the SNAPS project, sponsored by NAD and the National Institute for Alcohol and Drug Research (SIFA) in Oslo, where I have had the opportunity to discuss Nordic alcohol policy. I would especially like to thank Pekka Sulkunen for his leadership in the project and his mentorship. The library at CAN has been a tremendous resource, and I am once again grateful to Marie and Gunnel for their wonderful assistance.

Last, but not least, thank you to my families for their encouragement, and in particular to Tron for once again showing patience and understanding.

Uppsala March 1988

Caroline Sutton

Preface

From California's Wine Country to Sweden's monopoly

When I moved to Sweden from my own home town, just a short distance from California's renowned wine country (Napa Valley), there were many cultural nuances that intrigued and surprised me, but none so much as Swedish regard for alcohol. In particular, I was confronted with a very different conception of what was problematic in relation to alcoholic beverages. As a Californian, I was aware that drinking-driving was a social problem; "drinking and driving don't mix" was the phrase of the day, and campaigns were waged by local governments all over California to this effect. Beyond this deviant behavior, however, my consumption of alcohol and that of anyone else over the age of 21, was rather 'unproblematic'—both for myself and for the government. In Sweden, I quickly learned that my drinking—whether I got behind the wheel or not—was regarded as problematic for my neighbors and the state.

The different conception of alcohol became apparent the first time I tried to to purchase alcohol. After several attempts, I learned that I would not find alcohol at my local grocery, but would have to visit a monopoly store, called *Systembolaget* (and remember you must get there between 10:00 a.m. and 6:00 p.m.!). In these shops, there were always brochures on display that encouraged me to cut back my consumption. I was informed that my drinking contributed to a total level of drinking in Sweden; and that the more I and others drank, the more social, health and economic problems would threaten Sweden. Moreover, everyone I met—from taxi drivers, to guests I met at parties, to professionals in the field, and other academics—explained to me the necessity of the monopoly, since Swedes were a people who would "drink themselves to death" without controls; "just look at what happened in the 1800s", they would say. Indeed, every brochure I picked up pointed out that in the mid-1800s, before there was a *Systembolaget*, Swedish drinking was "out of control", and people were "drinking themselves to death". Alcohol, it was argued, had always been a social and public health problem, and it was for this reason that the state had introduced various controls.

My work on this topic initially began in 1993 and led to a masters thesis at Stockholm University. At that time, I was interested in how conceptualizations of alcohol as a social problem were changing in the context of Sweden's potential future as a member of the European Community. New voices, such as the Brewers Association, were appearing in the media and brought with them arguments for changes in policy. What I found to be even more interesting than this, however, was that the traditional supporters of Swedish alcohol policy referred to the drinking practices of the mid-1800s as evidence that policy today needed to be protected. Thus, although my thesis was concerned with changes taking place with integration, I eventually dug into history in order to try to understand why the 1800s should have such an important place in current discourse. In this scholarly adventure, I also discovered that even the recent history of alcohol in Sweden, i.e. since 1900, revealed some very interesting twists and turns. And, these twists revealed different notions about what precisely the problem was.

As a sociologist I recognized that there were two ways I could approach not only the incongruent views of my homestate of California and my adopted home of Sweden, but also the views put forth in Sweden over time. Either one view was 'true' and the others 'false', or there were quite simply different ways in which alcohol could be problematized. As Fahrenkrug (1991) has stated:

> Alcoholic beverages possess not only a chemical structure but also a social definition that is of importance for understanding the public perception of, and reaction to the use of alcohol. (p. 317)

Alcohol problems are embued with meaning through the social definitions that bring them into public consciousness. Since these definitions emerge from social interaction, they are susceptible to reconfiguration and reformulation. Hence, although alcohol might consistently be defined as a social problem, the way in which it is presented, justified and built-up as such, may vary over time and across space. It is this sociological problem that forms the object of investigation for my study.

Overview of the Dissertation

My investigation and analysis of alcohol discourse in Sweden has been organized in seven chapters. In the *Introduction,* I present a short backdrop against which my work should be viewed, followed by an overview of the main questions and problems to be dealt with in the dissertation. My approach to discourse analysis as well as my conceptual model are developed in *Chapter 1.* This chapter also includes a discussion of my method and selection of materials. Following this, and as a backdrop to the major empirical work in the dissertation, *Chapter 2* offers the reader a short summary and some analysis of variations in the definitions of alcohol issues that can be detected in alcohol discourse during this century. Following this, I have strategically selected three formations in the alcohol discourse and investigated shifts through comparing, contrasting and juxtaposing these with one another. Analyses of these are presented in Chapters 3, 4 and 5.

Chapter 3 largely concerns the 'expert' discourse generated by the medical community. In particular, I have been interested in juxtaposing one discursive formation in medicine, and its definition and model of alcohol issues, with that of a second formation. In a somewhat unconventional methodological strategy, I 'extract' these two formations from their context, in order to more clearly see the lines along which they are constituted. As a final discussion, the institutionalization of these formations in official discourse is also mapped out, as a means of better understanding the relationship between the two loci of discourse that are investiged in the dissertation, and to draw attention to similarities in how alcohol has been defined as a social problem in both.

Chapter 4 focuses predominantly on what I refer to as the public health and total consumption formation and how the discourse in this context formed an object for study and policy. In this case, it is the official discourse which is of primary interest, but expert discourse is also considered, as is the content of public information materials. This chapter identifies the mode by which social problems, and the alcohol problem in particular, have been constituted as indeed 'social' in the Swedish context.

Chapter 5 investigates very recent transformations in the alcohol discourse. In this case, a broader range of discursive sources is considered in order to capture potential shifts in the distribution of authority. In this context, the alcohol problem has been maintained as a public health problem inside Sweden, while an emerging challenge to this discourse, both inside and outside Sweden, has defined the Swedish system to counteract this problem as an economic issue. That is, the problem has been shifted into an entirely different arena in this discursive context. This had an impact upon the types of groups and individuals who can participate in legitimate discourse, who may produce 'facts', and in what ways alcohol consumption will be controlled and regulated.

Chapter 6 contains a resumé of the more salient aspects of the transformation of the alcohol discourse and a discussion concerning further applications of this approach for investigating alcohol issues in Sweden and the European Union, as well as in additional policy arenas.

Three appendices are also included in the dissertation. In *Appendix I*, I present the materials that have provided the data for the empirical analyses. *Appendix II* is also related to my method and methodology, and takes up questions related to working with the texts and data. Finally, *Appendix III* presents an overview of the events that are generally regarded as constituting the Swedish history of alcohol regulation.

Introduction

The Alcohol Problem in Sweden

Sweden boasts one of the lowest levels of total alcohol consumption per person per year in Europe, as well as worldwide. In 1995, Swedes drank on average, as little as 6.14 liters (Hein 1996), while their French counterparts drank 11.5 liters in 1994 (Folkhälsoinstitut & CAN 1996). Yet, alcohol is considered a major social problem in Sweden, and quite often as the most critical public health and social problem (Bergmark & Oscarsson 1990). Even to the outsider the social status of this problem is quite obvious (cf. Gould 1988). This is not due so much to the presence of intoxicated persons on the streets—although there is some of that—but to organized responses to a perceived problem, and collective 'stories' about why such regulation is necessary.

One of the important stories surrounding alcohol is the history of regulation. An important participant in Swedish history has been the temperance movement, which continues to maintain a presence in contemporary society. Over 20 organizations are registered as national organizations, with local chapters. Although organizations engaged in the movement have lost much of their former influence upon policy, they are officially recognized as an interest group and asked to comment on any proposed legislation.[1] In addition, most Swedes are also aware that teetotalers have traditionally been well-represented (if not over-represented, according to some) in the Swedish *Riksdag* (parliament). In 1951, as many as 43% of parliamentarians were registered teetotalers; today, only 6% claim to abstain from alcohol consumption (Lindblad & Lundqvist 1996: pp. 194–195), but many of these representatives participate in a cross-partisan parliamentary organization for teetotalers.[2] Traditionally, the most temperance-friendly political parties have been the Liberal Party and the Cen-

[1] According to the corporatist structure of Swedish political practice, any proposed legislation must proceed through a 'remiss' process whereby all interest groups are given an opportunity to comment upon such proposals. A number of organizations and entities are automatically recognized, and additional groups and individuals may also request the opportunity to respond. The most recent commission to study alcohol produced a series of reports in 1994. Nearly 100 organizations provided comments on the proposals layed out by the commission.

[2] For a thorough discussion of templars in the Swedish parliament this century, see Lindblad & Lundqvist (1996).

ter Party, but support for control-oriented policy has cut across party lines throughout most of this century.[3] It has also been customary that individuals holding the offices of the Minister of Social Affairs and the Director of the National Board of Health and Welfare are temperance friendly and support restrictive alcohol legislation.

Offspring of the temperance movement include a publishing company, SOBER, which publishes both temperance and scientific literature on alcohol and the alcohol problem in Sweden; an insurance agency, ANSVAR, which just recently opened its doors to moderate drinkers as well as teetotalers[4]; and a national temperance day, which falls on the observed religious holiday of Ascension Day.[5]

It is not only the presence of the temperance movement that draws attention to the social problem of alcohol. A number of institutions and practices also support the perception of alcohol as an important social issue. Until 1995, the Swedish government maintained a monopoly on the production, import, export, wholesale and retail sale of alcoholic beverages. After Sweden's agreement with the European Economic Space, EES went into effect in 1995, only the retail monopoly remained intact. Hours of sale are restricted through national legislation, and until recently the hours of sale at pubs and bars was also highly restricted across the country. The minimum age to purchase alcohol at a retail store is 20, and persons aged 18 and over may purchase beer and wine at pubs and restaurants, but may not purchase spirits until age 20. Advertising bans on alcoholic beverages have been in place since 1978. School children take part in obligatory education on alcohol and other drugs through the public school system, and public education materials are available at the retail monopoly stores that aim at educating adults on their own alcohol consumption as well as that of their children. In 1991 a Public Health Institute, *Folkhälsoinstitut,* was established, as a means of developing public information on alcohol consumption, among other issues.

In addition to the numerous state activities addressed above, alcohol forms an object for extensive scientific investigation. At present, alcohol is studied in various fields of medicine, psychiatry, psychology, sociology, social-psychology, economics, history, literary studies, etc. A number of researchers are also located at *Centralförbundet för alkohol- och narkotika upplysning*, CAN (the

---

[3] The Moderate Party has been somewhat less restrictive than other parties, although its official party-line, until only recently, has supported status-quo alcohol policy. During the 1990s, several right-wing protest parties also emerged, which openly questioned the traditional political line on alcohol. Among these, New Democracy won seats in parliament in 1991. These are further discussed in *Chapter 5.*

[4] ANSVAR met with financial difficulties during 1995, in part due to the fact that fewer persons abstain from alcohol today. In order to maintain its activities, ANSVAR was forced to introduce policy for moderate drinkers who take an oath not to drink and drive.

[5] The national temperance day provides a regular, institutionalized event for media coverage and public attention. Although this event generally receives attention in smaller, local papers, the two major Swedish newspapers in the capital city of Stockholm, have not covered temperance day during the last few years at least.

Swedish Council for Information on Alcohol and other Drugs), which maintains yearly statistics on alcohol consumption and drinking practices, together with the Public Health Institute (Folkhälsoinstitut) and provides research reports on specified topics of interest. CAN also houses one of Europe's largest libraries for alcohol and drugs.

Put concisely, there has been an extensive discourse on alcohol throughout the twentieth century. Alcohol is and has been regarded as a problem in Swedish society, and it would be very difficult to claim otherwise given the flurry of activity that contributes to presenting it as such. However, within the discourse on alcohol there have been variations in how this problem is presented and justified as such as I shall show below.

Swedish Alcohol History

The notion that alcohol is problematic is widespread throughout society. There are a number of 'facts' about alcohol that are collectively shared and 'known' as part of the common stock of knowledge (Berger and Luckmann 1966) in Sweden. One example of this collective knowledge is the history of alcohol consumption in Sweden and responses to this. This history is presented as evidence that alcohol constitutes one of Sweden's greatest social and public health problems, and as support for the claim that the state should maintain strict control over availability and therewith consumption in order to protect the population from potential health risks.[6]

In addition to structuring how historical 'events' are interpreted (and indeed, recognized as events), this conception of the Swedish problem also provides legitimacy for today's practices. For example, when the director of Sweden's alcohol retail monopoly, *Systembolaget*, met with skeptical EU parliamentarians in 1993 to convince them that Sweden should be allowed to retain this institution even after membership in the union, he argued that:

> The state, *for reasons of public health*, monopolized important parts of the alcohol trade. The underlying idea is that competition and private profit incentives tend to increase the sales of alcoholic beverages and thereby increase alcohol related harm (Romanus 1993; emphasis my own).

A key assumption in the statement above is that since it is the case that the alcohol problem is described as a public health threat today, it has been a public health problem at all times.[7] In contrast to this position, I will argue that

[6] For example, different 'natural experiments' are identified as events in this history. These natural experiments concern points in time when control measures were slackened and consumption levels increased. These events are well-known for the Swedish people, such that they do not even need to be mentioned by name, but merely alluded to.

[7] This is to say that the official and scientific discourses on alcohol construct a presentist history of the alcohol problem, and efforts to deal with it, assuming current knowledge as a point of departure. For a discussion of critical and effective histories contra presentist historical approaches, see Dean (1994).

public health has not always been the central theme in alcohol policy, nor has the role of the *Systembolag* been to protect public health. In my investigations I came across statements such as the following:

> *Medical statement from 1912*
> Alcoholism, which is not disease, is a minor problem compared to alcohol abuse in general. Most abusers are not real alcoholics, but their abuse is an expression of bad or crude habits (Alkoholen och Samhället 1912: pp. 188–89).
>
> *Medical statement from 1955*
> ... alcoholism, with respect to both its spread and social impact is fully comparable with tuberculosis, cancer and rheumatism (Myhrmann 1955: p. 1520).
>
> *Medical statement from 1982*
> There is a gradual transition from light to heavy consumers. An increase of total consumption for a population is accompanied by an increase in the number of people with heavy consumption and alcohol-related problems. If total consumption is decreased, the number of heavy consumers will also decrease and therewith the number of cases of alcohol harm (*Sveriges Läkarförbund* 1982: p. 2).
>
> *Official statement from 1948*
> Society's efforts to fight alcohol abuse should aim to affect both the states of illness and abnormality and environmental factors, which lead to or bring forth abuse (SOU 1948:23: p. 53).
>
> *Official statement from 1994*
> An increase in availability of alcohol is followed by an increase in consumption. The more alcohol is drunk in a society, the more people shift from moderate consumption to abuse. This also applies in the reverse, whereby the more difficult it is to obtain alcohol, the fewer the number of people who are harmed due to alcohol (Proposition 1993/94:136: p. 8).

Each of the citations above refers to alcohol issues as a social problem, and the need for measures to counteract this. However, each statement appears to refer to slightly different conceptions of what the object of regulation and investigation is. In the first medical statement, alcohol issues are a moral threat resulting from bad habits. In contrast, a doctor during the 1950s described the public problem of alcoholism as a widespread disease that could be compared to other known diseases such as cancer; suggesting a physiological location of the problem in the body. In the third medical statement, it is the number of heavy consumers and alcohol-related problems that is of concern, and this is seen as related to the total consumption of alcohol in a society. In the first official statement, found in a public document, the problem is caused by environmental factors outside the body and the person. In the final quote, alcohol issues are said to occur as more people drink more alcohol and find themselves in a 'risk zone'; it is alcohol itself which is problematic.

This quick comparison suggests that the definition of the problem, its causes and solutions have been the site of transformation and reconfiguration. At various points in time it becomes possible to conceptualize alcohol issues as a social problem in one way, and not another. It is this intellectual puzzle that forms the backdrop for the studies that follow.

The 'Social-ness' of a Swedish Social Problem

In my work I also aim to explore and identify in what ways the alcohol problem is 'social' according to the Swedish discourse on alcohol. In the United States, some scholars of social problems have argued that social problems are indeed 'social' because they are made meaningful by social actors who make claims about them (e.g. Best 1996, Conrad & Schneider 1980, Spector & Kitsuse 1973, Reinerman 1988). Social problems have also been seen as deriving their 'social' component from the narratives that have been constructed by social actors to describe them. In particular, deviant individuals or groups are defined as a threat to the social community through rhetoric, and a solution to their behavior is therefore transformed to a collective interest (Best 1987; Clarke 1975; Gusfield 1989, 1996). Indeed, these same claims could be made for the Swedish case of alcohol. In addition to these observations, however, I have also discovered other features of the Swedish social problem of alcohol that contribute to its status as a social phenomenon.

One feature of the Swedish discourse on alcohol issues that emerges in the studies of my dissertation is a concern for drinking as such, as well as alcohol abuse. This can be contrasted with a number of other western countries where a reference to alcohol issues, or the social problem of alcohol, is a reference to heavy or chronic drinking; i.e. what has been termed alcohol abuse, alcoholism, or chronic drinking at various points in time. In Sweden, however, "The alcohol problem has been regarded as sometimes the consequence, sometimes the causes or symptoms of alcohol abuse." (Rosenqvist & Kurube 1992: p. 67). Moreover, while chronic drinking has been a point of concern in Sweden, drinking as such has also formed an important point of regulation. Drinking as such, has been viewed either as a port of entry to heavy drinking, or in most recent discourse, as in and of itself problematic for the individual and society. This means that in addition to debate and research concerning treatment of heavy drinkers, Swedish research and legislation has also been concerned with the drinking of all citizens and the relationship between moderate, 'normal' drinking and heavy drinking. As the reader will detect through my work, this relationship contributes to sustaining universal policy measures to combat alcohol problems.

Although this duality of alcohol discourse is perhaps most clearly articulated in Sweden, it is also found in Norway and Finland, and can likely be related to the basic parameters of the provision of welfare in the Scandinavian welfare states that proposed an egalitarian individualism (Sulkunen 1991). Specific projects within the welfare state have aimed to equalize otherwise unequal groups, classes, the disabled, the sick, the elderly, etc., through universal policy measures rather than residual programs (Esping-Andersen 1990). In addition to universal rather than residual policy, I shall identify several other features of Swedish discourse on social problems that contribute to maintaining alcohol issues as a collective rather than individual problem.

My interest in studying the social aspect of the alcohol problem has also meant that I have limited my analysis and empirical data base to studying what is collectively defined as problematic. This means that I have largely omitted the study of treatment and alcohol abuse after the 1960s. It was at this time that the two issues became distinguished in official discourse. Such a move also follows established research traditions in Sweden, where there has been a division of labor among social science researchers. This division is drawn between alcohol consumption and alcohol policy on the one hand, and alcohol abuse and treatment on the other.

Social Problems and Social Research

My own work departs in several ways from conventional approaches to studying the alcohol problem in Sweden. As background to the work at hand, a brief overview of how social problems have generally been studied and legislated in Sweden is useful. Later I will contrast my own approach against this backdrop.

According to the conventional approach, social problems are defined in relation to an official definition of *welfare*. Welfare concerns a standard of living that is constituted by both a minimum economic standard as well as a minimum quality of life based on personal resources (Elmér 1989). Formal social policy goals have been established within several social policy domains.[8] Each goal is operationalized by the state or local authorities[9], such that minimum, measurable standards are identified. Typically, a social problem in Sweden is defined as a situation in which the expected (quantitative or qualitative) minimum set by social policy goals is not met (ibid. p. 14).

As the social policy goals of the welfare state point to, in the Swedish context, what are often viewed as private needs or issues in other national contexts, have been viewed as social concerns. Although these concerns are ex-

---

[8] Generally, nine social policy goals are cited in welfare state literature. These are: 1) health and availability of healthcare; 2) occupations (sysselsättning) and labor relations; 3) economic resources and consumer protection; 4) knowledge and educational opportunities; 5) family and social relations; 6) housing and proximity to services; 7) recreation and culture; 8) personal safety and security for property; and 9) political resources. These goals derive from a standard of living study carried out first in 1965 by Sten Johansson (see Johansson 1972), which has been followed up several times since using the same operationalization of welfare.

[9] Where these goals are established is dependent upon how the relations between levels of government are constructed at different points in time. Traditionally, policy goals have been highly centralized, but over the last decade there has been a trend towards decentralization of both services and authority over defining policy standards.

tensive in Sweden, they derive from some similar assumptions found among those states concerned with social policy. For example, an important latent assumption of welfare discourse is that social and private life can indeed be rationally regulated, planned, and formed through social policy. It is a modern discourse that provides parameters for cognizing social life and social issues, in terms of progress, individualistic universalism and nationalism (Sulkunen 1991). Put another way, there is a propensity to identify conditions as public or social problems and moreover to recognize public institutions and administration as the appropriate arena to deal with these issues, reflecting a "... sense of progress according to which life's difficulties are inherently remediable" (Gusfield 1989, p. 431). The welfare discourse constructs progress as achievable with the help of rational planning and social engineering to regulate the mechanisms behind social life. As such, the social domain is treated as a great domain of objects and potential objects for control and regulation (Cohen & Arato 1991, p. 284)[10], or 'social steering' as this has been referred to in Sweden (Olsson & Therborn 1991)[11]. Moreover, the discourse also assumes the normative position that social life not only can be regulated, but *should be regulated.* This also implies a social responsibility, to be assumed by the state or professional groups, for "resolving the resolvable" (Gusfield 1989, p. 432).

An important point that will be emphasized in the forthcoming analysis is that social policy has not proceeded alone in this endeavor. It has relied heavily upon science and expertise to guide the development of 'rational' policy.[12] In fact, it has been observed that social science, and Sociology in particular, are historically linked to social policymaking and practices in Sweden.[13] Or as Fridjonsdottir (1991) describes the emergence of Sociology in Sweden, "a fortuitous combination of academic and socio-political interests" (p. 250). One expression of this link is detected in the cooperation of scientific 'experts' with governmental investigative commissions. Such commissions are generally established to investigate social issues, evaluate heretofore policy, collate knowledge about them, and make recommendations for future policy directions. 'Experts', including scientists, often take part in such commissions, either as members of them or by undertaking requested studies to support commission work. This tradition has led some to argue that the history of Sociology is integrally linked to the history of commission work (Therborn 1973), and to the development of what was referred to as social engineering

[10] There is a growing literature on this topic, based on a theory of governmentality that derives from Foucault. See for example Rose (1992, 1996).

[11] Olsson's and Therborn's collected volume on social steering and social development investigates how regulation has been manifested in a number of social policy arenas.

[12] The relationship between expert knowledge, an epistéme (Foucault 1971) and liberal forms of government such as the welfare state has been studied as a more general phenomenon. See for example Rose (1996).

[13] Although many universities in western countries have Social Policy Departments, Sweden has not developed such a field. Rather, special professorships in applied policy areas within Sociology or other fields appear to fill policy-analysis needs.

(Jonsson & Tåhlin 1987).[14] In the area of alcohol, such commissions have been important arenas for influencing the 'governing images' of alcohol problems (Rosenqvist & Kurube 1992).

In addition to providing support and giving shape to legislative developments, the Swedish state plays an important role in constructing the means for conducting further investigation of various social policy issues. Research departments, scientific specialties and professorships are established through social policy legislation. In turn, the scientific community is expected to accumulate and share knowledge about the social issue and provide a scientific basis for the construction of further social policy.

Two consequences follow from this practice, which are relevant for the current discussion. The first is the institutionalization of policy domains. Social issues like 'alcohol problems' generally occupy a permanent or semi-permanent place on the policy agenda, as well as within research. Of more immediate consequence to the dissertation here, is how this practice has shaped social scientific investigation of social problems and the 'alcohol problem'. Sociology and the study of social policy is largely an empiricist field that is data-oriented; it often focuses on specific public concerns and policy goals and aims to develop results that could be used by the state (Jonsson & Tåhlin 1987). Investigation focuses on such issues as: establishing quantitative expectations for welfare; identifying the mechanisms operating behind social life and social issues; developing methods for 'accurately' measuring and studying these mechanisms; and the development of rational measures for intervening in social life and preventing or eliminating social problems.

The position described above entails a commitment to several basic assumptions about the 'nature' of the alcohol problem. First, for both these arenas, the alcohol problem is assumed to be an objective phenomenon. It 'exists' and through establishing and identifying proper 'indicators' it can be known and studied. Second, the relationship between the alcohol problem and research, and indeed policy which seeks to alleviate the problem, is assumed to be an independent one. The problem resides outside those efforts that are made to describe, theorize about, and regulate it; it is exogenous to these processes. This means that *the relation between research and its object is not problematized.* Third, the 'nature' of the problem remains the same regardless of human intervention. There may be fluctuations in the incidence of the problem, but the 'essence' of it remains the same. All three of these methodological commitments will be problematized in the dissertation. The third point, regarding the stability of the alcohol problem, forms the major focus of my investigation.

[14] Sociology was developed in Sweden in the 1940s and 1950s, and was established as an academic discipline in 1947. For an overview of Swedish Sociology, see Allardt et al. 1987.

Policy Variations and the Social History of Alcohol in Sweden

Not all research in Sweden has been oriented to the empiricist study of the alcohol problem as such. A large body of work has also dealt with the social history of regulation with respect to alcohol. [15] A common historical approach is to focus on the interests of various groups involved in the alcohol arena as a means of explaining why the Swedish system has developed as it has. For example, both Rothstein (1992) and Johansson (1995, 1997) point to Swedish corporatist political culture as an explanatory theory for the development of policy. The structure of social life, and the organizations that this gives rise to, as well as the power relations between these, are seen here to play an important role in the collective struggle to shape and produce social legislation. In a similar vein Nycander (1967/1996) and Svensson (1973) consider the rise and fall of the temperance movement among competing interests. These works emphasize the complexity of political discourse by identifying the many actors and interest groups involved in debating alcohol questions. Moreover, they draw attention to the fact that the system constructed to resolve alcohol issues is highly political, and context-dependent.

Additional issues dealt with in the social history of alcohol include the emergence of the regulation system in Sweden (Nycander 1967/1995, Bruun & Frånberg 1985), the history of consumption (Helling 1987), the role of the temperance movement in constructing a political arena around alcohol (Svensson 1973), the history of key institutions (Ragnarsson 1993), the history of treatment (Rosenqvist & Kurube 1992; Rosenqvist 1985, 1987), the impact of cultural orientations upon drinking practices (Gustavsson 1991), local variations in controlling and regulating alcohol (Frånberg 1983, 1985; Uusitalo 1998) and the history of the brewing industry and its attempts to influence policy (Hamberg 1985).[16]

As noted above, it is commonly assumed in alcohol research that the regulation system that was constructed in Sweden is only one of a number of potential systems that could have been constructed. This position is also adopted in the official history of Swedish alcohol, which builds on several of the texts cited above (e.g. Bruun & Frånberg 1985, Nycander 1967, Helling 1987). In texts such as informational brochures and commission reports, eras of liberal and control-oriented policy are identified. Different strategies are related to these overarching orientations and offered as explanations for shifts in policy.[17] While such researches and narratives draw attention to the variability of one aspect of alcohol issues—the social response to them—researchers and

---

[15] Internationally there have been several approaches that are common: Marxism, industrial discipline, culture, and discourse (Barrows & Room 1991).

[16] An additional historical work is Rydbeck's (1995) literary study of temperance litterature between 1896 and 1925 in Sweden.

[17] Appendix III contains a timeline of events that are generally recognized as consistiuting the Swedish alcohol history.

legislators have largely assumed that the problem itself—i.e. the object of research and legislation—is objective and invariable. The actual ways in which the alcohol problem is defined and conceptualized is largely left unexplored in the Swedish literature. Indeed, few works have actually examined or discussed the formulations of the problem that have been espoused by various interest groups.[18]

Asking these types of questions is important, because the 'nature' of the problem has important consequences for a host of practices. How moneys will be spent, at whom policies are aimed, whether a 'problem drinker' will be helped, treated, cured or incarcerated, who will be treated, which institutes will be developed, what questions will be asked, what instruments are appropriate and 'correct' for studying the problem, who will be blamed and held accountable when drinking becomes problematic, etc. are all linked integrally to how alcohol issues are conceptualized as a social problem.

My own work will contribute to filling this gap in examining variations in the social reaction to alcohol in Sweden; it is aimed precisely at investigating and better understanding variations in the perceived object of analysis through a socio-historical analysis focused on contemporary history. In this way, my work contributes to this arena by providing a compliment to an otherwise one-sided study of policy outcomes.

Towards an Alternative Set of Questions

My empirical work is concerned with what is taken as knowledge about alcohol, which is located in formal statements about alcohol, especially official or scientific ones. I seek to detect how conceptualizations of the alcohol issues , alcohol problems as an object, have shifted over time, such that they reflect very different perspectives on what exactly is fundamental with respect to alcohol. For this reason, the questions posed in the dissertation are not aimed towards the 'object' of alcohol problems, but are turned back towards the discourses, and production of knowledge about this object. I investigate how alcohol issues have been conceptualized and constituted as a social problem during this century, through three studies in discourse on alcohol in Sweden. Some of the research questions that have shaped my investigations are:

- How is alcohol conceptualized, problematized and justified as a problem in Sweden? i.e. How is alcohol constituted as a problem?
- How has this shifted over time?
- What kinds of assumptions underlie the conceptualization of the problem?
- What do legislation and science have to say about the 'nature' of the problem?

[18] One exception is Abrahamson (1989) whonpoints out that the nature of treatment programs, as well as society's position on involuntary care, has fluctuated in step with shifts in how the alcohol problem has been defined.

- What consequences does this have for the solutions proposed to deal with the problem?
- Who is regarded as an authoritative expert in relation to the problem?
- In what ways do scientific models and concepts contribute to the definition of alcohol issues as social problems?
- What is the relation between the questions posed by researchers, their latent theoretical commitments, and the definition of the problem at any given point in time?
- How do the statements about alcohol at a given time relate to one another?

In order to address these questions, I have adopted a constructivist approach to social problems that builds on a research tradition within alcohol studies that has provided a counterpoint to strictly empiricist work (e.g. Conrad & Schneider 1980; Gusfield 1967, 1981, 1989, 1996; Levine 1978, 1984a, 1984b; Mac Andrew & Edgerton 1969; Reinerman 1988, 1993; Room 1978, 1984; Schneider 1978; Wiener 1981). My work is also informed by discourse analysis, which suggests that the social world is knowable through what is said and written about it. Statements about alcohol appear as 'reality' and 'truth' (Brown 1989: p. 188). Discourses and social constructions do not indicate themselves, but appear as the 'natural order of things' (Berger & Luckmann 1977). Hence, the various approaches to discourse analysis utilize conceptual frameworks that allow the researcher to problematize the many unexamined assertions that are the object of analysis. In my work I have focused on detecting definitions of alcohol issues. Here a definition is an analytic tool used to denote socially constructed 'images'(Room 1978; Best 1987, 1995) of the alcohol problem. I have operationalized definitions as consisting of several components that can be detected in statements about alcohol. The most important components are: causal stories, stories of threat and harm, the dispersion of the problem, the distribution of authority, and solution complexes. These are defined and discussed in *Chapter 1.*

CHAPTER 1

Problematizing the Alcohol Problem

A Conceptual Framework

My research focuses on variations in the way in which alcohol has been defined and problematized as a social issue in Sweden, and in particular on the ways in which alcohol has been presented and justified as a problematic phenomenon. The main objective of this chapter is to present the concepts and methodological strategies that were adopted in the course of working with the empirical materials, and how these relate to the detection and deconstruction of problem definitions in scientific and legislative texts.

The Social History of Alcohol Issues

In the *Introduction* I provided a brief overview of some of the more common socio-historical approaches to discussing alcohol in Sweden. It was noted that while such studies have recognized the political and variable quality of regulation systems to deal with alcohol issues, they have not problematized the object of these systems. In contrast to these, the approach I have adopted allows me to focus more specifically on: 1) the interpretations of alcohol issues rather than the objective 'facts' associated with alcohol, and 2) the discontinuities rather than the continuity in defining the object of regulation and investigation. As such my work builds on a tradition of alcohol research that has been rather uncommon in Sweden, but which has been established elsewhere, particularly the United States (see *Chapter 1*).

One counterpoint to the empiricist tradition, is the social construction of social problems, which stems from the value-conflict school (Fuller & Myers 1941), and later labeling theory (Lemert 1951) or interactionist perspective (e.g. Becker 1963, Blumer 1971). From this perspective, what is of interest is the fact that conceptions of social problems or deviance emerge and develop independent of the objective conditions they are thought to give rise to. As Reinerman (1988), in his study of the case of Mothers Against Drunk Driving has phrased it, this tradition "... has focused on the claims-making activities and structuring of practices that, whether or not 'objective' human suffering exists or is rising, constitute the sine qua non of a social problem" (p. 92).

According to this cadre of researchers, the status of a phenomenon as a social problem does not arise by virtue of some intrinsic or essential quality of that phenomenon. Rather this status comes about because groups identify a phenomenon as problematic and demand that "something be done" (Spector & Kitsuse 1973). Following the work of other social constructionists studying social problems, these analyses have centered upon the struggle of various interest groups to draw attention to a phenomenon and to rally political and professional commitment to resolve it. Often, these studies take the form of case studies that follow the emergence of a social problem or arena (see e.g. Wiener 1981). This draws attention to the role of interest groups and social movements that contend for ownership of a problem and the power to define and give public prominence to it (ibid.). On this reading, then, the alcohol problem is a product of human subjectivity and social practices.

An example of this type of work is that of Schneider's (1978) and Conrad and Schneider's (1980) studies of deviant drinking as disease. Both works argue that alcoholism is not 'objectively' a disease, but is a "social accomplishment". Schneider's work draws attention to the use of labels and the monopolization of such labels as a means of determining 'ownership' of the issue. Conrad and Schneider's critical analysis places the discourse of alcoholism in the United States within the context of a trend towards medicalizing deviant behavior in general. The medicalization thesis, as in Schneider's earlier piece, as well as the work of others following the same interpretation, emphasizes the 'who' in alcohol constructions, especially those "who should have the legitimate jurisdiction over the definition and treatment of the symptoms of acute intoxication or alcohol poisoning or of the physiological consequences of chronic heavy drinking." (Conrad & Schneider 1980: p. 73). Their work lends understanding to the factors influencing the ownership of social problems. In the case of alcoholism the major entrepreneurs were not only the medical community, which was supported by the establishment of a national research center devoted to alcoholism, but also the Alcoholics Anonymous movement and later the alcohol industry and a variety of interested non-medical persons and groups, who regarded the medicalized definition as in their interests (see also Appleton 1995). As Conrad and Schneider (1980) themselves point out, their work is important since they provide an historical account that suggests that it is not only shifts in definitions that take place, but also a shift in morality over time (p. 2). However, by looking at the meta shift in conceptualizing social problems from religious to legal to medical frameworks, Conrad and Schneider's work misses the variations within medicine that can take place.

Elsewhere, the type of approach exemplified by Schneider and Conrad and Schneider has been adopted in order to focus on the process of defining a phenomenon. Such an approach is interested in the "crusade against" alcohol issues (Reinerman 1988: p. 114), and often draws attention to power relations particularly with respect to the ability of a single group, such as medicine, to dominate claims-making. This domination is provided as an explanation for the specific definition that gains currency. Additionally, these works draw attention to factors in the environment, such as the establishment of specific research institutes that support some claims as opposed to others. Although these works emphasize that the problem is a social accomplishment rather than an objective fact, the resulting construction is somewhat static. We do not see the potential variations of the conceptualization within the medical discourse, since they are often focused on how a single definition gained currency; i.e. the single event of 'discovering' a social problem.[1] The variations that do emerge with this approach concern the different definitions that are espoused by different interest groups, while variations over time have received less attention.

A second approach to the study of how social problems are defined is apparent in a short piece by Rouse & Unnithan (1993) who are specifically concerned with the definition of alcoholism and problematize this through a cross-national comparison of discourse in the United States and the former Soviet Union. These researchers shed light on the context-dependent character of problem definitions, within the medical community, by locating the more specific definition of alcohol issues within the Protestant ethic and proletarian ethic respectively. The Protestant ethic, as analyzed by Weber, involved a calling to do God's work, a work ethic that required individuals to labor for the glory of God, and the notion of a predestination. The proletarian ethic was inspired by Lenin, and involved a socialist calling, the idea of a consciousness and the sacredness of labor, as well as placing the needs of the group before the needs of the individual. Rouse and Unnithan argue that these frameworks provided terrain for defining the problem. Interestingly they discovered that one finds evidence of both a medical model and a moral model to describe alcohol problems and that these two models were "essentially similar" (p. 221) in both countries despite the differing contexts, and bases for legitimization.

Rouse and Uunithan provide some basis for comparing and contrasting different discourses on alcohol. However, their work is limited in that it does not compare these discourses over time. It would be interesting, for example, to investigate whether the medical and moral models detected in the former Soviet Union and the United States have been fairly stable, or if variations could be found. In *Chapter 3,* I will investigate Swedish medical discourse on alcohol problems over time, and note that different medical models can be located. This implies that there is not one single medical model, but the potential for multiple models.[2]

[1] Elsewhere I have argued that this approach seems to derive from the American context, and political practices, where social problems can be more short lived than those in Sweden (Sutton 1996).

[2] This is supported by Karin Johannisson's (1997) work on the body, and medical history. According to her, medicine and approaches to medicine and illness have different "cultures" and different "grammars". Appleton (1995) also points to competing models within medicine in her critique of the medicalization thesis, particularly as it has been applied in alcohol studies. She argues that these analyses have ignored what is referred to as 'alternative medicine' which she claims could offer some important insight into why alcoholism can be considered a disease despite the fact that it does not meet the established medical criteria for disease.

An important and influential body of work that has contributed to the social constructionist approach to alcohol issues is supplied by Joseph Gusfield (1967, 1975, 1981, 1996) , whose work links social constructionism to cultural analysis. On Gusfield's reading, there are a "plurality of possible realities", and with each reality a "world of fact is posited" (1981: p. 9). Building on a dramaturgical and rhetorical analysis, much of Gusfield's work has focused on the struggle to define a phenomenon as a public problem in a specific way through a symbolic system of meanings and actions. He has examined both the construction of consensus (1981), as well as the hegemony of the field (1996). In Gusfield's work the variability of the object of regulation becomes apparent through his mapping out of the competing narratives within the political arena. At the same time, his work also points to the way in which this contest over meaning takes place within basic parameters that exclude other ways of thinking. For example, he points out that all participants in the discourse surrounding drinking-driving as a public problem, assume that alcohol alone constitutes the problem; as he argues:

> ... the system of asking questions, excludes alternative ways of asking. Thus the auto itself—its design and mass consumption—is *not* viewed as a possible source of accidents that are capable of being controlled. Neither are such variables as age or nonintoxicated conditions of the motorist (sleepiness or emotional distress, for example). Nor is the interaction of variables displayed. Alcohol alone is singled out as *the* cause (p. 187).

A second aspect of Gusfield's work that is revealed in the excerpt above is his recognition of the importance of science, which he refers to as an 'art', in shaping conceptualizations of alcohol-related problems, in ways that extend beyond the boundaries of medicine. This suggests that science is not outside the processes of society and social problems, but an integral part of them.

Levine's now classic piece (1977), "The Discovery of Addiction" , as well as his study of the temperance movements in the United States (1984a) provide examples of discourse analysis that illustrate the variability of legislative and scientific objects over time.[3] These works follow the conceptualization of habitual drunkenness across two epochs in order to trace the genealogy of a 'new' and more medically-oriented conceptualization of drunkenness. A similar study is also provided by Baumohl and Room (1987), who trace the development of treatment facilities for inebriates before 1940. While their work is not specifically constructed as a discourse analysis, Baumohl and Room compare and contrast different models of institutional treatment and link these to broader social discourses and ideologies. Here, there is evidence of variation both over time, as well as across a single space in time.

---

[3] Levine's work is also of interest to the work at hand since he points to the emergence of yet another coneptualization, or discourse, on drunkenness that would center on public health (1984a), and which he later problematized by investigating official texts produced by the international research community (1984b).

In Europe there have been fewer works that focus on the social interpretations of alcohol issues. A noteworthy exception to this trend is an influential piece for the work at hand, Bergmark and Oscarsson's (1991) essay on the rhetoric of the Swedish alcohol discourse. Their work identifies some of the rhetorical devices that are consciously and unconsciously used to shape our understanding and conceptualization of alcohol as a social problem in Sweden. More specifically, they investigate the dominance of the total consumption model and public health perspective in the discourse of the 1980s (see also *Chapter 4* this volume), and draw attention to the discursive basis for legitimacy in this discourse.

While Bergmark and Oscarsson draw attention to the legitimacy surrounding administrative practices, Elmér's (1983, 1993) discussions of alcohol discourse in Sweden shed light on variations in how the subject of drinking narratives has been constructed at different historical junctures. Although he does not refer to social constructionism, per se, Mäkelä (1983) also points to the variability of social conceptions of alcohol problems in the Scandinavian countries, and argues that the definition of alcohol as a problem has been more dependent upon society's collective tolerance of consumption than upon the actual level of consumption or its prevalence in society. His work focuses on "when and under what conditions alcohol is defined as a social problem" (p. 12), and identifies several variations. Simpura (1987), Abrahamson (1989), Simpura and Tigerstedt (1990), Karlsson (1997) also provide insight into the relationship between the conceptualization of problems and the practices that are adopted in response to them and provide support to the work at hand.

A study that has inspired the current work, and which focuses upon contemporary history is Fahrenkrug's (1991) study of "varying contemporary conceptualizations of the alcohol question and the solutions that were to be derived from them" (p. 315) in Nazi Germany between 1933–1945. Within this space, Fahrenkrug identifies two different definitions of alcoholism that appeared simultaneously within the Nazi discourse on alcohol. Fahrenkrug's work shows how each definition was related to its own causal story and associated with a distinct set of practices, at the same time a logic was constructed between them that allowed the two models of alcoholism to coincide.

Social constructionist approaches to alcohol share several common points of departure. The first is that they raise questions concerning the universality of alcohol issues, and even the effects of alcohol (MacAndrew & Edgerton 1969). In viewing social problems as a social construction, they draw attention to the fact that alcohol could be 'thought' differently. Second, they shift scientific gaze from the problem itself, to conceptualizations of this problem, and to the variability of these. In this sense, we cannot say that empiricists and constructionists are looking at two sides of the same coin; they are concerned with studying two different things (Best 1995: p. 75). Third, variations in conceptions are understood in relation to the processes by which our understanding of alcohol is socially constructed through social interaction, discourse or practices. This means that studies are not strictly concerned with those that display the problem, but with all those who are interested in it, work with it and talk about it, and thereby justify phenomena as problems. In this sense, such works also problematize the relationship between science, legislation and social problems.

My work assumes a somewhat middle position among these approaches. Similar to Fahrenkrug, I am interested in contemporary history, and in how alcohol issues are constituted as an object of legislation. At the same time, I employ a form of discourse analysis that is reminiscent of Levine's work, whereby I investigate the construction of alcohol issues as a social problem over a longer period of time. However, rather than investigating a single major shift between two epochs, I will be exploring variations within the second epoch identified by Levine. That is, within what some have referred to as the "modern epoch" (e.g. Foucault 1977), I will be looking for variations in how alcohol issues have been defined. Finally, rather than viewing definitions in the context of the various interest groups, I am interested in those conceptualizations of alcohol that become dominant in society. In particular, I will examine collective statements about alcohol as a social problem that can be located in legislation, commission reports and public information materials.

Working Terms and Concepts

Social constructionist approaches have been concerned with the claims made about alcohol, which define the phenomenon in certain kinds of ways. In this sense, such studies investigate the *field of knowledge* (Foucault 1977) that constitutes alcohol issues as a social problem. A field of knowledge is a conceptual space rather than an actual space, which encompasses what can be thought, stated or formulated about alcohol within a specific context and by whom (Foucault 1978: p. 18). The field takes the form of a web of facts, relationships, practices and statements that refer to one another and thereby constitute a more or less coherent image of alcohol issues.

Since alcohol has been defined as problematic for such a long period of time in Sweden, certain claims and knowledge about alcohol have come to dominate key social arenas, and as such, they do not appear as claims, but as the unquestionable 'reality' of the problem. The field of knowledge about alcohol is enacted in part through the definitional interpretation of reality by means of *discourse*. In my work I have defined discourse as *a social dialogue, that takes place in the form of spoken or written statements concerning alcohol issues as a social problem*. It is through this discourse that the problem is or becomes, 'knowable', i.e. discourse offers us a way to think about and conceptualize alcohol (while also excluding other ways of thinking and knowing). Texts and statements produced by the medical and legislative communities, which are the primary sources of data for the studies at hand, offer society a collation of what is 'known' or should be 'known' about alcohol and its 'true' nature. Other agencies, groups and individuals are involved in spreading this knowledge.

Within the broader discourse on alcohol, variations on how the phenomenon has been problematized and justified can be detected. This is to say that the problem has been defined, in different ways within different historical contexts. Within the frame of a definition, the statements of a discourse appear to conform to certain principles or an inner logic by which one statement is regarded as related with the next. This logic, or *rules of formation* (Foucault 1971), structure discourse, giving it a certain regularity. In this sense, we can speak of a *discursive formation.* The formation implies the combined relations established between statements, concepts, theories, etc. in time and context (see Foucault 1972: p. 38; Tilley 1992: pp. 294–297). The term discursive formation refers, then, to a form of social order that is primarily located on a conceptual level, but which has important consequences for material practices as well.

Discourse analysis is often associated with a critical form of socio-historical analysis. One of the linchpins of this approach is an attempt to maintain a nonlinear perspective on history and social change. As such, it is concerned with problematizing "horizontal totalities such as society or period" (Best & Kellner 1991; p. 43). Thus, in the context of my work I recognize that a discursive formation is a conceptual space that is penetrated by concepts, statements, etc. that can stem from sometimes different 'genealogical' trees, *but which combine at a historical moment in a unique configuration.* A discursive formation belong to a series of discourse identified by the analyst. I use discursive formations to periodize time rather than starting with the periods (based, for example, on shifts in political power, changes in levels of alcohol consumption, etc.). This means that formations can appear at different points in time or parallel to one another; and that they contain a distinct logic and story within a historical context, but also belongs to a broader story within which concepts and practices may appear, retreat, be excluded and reappear.

The regularity of a discursive formation emerges both out of the positive rules that proscribe models and theories for interpreting reality, as well as through a "policing of statements" (Foucault 1978/76: p. 18), whereby certain types of information, 'facts', or statements are rejected and excluded from the right to expression, because they do not confirm or contribute to the 'true' and 'serious' discussions of the 'problem' (Foucault 1971). Moreover, different professions or individuals are also excluded from the discursive community for the same reasons (ibid.).[4] Certainly there are voices and claims that would challenge the dominant discourse, but these do not find expression within the confines of 'serious' discourse.

The practice of exclusion suggests that discourses have *limits* or *boundaries.* Best (1987) has pointed out that one of the modes by which a boundary is sustained, is through the adoption of a *definition* of alcohol as a public pro-

[4] See next page.

blem. A definition, "identifies a phenomenon, setting its boundaries or domain." (Best 1987; p. 104). Although this is not always stated explicitly in the discourse, a definition is evident at any given moment. The definition provides an "operative reality" (Brulle 1993) that provides the basis for interpreting new information (as 'true' or untrue discourse), for judging what can be said, when, and by whom. Its practical consequence is that "Someone who understands a definition can examine phenomena and determine which do, and which do not, fall within the defined category's domain" (Best 1987: p. 104). That is to say, the problem definition entails parameters, which provide clues as to whether or not a condition or remedy for that condition shall be considered under the umbrella of 'alcohol problem'. Furthermore, as we saw from Gusfield's example of drinking-driving, problem definitions highlight some aspects of a situation, while detracting or overshadowing other aspects.

In addition to identifying the domain of a specific category, the definition is also important as it links the discourse to a number of practices related to treatment, regulation and punishment (Gusfield 1981) by establishing an inner logic between these. As Weiss (1989: p. 97) notes, problem definitions are not "merely a label for a set of facts and perceptions." but a "a package of ideas" that provides the basis for generating a discourse on the alleviation of a condition. In particular, the definition often relates to different institutional arrangements for managing and regulating the problem.

Important to note is that these boundaries are not constituted once and for all, nor are they 'obvious' in relation to a given 'problem'. Discourses are embodied by human agents (Burns and Sutton 1996). Boundaries are, therefore, often the object of much dispute, struggle and negotiation as different communities consciously and unconsciously redefine them. Social movement organizations, for example, have been cited as locations for the embodiment of the struggle to problematize an issue or to redefine the terms of discourse (e.g. Brulle 1993, Gusfield 1967, Reinerman 1988).

Although this struggle over boundaries is not the object of analysis in the

[4] The example of the 'discovery' of the positive effects of red wine provide an example. For quite some time researchers in France, the United States and other countries have argued that red wine is good for the heart; this alternative 'knowledge' emphasizes alcohol's positive affects upon health rather than its negative ones. In Sweden, these 'facts' were regarded for a long time as 'false' or 'misleading' and were hence excluded from government reports on alcohol, from public information materials, and other serious discourse. Likewise, the Brewers Association was excluded from serious discourse during the last five decades until only recently. The organization was regarded as 'impartial' and 'lacking objectivity' since it sought to profit from others' alcohol consumption, a practice which is related to immoral positions according to the current discourse. When it became known that Sweden would enter negotiations with the European Union (then, European Community) for membership in the community, the Brewers Association commissioned a study of illegal distilling and smuggling. This report indicated that illegal consumption of alcohol might be as much as 40% of registered sales. The information was upsetting to European Brewers who saw Sweden's illegal market as a threat to their own market. The information was initially rejected in Sweden, but later entered official discourse after a Danish paper covered 'the story'. However, the government commissioned its own investigation of the illegal market, and argued that the Brewers figure was much exaggerated. Chapter 6 will return to this discussion (Sutton 1996).

current dissertation, it has consequences for the definition of the alcohol problem. Namely, as the boundaries of a field of knowledge are disputed and repeatedly redrawn, the definition of alcohol as a public problem is also reconfigured. Sometimes it is precisely the definition of the alcohol problem which is wielded in discourse as a challenge to the dominant discursive formation (e.g. Edelman 1988, Stone 1989, Weiss 1989). In other instances, the definition shifts slowly in relation to subtle changes in theoretical or legislative statements.

Conceptual Framework and Method for Detecting Formations

Because discourses and social constructions often appear as the 'natural order of things' (Berger & Luckmann 1966), it is necessary to utilize a method for detecting them. Such a method operates to problematize the taken-for-granted assumptions that shape reality and allow us to objectify objectifying practices (Bourdieu 1990). There is no established method for discourse analysis at a macro, or formal, level of knowledge production. Rather, approaches have varied in relation to the specific questions posed by the researcher. For example, in their work on how protest is constructed by social movement actors in relation to events, Snow and Benford (1992) deconstruct discourse by looking for "master frames"; while others seek out "cognitive schemata" (Johnston 1995), or "narratives" and "narrative types" that allow typologies to be constructed. Gary Fine (1995), for example, identifies three types of narratives by which movement organizations describe social threats: horror stories, war stories, and happy endings. In his work on "Constructing the Missing Children Problem", Joel Best (1987) seeks out the rhetorical structure behind statements by various groups on the issue of missing children by identifying three 'elements of claims': grounds, warrants and conclusions. These conceptual frameworks allow the authors to 'grasp' the discourse and make it visible and researchable.

In my approach, I have focused on detecting *definitions* of alcohol issues. In this case, a "definition" is an analytic tool introduced by the researcher to denote "images" of the social problem (Room 1978, Best 1995). Definitions are generally not expressed in the discourse in an explicit way, but can be constructed by the researcher by using various cues. In the following work, I have operationalized definitions as consisting of several components that can be detected in statements about alcohol. The most important components are: Causal stories, stories of threat, the dispersion of the problem, the distribution of authority, and solution complexes.

Causal Stories

Statements about alcohol issues contain implicit and explicit assumptions concerning the cause of alcohol issues. Causal stories are composed narratives that "describe harms and difficulties, attribute them to actions of other individuals or organizations, and thereby claim the right to invoke government power to stop the harm." (Stone 1989: p. 282).[5] Causal stories are found in both the official discourse, which uses a notion of cause in order to establish legitimacy for a specified course of action (or inaction), as well as in scientific discourse, which approaches cause as either a puzzle to be unraveled or as a basic assumption upon which research is conducted. Where policy is based on expert knowledge, assumptions concerning cause have important ramifications since scientists make choices concerning what causes will be studied and hence promoted (Manning 1985: pp. 25–27).

Notions of action and blame are linked to the identification of cause. The essence of 'what has happened', i.e. where the action lies, is implied through the cause. Blame, with respect to the individual's culpability, is related to the notion of whether will can be attached to the action (Stone 1989). For example, Joseph Gusfield's well-known study of drinking-driving in Southern California illustrates the relationship between cause and blame.

> Fixing responsibility for preventing accidents by laws against drinking-driving involves seeing drinking-driving as a choice by a willful person. Seeing it as a medical problem involves an attribution of compulsion and illness (1989: p. 6).

He notes that while drinking-driving is described as a situation in which 'killer drunks' get behind the wheel, the problem is understood as deviant behavior on the part of irresponsible individuals who ideally have a will. If, however, one considers an alternative set of explanatory factors such as: the lack of a public transportation infrastructure, long distances between bars and housing areas, etc. then it is not the individual's will that has gone wrong. Rather, cause and blame are transferred from the individual to government, for instance.

Causal stories are important definitional components where intervention, especially by the state, is demanded or expected. State intervention can only take place if a space has been constructed within which its activities are constructed as capable of achieving specified outcomes; that is, human intervention

---

[5] Stone's work shows how causal stories are used as weapons by claims-makers to gain control of a policy agenda. The structure of causal stories is emphasized in her work, particularly the difference between causal stories that locate will within the 'natural' sphere and those that locate it within the 'social'. In the natural sphere, occurrences are "undirected, unoriented, unanimated, unguided and 'purely physical'" (1989: p. 282). In contrast, the social sphere is a world in which there is will, and where occurrences are the result of control and intent by humans. The distinction between these two worlds is important because they appeal to very different interpretaive frameworks and expections concerning what constitutes an adequate understanding of the cause of events. In the study at hand, it would be important to point out that causal stories are also the product of competition between claims-makers. In this sense, causal stories as a component of the problem do not lose their significance once the problem has hit the political agenda.

must be deemed reasonable and possible according to the causal framework (Stone 1989). This also means that causal explanations must be seen as reasonable in the context of how authority is distributed and what solutions are proposed.

Stories of Threat

Threats say something about the 'nature' of a problem, who is affected by it, and the consequences of a problem's continued existence if left unattended. Social problems are presented in the form of some 'type' (Clarke 1975) such as: moral, religious, political, personal, family, economic, and health.[6] Put another way, it is "not just that X is a problem, but X is a problem of a particular sort." (Best 1995: p. 8). The type of social threat that is linked to a social problem gives an 'orientation' to the problem by indicating or providing an 'assessment of the sort of problem it is' (Best 1987). Since morality and politics are regarded as collective goods, a threat to them implies a social concern rather than an individual concern. In addition to being defined as collective goods, social orders are generally assumed to constitute a 'natural order'; and as threats to this, social problems appear as not only dangerous, but also unnatural.

The structure of the threat potentially constructs a social component of the social problem by identifying the basis for a collective interest. The threat identifies 'who', which group or groups, are affected by the existence of the problem and identifies who or what poses such a threat. While most research on social problems has highlighted the narratives by which individuals have been defined as posing a threat to the social order, I will also be arguing in my work that the social component of the problem can reside on either side of the formula for the threat.

A threat is also established through the presentation of statistics and other evidence to substantiate the present condition and determine its 'extent' (Best 1987). This evidence is also used to predict what might happen if it is not counteracted, and contributes to an image of the problem as a consensus issue, since few would stand up and say they are 'for child abuse' (Gusfield 1989).[7]

---

[6] The social order is formulated in different ways at different times. Theorists of social problems have pointed out that social problems have been presented as moral (religious), legal and later medical problems. This could be interpreted as threats to moral, legal and health orders. Today, we tend to see an emphasis upon health, eonomic and legal orders.

[7] In my work I will not be focusing on this aspect of the construction of a threat. Bergmark and Oscarsson (1991) provide some discussion of this, as they note the kinds of statistics and 'facts' that are cited repeatedly in Swedish discourse in order to substantiate claims for new measures to deal with alcohol problems. In addition to this, I have pointed out elsewhere that the Swedish discourse refers to 'natural experiments' to substantiate the claim that when restrictions are relaxed in Sweden, consumption of alcohol increases, and more alcohol-related problems arise as a result (Sutton 1996).

Dispersion of the Problem

Statements about alcohol construct and refer (implicitly and explicitly) to categories, types, conditions, aspects, cases, etc. by which the larger problem is broken down into manageable pieces of a puzzle. As Foucault has argued:

> [Discourse] organizes the document, divides it up, distributes it, orders, arranges it in levels, establishes series, distinguishes between what is relevant and what is not, discovers elements, defines unities, describes relations (1972: pp. 6–7).

The practice of dispersing the problem involves the imposition of values, comparisons and categories which contribute to 'translating conditions into social problems' (Kingdon 1984: p. 116). This dissection of the issue, contributes to cordoning the phenomenon off, establishing its boundaries and limits, from other parts of social reality that are not problematic by "realizing differences and distinctions" (Brown 1990: p. 191), as well as determining the internal relations among concepts, objects, subjects, etc. that belong to a discourse.

If we look, for example, at Figures 1 and 2, different conceptualizations of alcohol issues emerge. The first figure (see Figure 1) is of a scale of temperance progress formulated by Benjamin Rush in 1790, who regarded drunkenness as a "disease of the will" (Levine 1978). In Rush's formulation, the type of beverage is important, and provides the basis for constructing a classification system whereby different drinks were linked to temperance while others led to intemperance. Intemperance was further divided according to three series: vices, diseases, and punishments. A logical relationship was established, for example, between the consumption of "bitters infused in spirits", fraud, pains in the limbs, and time in jail. This image can be contrasted with a diagram by Jellinek in 1952 (see Figure 2). According to this dispersion of the problem, the type of beverage is irrelevant. For Jellinek, the heart of alcohol issues was alcoholism, defined as a disease, characterized by a "loss of control" over one's drinking. In this image, the key to dispersion is the disease as a progressive illness, which played itself out in somewhat predictable ways in alcoholics regardless of choice of beverage. Stages of this illness were identified, and different 'symptoms' or 'evidence' of disease were associated with each phase. The dispersion of the problem in each case is related to what is considered the essential aspect of the alcohol problem. In turn, the construction of classifications contributes to an objectification of the 'problem' as scientific and 'objective'.

For the discourse analyst, what is of interest is to first identify what divisions and similarities are made, and second to unravel the logic by which these divisions are drawn and by which objects and subjects are linked to one another, or proclaimed dissimilar. This is an important aspect of 'freeing' statements from the "groupings that purport to be natural immediate, universal unities" (Foucault 1972: p. 29).

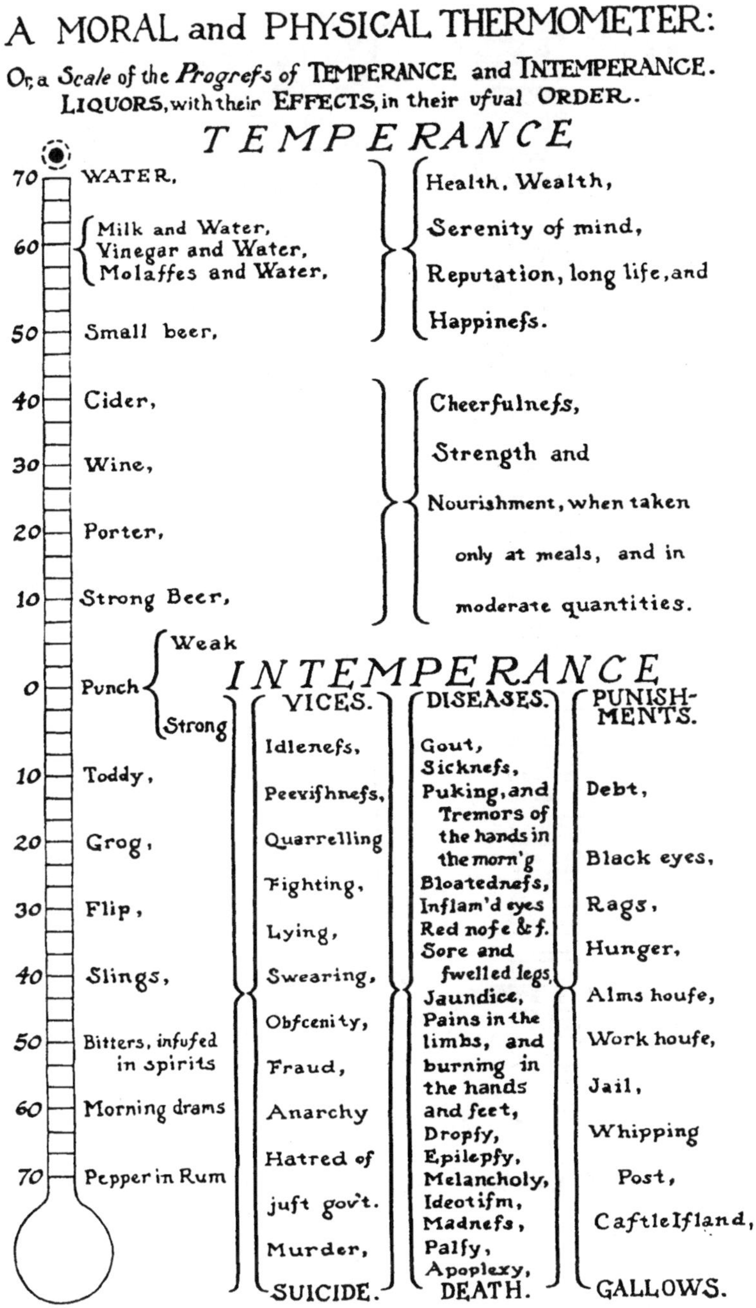

Fig. 1. The dispersion of alcohol problems and resolutions according to Benjamin Rush. From Rush, B. *An inquiry into the effects of ardent spirits upon the body and mind,* 1790. Thomas & Andrews.

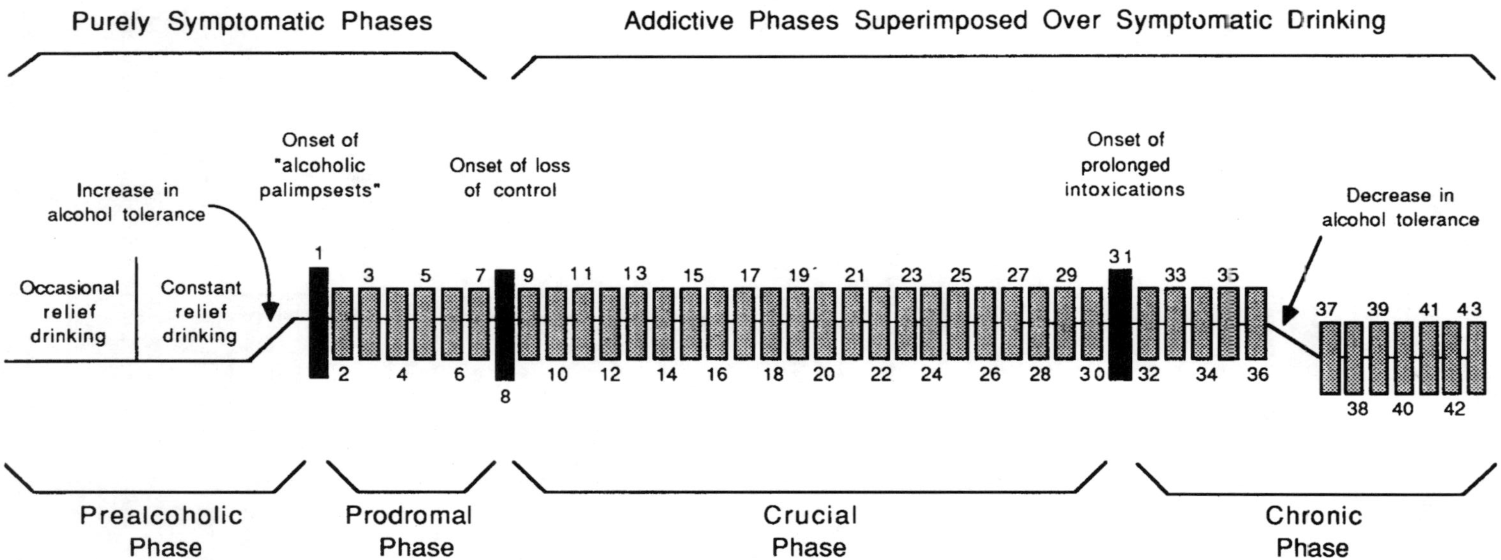

Fig. 2. The dispersion of the disease of alcoholism and the phases of alcohol addiction according to E. M. Jellinek. From Jellinek (1962) "Phases of Alcohol Addiction" in *Society, Culture and Dringking Patterns,* Pittman, D. J. and C. R. Snyder (Eds.), p. 360. New York: John Wiley & Sons, Inc.

Distribution of Authority

In relation to social problems and their resolution, there are many tasks to be carried out. Some examples include: the production of knowledge or facts about the problem, spreading these facts, administering solutions, and bringing attention to related issues, among others. Authority for assuming "ownership" (Gusfield 1989) for one or several of these tasks is distributed through the macro discourse on social problems.[8]

One of the more important tasks, and one which is specifically studied in this dissertation, is the production of knowledge and professional claims to 'truth' by the scientific community. Within the context of modern government, and the governing of citizens within the Swedish welfare state, in particular, 'science has become incorporated into strategies of regulation'; "government is dependent upon the production of truths that realize in a concrete form what is to be governed" (Jagger 1997: p. 447–448; see also Rose 1991). However, these claims to truth do not operate in a vacuum. The medical community, for example, can not simply argue that alcohol issues 'belong' to a medical arena of phenomena, and thereby secure their position (Schneider 1978). Such claims must be recognized both inside and outside of medicine (Sutton 1995).

Authority for some aspect of the problem is not always sought as pointed out by Gusfield (1981) and others (see e.g. Morgan 1980). In many cases the problem and causality can be constructed such that a party other than the state, or a profession is awarded responsibility. For example, the problem may be depoliticized, by defining it as a disease, in a text produced by the government, thereby deferring state responsibility and accountability at a time when there are little funds.

The production of knowledge and statements of 'truth' are only one task that must be carried out. Social problems are also accompanied by the need for professionals to apply solutions. This group of professionals, or the 'troubled persons professions', are assigned authority over "bestowing benevolence on people defined as in need." (p. 432). The administration of practices for resolving issues has often been in the hands of medical professionals, but in Sweden and the other Nordic countries, it has been observed that there is evidence of a "non-medical model" (Bruun 1971, see also Takala & Lehto 1992). According to this division of authority, the state has assumed a great deal of responsibility for organizing solutions, but the treatment of persons with chronic drinking problems has been shared among different groups, not only the medical community. In addition, since the problem itself has not strictly been related to alcoholism, but also drinking as such, other types of administrative institutions and groups have been brought into the field of authority. These initial observations will be further discussed in the dissertation.

[8] On another level of discourse the distribution of authority is often an object of conflict as groups vie to either assume ownership or disassociate themselves from tasks that the government or others wish to bestow upon them. Analyses that focus on the professionalization of different groups, focus on the distribution of authority, for example, and how collectives consciously and unconsciously strive to define the boundaries for this.

Solution Complexes

Solution complexes concern how the resolution of a social problem is constructed. A solution complex can take the form of a set of institutional practices (e.g. a state retail monopoly for alcohol), but it can also concern a formulated strategy, on a theoretical level, for how a social problem should be dealt with.[9] This means that a relatively stable practice such as a state monopoly may take on a 'different' role within the context of a shift in strategy, although its physical form appears similar. Solution complexes are also linked very closely to the distribution of authority since a selected institutional setting often implies work to be carried out by professionals located there.

Joseph Gusfield has pointed out that "To give a name to a problem is to recognize or suggest a structure developed to deal with it" (1989: p. 432). I want to suggest here that we can also perceive of the reverse condition; that is, to suggest a structure is to give a name to a condition.[10] It is not always the case that the identification of a problem precedes the solution that is developed; rather, it can also be the case that solutions or institutions that are already in existence or proposed are linked to problems aposteriori. In this linking, the problem and solution may be reconstituted in their relationship to one another. Just as texts share an intertextuality in a discourse, solutions too, do not emerge as completely new upon the horizon, but refer to past and present practices. In the Swedish case, this is seen most clearly with respect to the state retail monopoly for alcohol. Although it was initially established as a means of controlling purchases by individuals, it is currently regarded as a means of protecting public health.

Studies in the Swedish Discourse

The empirical and analytic discussions of the dissertation are based on three studies of formations in the Swedish alcohol discourse over time. While each of the studies was conducted based on the same method for detecting definitions (see above), the methodological principles and strategy for selecting data have been slightly different in the three cases. For this reason, I will discuss each chapter separately.

[9] These tasks do not necessarily result in an effective resolution. Their importance to the problem is established through rhetoric, not strictly through their rates of success.

[10] A common assumption among policy analysts and a number of social constructionists studying social problems is this temporal relationship between problems and solutions. For example, Weiss (1989) combines policy analysis with social constructionism by exploring the relation between how conditions are defined and policy outcomes. She argues that problem definitions can be presented and redefined at various stages in the policy process, but "At whatever stage a new problem definition gains significant support, it shapes the ensuing action. It legitimates some solutions rather than others, invites participation by some political actors and devalues the involvement of others, focuses attention on some indicators of success and consigns others to the scrapheap of the irrelevant." (p. 98). My point here is not to question the validity of this statement, but to argue that discourse analysis, with its emphasis upon intertextuality, points up that this relationship can be conceived in quite the reverse manner.

One general comment should be made. The Swedish alcohol discourse is a complex discourse and political arena, where many different "interest groups" meet and compete to define reality. Among some of the key groups that have previously been identified are: temperance movement organizations and individual members (Svensson 1973, Nycander 1967/1995), economic interests (Bruun & Frånberg 1983, Johansson 1995, Hamberg 1985), professional groups and administrative personnel (Rosenqvist 1985, 1987; Rosenqvist and Kurube 1992), and others. Given more time and resources, a complete analysis of the discourse would have included several of these locations; and indeed, I will be suggesting how such a task might be carried out in *Chapter 6*. Given the constraints upon time and resources that surrounded the current project, I chose to concentrate my analysis primarily upon statements generated within two loci: the official and the medical. These are further discussed below.

Studying the Medical Discourse

As one means of locating a point of entry into the Swedish discourse on alcohol, I decided to focus on one specific group that had been engaged in alcohol questions throughout the twentieth century. Moreover, I wanted to select a source of discourse that had contributed to shaping the models and knowledge associated with alcohol as a social problem. Although it was tempting to select the temperance movement, about which several studies have been conducted, I chose instead, the medical community. There were several reasons for doing so. First, during my initial investigation of discourse about alcohol in Sweden in 1993, I interviewed several representatives of organizations within the temperance movement. I discovered that these representatives borrowed knowledge produced by researchers in the social science and medical fields in order to describe the problem and argue for solutions. This could also be seen in the membership magazines of the respective organizations. From this, I deduced that although the temperance movement had had an influence in shaping policy and definitions of the problem earlier in this century, it had not maintained this authority. Second, temperance organizations were largely absorbed into the state apparatus following World War II (Olsson 1998); they have been institutionalized and in many ways disarmed, such that they may react to policy by way of commenting on proposed legislation, but participate less in directly shaping it. For both these reasons, the movement was less interesting for the studies at hand.

Rather than studying the temperance movement, I chose to study the medical discourse on alcohol. This source of discourse is interesting for several reasons. First, the medical community and medical professionals have been active participants in discussing and debating alcohol problems and resolutions to deal with the problem throughout the twentieth century. This is not surprising given that rational policy has been based on scientific knowledge in the context of the Swedish welfare state (Hugemark 1994). Second, precisely because this is the case, it is important to study what science has contributed. Although research has considered the role of the temperance movement in the early phases of building alcohol policy, only one minor work has been conducted to examine the role of medicine specifically (Rosenqvist 1987). Science has largely been viewed as a subject position outside of the alcohol policy arena, from which other actors can be viewed and studied; it is time to put science into the field.

The medical discourse is presented in *Chapter 3*. I have defined the medical discourse as statements and texts that are generated within the medical profession or its settings. Such statements can generally be found in bonafide expert reports that are recognized within the medical profession as satisfying medical criteria. Of course, there may be disagreement or debate concerning hypotheses or theories; and these, too, contribute to constructing the parameters of discourse within which this debate will take place (e.g. what kinds of things may be questioned, upon what grounds, who may question it, etc.).

My method of analysis in this chapter was to "extract" two formations, from their historical and discursive contexts, in order to juxtapose them. The purpose of this was to allow me to more clearly detect the lines along which they were constituted. Following from this, my data selection for the chapter aimed to pierce two different moments in time, where I knew from previous exposure to the discourse, different conceptualizations of alcohol problems were likely to emerge.

The first formation, which I refer to as the *alcoholism formation*, was selected based on previous readings in the field.[11] Other researchers have noted that towards the end of the 1940s a stronger leaning towards formulating alcoholism as a disease emerged (see e.g. Abrahamson 1989, Elmér 1993, Rosenqvist & Kurube 1992, Stenius 1996). Among other evidence, these researchers point to a 1948 public commission report in which a stronger emphasis is placed on medical treatment and knowledge. It is unlikely that the state would begin to support a disease orientation to the problem if the medical community itself did not support the idea, and it was therefore deemed reasonable to begin my study of medical discourse on alcohol problems with 1948. In addition, it was known that the World Health Organization also adopted a disease-orientation to alcoholism during the 1950s following the wide acceptance of Jellinek's work on *the Disease Concept of Alcoholism.* It was thought that a ten-year period, the 1950s, would provide enough data to establish the limits of the discourse. In order to ensure that this was covered, I extended the study to cover from 1948 to 1962. Later, it was also decided to follow-up my study by also considering the years 1963–1979 (see below).

Data for the study was collected from *Läkartidningen*, the official journal

[11] I knew that the earliest period of the 20th century presented one type of medical appraoch to alcohol issues, according to which medical professionals were involved in administering solutions but did not deem the problem as strictly a medical phenomenon. (Rosenqvist 1987). Selecting an episode after this period, provides a basis for later relating my work to Rosenqvist's in the future.

for the Swedish Society of Medicine, which includes both medical advances as well as discussions of political issues of interest to the medical community (see *Appendix II* for further discussion). Between the years 1948 and 1962, 111 articles were identified that were related to alcohol (three articles were omitted from the study since they did not deal directly with alcohol in Sweden). It should be noted that until 1950, primarily one man, Alfred Petrén, contributed to the journal. His main subject of discussion was the administrative practices related to where alcoholics would be treated and in what ways the local temperance boards could make better use of physicians, through allowing house calls, for instance. In 1950, the first article related to pharmaceutical use in treatment appeared in the data, and increasingly after this time, the contributions to the discourse were made by a larger number of medical professionals. Moreover, these articles increasingly debated the status of alcoholism as a disease and defined both the disease and the role of medical professionals in relation to it. Also included in the study is a review piece by Carl Henry Alström, which was contributed to a book on *20 års medicinsk forskning* (20 years of medical research) in 1965.

The second formation of medical discourse was identified as falling from approximately 1982 to the present. Based on knowledge of the discourse, 1982 was selected as a point of departure for studying the second formation, as it was in this year that the Swedish medical profession presented an important position piece, *Läkare om alkohol* (Doctors on alcohol), which was widely cited thereafter in both the medical and official discourses. My examination of *Läkartidningen* began initially with 1980, again, as a means of assuring that 1982 was a good starting point. This study was later complimented with a further investigation of texts presented between 1962 and 1982. It was found that although the important position piece was presented in 1982, it was not until the late 1980s that the second formation really took shape and came to dominate the discourse. Between 1980 and 1995, I identified 246 articles that provided the basis for the discourse analysis. Over 50 articles per year were contributed in 1980 and 1981. For these years, I selected every third article listed in the subject index, as well any pieces that mentioned public health specifically (book reviews were excluded, as were any letters to the editor that did not deal specifically with policy or public health). In addition, this study was complimented with several collections of pieces that were presented at conferences held among the medical community, including *Risken att bli alkoholist* (1982), *Alkoholpolitiken och forskningen* (1984) and *Problemet Alkohol* (1986). These latter texts were, and are, widely cited in the official and medical discourses.

Studying the Total Consumption and Public Health Formation

As Levine (1984b) has demonatrated, one of the ways in which the reality of alcohol problems is constructed is through the production of 'consensus statements', or what I refer to as 'collective statements' about the problem. Levine's own study concerned the production of a document, following an international conference on alcohol problems, that would summarize what all researchers in the field 'knew' and agreed upon. Similar types of collective statements can be found in Sweden. In some cases these are found among professional discourses, as will be taken up in *Chapter 3*, but they are also found among the broader political arena where collective statements are produced as statements of what all interest groups and researchers 'know' and agree upon. In Sweden, the political process of constructing legislation generally follows a common pattern. A social policy area or problem is investigated by a parliamentary or government appointed commission that then makes policy suggestions in one or several reports. These reports are circulated, in what is known as a 'remiss' process, among recognized interest groups and other interested parties, who will then comment upon them. In the final bill, references are made to the comments of these parties and the ways in which the bill differs from proposed legislation is discussed in relation to these comments. In this sense, commission reports and legislation can be viewed as collective statements since they are viewed as emanating from the collective of groups involved in an arena. They consist of a recognized set of statements that thereafter provide the basis for continued public discourse (even if this discourse challenges these statements), and in this way, form cultural artifacts.

In *Chapter 4*, where I focus more on the official discourse, I have primarily relied upon propositions to laws, commission reports preceding laws and several additional governmental reports as sources of official discourse. Specifically my analysis included five propositions[12], nine public commission reports, three governmental reports, and three reports by the National Board of Health and Welfare. Although my strategy for the official discourse has been to hone in on 'artifacts' of official discourse, I have not limited my analysis to these texts. My analysis also builds on a review of the customer magazine of the *Systembolag* from 1989–1995[13], especially articles written by the director Gabriel Romanus, a series of public information materials distributed at *Systembolaget* (e.g. *Bakgrund, Vid dina sinnens fulla bruk*), and several key research reports by scientists that are repeatedly cited in the official discourse (e.g. Bruun et al. 1975, Edwards et al. 1994, Holder & Edwards 1995). This is also in line with a shift in methodological strategy in this chapter, whereby I have tried to follow the discourse itself and how it establishes 'key texts', classic pieces, and 'roots'/foundations.

[12] The propositions for laws rather than the laws themselves have been studied here for two reasons. First, propositions generally include argumentation and justification for any proposed shifts in laws, while the laws themselves do not. Such argumentation provides a much clearer view of the components of problem definitions. Second, propositions also include a discussion of the preliminary reviews (remiss) of laws and policies, supplied by various interest groups.

[13] This builds on a review of this magazine carried out in conjunction with two earlier research projects. See Sutton (1993, 1996).

Swedish Discourse and the European Union

In *Chapter 5*, which deals with Sweden and the EU, my investigation of the discourse was broadened to include additional loci, including both institutionalized statements of discourse, as well as some of the more spontaneous forms for discourse. Data sources included a departmental report and proposition for establishing a new alcohol control board, three legislative propositions, a review of the debate pieces in the Swedish newspaper *Dagens Nyheter* between the years 1989–1995 (37 pieces),[14] EU related articles in the customer magazine *Uppdraget* for the same period (25 pieces), 2 letters exchanged by the Swedish government and the European Commission, 2 Communications by the Commission, a Bulletin of the European Community from 1992 where the Swedish membership application was initially discussed, and informational materials supplied by the *Systembolag* concerning how the monopoly would be affected by Swedish membership in the EU. These materials allowed me to investigate how the situation was defined on two levels: 1) how the problem was defined and re-defined inside Sweden; and 2) how the situation was defined and re-defined outside Sweden. This chapter also includes an epilogue which builds on two texts generated by the European courts.

The medical discourse also figures in the discourse discussed in *Chapter 5*. In this case, data on the medical response to this, was extracted from the following sources: four EU-related articles in *Läkartidningen* between 1989 and 1995, four debate pieces written by medical professionals in the two major Swedish newspapers *Dagens Nyheter* and *Svenska Dagbladet*; two pieces written by medical doctors in collections by the temperance publisher SOBER (Andréasson 1992, Rydberg 1996); and a letter submitted to the government by a group of doctors warning about the dangers of liberal alcohol policy in the context of EU membership.

---

[14] A less systematic media review of EU related articles was conducted at an early stage in the research process in order to gain knowledge of the field. This review was based on articles found in the newspaper clipping archive at CAN library in Stockholm, and consisted of reviewing pieces under the subject headings, "alcohol policy", "debate", "EU" and "EG".

CHAPTER 2

Formations in the Swedish Alcohol Discourse[1]

This chapter is presented as a backdrop for the analyses that follow in *Chapters 3, 4 and 5,* and is intended primarily for readers unfamiliar with the Swedish case of alcohol. The content is historical, but this history differs from the official alcohol history presented in public reports and referred to in research, since I will be looking for discontinuities in the how the problem has been perceived rather than continuities. My analytic focus is primarily concerned with the official discourse, as defined in *Chapter 1*, as well as the medical discourse, although I shall also touch upon definitions of the problem that were found in other sources of discourse.

Early Alcohol Discourse

An open field

Looking at the register from the Swedish parliament, one sees that there are few hints of legislation and proposals to deal with alcohol as a public or social problem.[2] It was not until the first decades of this century that the alcohol question was politicized and defined as an object for public policy (see also

[1] The background information presented in this chapter is based on both primary and secondary sources. Secondary sources included socio-historical analyses of the Swedish alcohol history or parts of this history such as Abrahamson (1989), Bruun & Frånberg (1985), Elmér (1983, 1993), Rothstein (1992), Johansson (1995, 1997), Rosenqvist (1987), and Stenius (1996). Primary sources included govenrment reports and propositions; see *Appendix I* for a more complete listing. I am aware that by using secondary sources to develop the story in this chapter I am deviating from my use of texts in the remainder of the dissertation. In this chapter I borrow from Swedish research, in order to present this background, although in some cases I draw some conclusions that the authors themselves might not. In the remainder of the dissertation Swedish research is not used as a secondary source, but as data.

[2] As a means of verifying that all propositions and government documents were included in the analysis, I reviewed the Riksdagsregister (Register for Parliamentary actions) for the years 1900–1996.

Johansson 1997).[3] Earlier attempts to politicize the question were made by temperance societies[4], among others, but the vast majority of legislation concerned alcohol as a commercial good and focused consequently on taxation and importation of spirits; taxes were aimed at the producers, not the consumers. This was more in the interest of building up the state coffers than to steer consumer behavior.

One exception to the lack of public measures to deal with alcohol and alcohol problems, concerns the spread of information on the risks of alcohol. As early as 1844, a political debate concerning public funds for the spread of informational materials on alcohol's negative effects placed alcohol issues on the public agenda. Funds were allocated to temperance societies and their campaigns (e.g. to *Svenska nykterhetssällskapet*) for this purpose (Rothstein 1992: p. 138). As part of this endeavor, the *Centralförbundet för nykterhetsundervisning bland ungdomen*, CFN (Central association for temperance education among youths) was established by the temperance community. The work of this organization took up issues that were discussed among society, but were not incorporated into a publicly organized (i.e. state-administered or directed) solution to alcohol problems.

Despite this early absence of official legislation, and a structured policy arena around alcohol, by 1920 the state was clearly involved in intervening in alcohol issues in order to meet the claims of various groups, and an administrative system was in place. Before this, the nature of state intervention was not clear cut from the outset, but debate took place during these first decades concerning how the problem should be defined, by whom, and to which types of institutions it would be linked.

The Threat and Causes of Intoxicated Behavior

To grasp the significance of latter definitions of the drinker, and to understand what it is they have in common, it is important to first take a few steps back, and discuss even earlier definitions of alcohol-related behavior as these views continued to appear in different ways. From approximately the middle ages to the turn of the century one can detect references to "the drinker's" behavior as "immoral, caused by the devil, and worthy of a place in Hell" (Elmér 1993: p. 4–5).[5] Inebriation that was experienced as problematic was something mystical, a possession by the devil and evil forces, the result of an inertia outside

[3] It would be appropriate to state that alcohol was defined as a social problem prior to this century. It was regarded as problematic by different groups of people, among others temperance societies, and was dealt with in various circles, including labor groups. However, this strategy is different than that adopted after 1900 when public institutions are regarded as appropriate instruments for dealing with 'drinkers', and an 'official' discourse on alcohol troubles emerges.

[4] Before the turn of the century, the temperance societies were not concerned with absolutism. Their work was largely focused on spirits drinking, a practice of the lower classes.

[5] This formulation of the subject is likely a common one among pre-modern discourses on alcohol troubles. Sprode 1997, for example, detects similar formulations of the drinker in Germany during the same period.

the confines of society. The drinker himself could be culpable if he had been weak to temptation. Consequently, 'drinkers' were not regarded as potential subjects of reformation, and attempts were not made to control such behavior. Rather, 'drinkers' were excluded in various ways from society, and confined, in much the same manner as criminals or the insane. Commonly, they were isolated in asylums, where they could not be a burden to others, or threaten public safety and order. As such, solutions at this time aligned alcohol problems more closely with criminality and insanity, than those suffering from cancer (as discourse would later suggest).

Not all consumption constituted 'drinking'. Quite the contrary. As Elmér (1993) points out, alcohol consumption in regular doses was considered healthy, and even important for carrying out heavy physical labor. Children were often given daily doses of spirits along with their morning bread. The problem was not in the bottle, so-to-speak, but in the man.

The term 'drinking' was applied to describe the actions of the deviant drinker, as something distinct from 'normal' practices of ingesting alcohol. As in the United States, the use of the label imparted a moral judgment upon the individual who could not resist the 'love of liquor' (cf. Levine 1978). This terminology and type of statement is evident in legal texts as late as 1909, by which the term used to distinguish the group of perpetrators is "drinkers" and other language such as "drinking" is used.[6] Even later, the moral aura surrounding 'drinkers' is evident in the first law on the treatment of alcoholics presented in 1913 (see below). However, after 1912 these terms began to be replaced by "alcoholics" and "alcoholism" in various contexts, although the moral impact of the former terms continued to proliferate. The emergence of the new terms paralleled a trend towards distinguishing this group of persons as a more specific object of concern (i.e. not just another form of insanity).

Formation 1: Poison or Person?

The Poison of Alcohol

As in many western countries, an active temperance movement sought to define alcohol conditions during the latter half of the nineteenth century and into the twentieth. In the Nordic countries[7], the temperance movement played an important role as one of the forces shaping society during the pre-welfare state discourses early this century, and providing a vision for the good society (see

[6] See for example: 1903 A.K. n:r 67; 1903 Prop. 1:8,293,294; 1904 A.K. n:r 87; Prop. 1:6,300,302; 1905 A.K. n:r 155; 1905 Prop. 1:6, 230,231; 1906 A.K. n:r 93; 1907 n:r 15, A.K. n:r 140; 1908 Prop. 1:6, 146, 152, 155; 1908 A.K. n:r 91; 1909 A.K. n:r 154; A.K. n:r 5.

[7] The Nordic countries—Sweden, Denmark, Finland, Norway and Iceland—are generally viewed as sharing a closely intertwined cultural and historical heritage. With the exception of Denmark, they have also shared similar institutional solutions to alcohol problems, which have focused on universal measures as opposed to strictly dealing with alcoholism or alcohol abuse.

e.g. Olsson 1990, Reuter and Tigerstedt 1992). As one of three major movements at the turn of the century[8], absolutists succeeded in linking a vision of an alcohol-free society with the emerging discourse on democracy. As such, temperance constituted one of the key elements and symbols of a collective vision of the 'good life' (Sulkunen 1991).[9]

As one of the first organized collectives, it comes as no surprise that temperance activists were among the first to present a definition of the temperance problem and propose solutions to it. The most devout and absolutist members of the temperance movement defined alcohol as a poison. Accordingly, it was the beverage itself that was the causal agent in relation to the problem, and not the man. One of the consequences of this definition was that teetotalers did not distinguish between moderate drinking and problematic drinking, or good and bad drinking. As a poison, alcohol consumption was dangerous even in small doses. In her analyses of the literature produced by the early temperance movement, IOGT, Kerstin Rydbeck (1995) notes, for example, that according to teetotalers "Moderate drinking was unthinkable, as all who tasted alcohol became shortly thereafter slaves to a dependence that was impossible to break free from." (p. 275).

But alcohol was not simply frightening because it could poison the body. What was more threatening was that alcohol took hold of the drinker and lured him into uncontrollable consumption; and once one had been captured by "King Alcohol", there was no escape according to this interpretive frame. It was said that alcohol's stronghold could not be overcome with merely one's own will; nor with solidarity and support from others. The alcohol 'thirst' was a mystical force, and one's freedom from it was also a mystical process, that often involved the divine intervention of God. [10]

In addition to destroying the will of the drinker, alcohol was also a threat to society. Drinking was described as leading to many forms of misery including poverty, crime and illnesses or malnutrition for the 'drinker' and his family (Rydbeck 1995; p. 277).[11] This description fit well with the broader discourse

[8] The Labor Movement, which became institutionalized as the SAP, and the Free Church Movement were the two other forces at this time. For a discussion of Swedish social movements and the evolving welfare state, see Lundqvist (1977); Olsson 1990 also discusses the role of temperance and the other two movements in the evolving welfare discourse. In Olsson's work the links between these movements is very clear. Some of the most active members of public debate on social life were members of the temperance movement.

[9] Eriksen (1988) points out that temperance was not only related to the notion of refraining from alcohol consumption, but was a more general modern project or way of life; it was an ideology that emerged in different cultural contexts, in part related to the religious form of Christianity adopted.

[10] As Rydbeck also points out, the early temperance movement did not function as today's Alcoholics Anonymous or 'Links' (länkarna), as a place to which problem drinkers could turn. Rather, temperance groups were sought out by those who had already managed to embark upon a 'sober' life. The organization was more commonly regarded as a means of avoiding poor company and the risk of falling into the trap (again).

[11] This definition is not so very different from how the alcohol problem is described today (Abrahamson 1989). Both then, and now, various social ills and problems were viewed as a consequence of alcohol consumption.

on poverty and social ills that was taking place at the time (ibid.). This discourse was framed foremost according to social Darwinism, and argued for a 'race hygiene'. In this sense, the discourse built on broader interpretive schemes at the time that emphasized the 'inheritance' of poverty and social ills between generations (Johannisson 1993: p. 65). Temperance organizers incorporated these ideas into their own discourse on the social ill of alcohol, noting that, "Children of alcohol abusers were regarded as running a many times larger risk than other children for contracting different illnesses, such as epilepsy, and a predisposition for tuberculosis." (Rydbeck 1995: p. 278).

The solution proposed by temperance supporters was in line with their definition of the problem as poison. Since even one drop was dangerous, nothing short of a full prohibition was an acceptable solution. Although the movement was constituted by different organizations, each with its more specific ideology, participants across the movement agreed upon the need for prohibition as a solution to achieving their goal of an alcohol-free society. Temperance members organized a private referendum in 1909 following a major strike. During the strike alcohol was prohibited for several days, and as a result, the incidence of public intoxication saw a dramatic drop. This was used by the movement as evidence of both the nature of the problem as poison, and the potential of prohibiting alcohol as a solution. In 1909 enough signatures were gained, and the temperance commission found it useful to hold a public referendum on the question of prohibition in 1922.

Extensive campaigning, posters, and informational materials were produced by both sides.[12] Despite a close run, prohibition supporters lost and an alternative system was put in place. As I shall narrate below, this alternative system was supported by the medical community and others who argued that there was a problem, but that it was not one of poison. Their position was supported through an alternate set of facts and experts, and ultimately led to a very different solution to the problem.

Emergence of an Official Discourse on Temperance

Certainly there had been a legislative discourse during the 1800s that dealt with regulation of the malt-drinks industry and spirits production. However, it was not until the 1900s that legislation began to deal specifically with the problem of drinking as an object of regulation, and the persons who consumed alcohol as targets of such regulation. Hence, one of the important discursive trends, or initial tasks, that can be detected during the early decades of this century is an attempt to define the temperance issue or question as something distinct from other categories of social problems and concerns.

[12] As Johansson (1995) states, the mediation of the issue was very modern in its use of printed materials, posters, and other mediums to spread the message. The campaigns waged by both sides are impressive even by today's standards.

Initially, the temperance issue was raised in the context of poor relief and related legislation. A specific group within the poor, 'drinkers', were regarded as consuming a large proportion of available funds. Leaders of the various municipalities met at a conference in 1906 to discuss the 'burden' of drinkers on their local budgets, among other issues (Rosenqvist 1985, Elmér 1993). Following an appeal to the government by this group in 1907, a commission was established to investigate the issue. What emerged here was an attempt to define this condition as something distinct from other forms of poverty. The group of 'drinkers' constituted a unique category that in turn demanded a unique set of measures and practices. This operated towards the construction of a new object of reform, and a 'new' category of individuals requiring assistance, with appropriate administrative practices and professionals. Concurrently, it contributed to a more strict boundary around objects of regulation for social assistance programs.

The question of a new temperance law was dealt with in the context of the parliamentary committee for poor law, and resulted in the first law for the treatment of alcoholics in 1913 (*Lag om behandling av alkoholister* 1913). As can be detected in the following excerpt, the poor relief authorities regarded such drinkers as a burden, and an unnecessary one:

> If it is found that a person is prone to drinking and as such is a danger to another person's personal safety or own life, or leaves his wife or children, whom he is responsible for supporting, without means or deserts them entirely, or is a burden to the poor relief authorities or his family, then according to the statutes of this law, he shall be taken into the care of the public authorities to be treated for alcoholism (1913 *Lag om behandling av alkoholister, paragraph 1*).

Those "prone to drinking" were a burden both with respect to their own destitute situation, but also because they left their wives and families in financial ruin who became cases for the poor relief authorities.

One of the divisions drawn up in this first law, and which is repeated in a revision of the law in 1931 (Kungl. Maj:ts proposition nr 164), is the potential danger of drinkers to their families and to society. This is also detected in the excerpt above, which refers to a person who is "prone to drinking" and "as such is a danger to another person's personal safety". Again, this formulation of the problem contributed to cordoning it off from other social assistance concerns. The difficulty with this class of persons was not that they were in need of financial help, but that they were a threat to public safety (see also discussion in SOU 1948:23, pp. 57–58). In fact, it appears that the law assumed that 'drinkers' were capable workers, who should not be in need of assistance; that is, they were not worthy of assistance. Becoming a "burden to the poor relief authorities" did not warrant assistance, but provided grounds for being taken into compulsory care.

This first division, or principle for distributing the problem, constructed two categories of drinkers, those that were 'dangerous' and those that were not or who were less dangerous. A second division that can be detected is that between 'drinkers' who admitted to their problem and submitted themselves to treatment, or who could be reckoned with such that they recognized the issue for themselves; and those who did not admit to their condition. For example, the committee emphasized that it was important to provide the necessary legal framework so that 'drinkers' could be taken into compulsory care. However, this was not to take place until all 'help' measures had been exhausted. Such measures included, encouraging an alcoholic to join a temperance organization, securing a job for the drinker, persuading him to relocate or change jobs, preventing him from purchasing alcohol, or encouraging him to seek voluntary admittance to an alcoholic facility (pp. 26–28). Thus, the distinction between types of drinkers was related to a distinction in reform measures.

Responsibility and authority for identifying problem drinkers demonstrates an interesting coalition between the state, the church and medicine. Authority for administering solutions and professional intervention was not delegated to poor relief committees, but to clergyman and medical advisors who were identified as the gatekeepers to rehabilitation. Families and loved ones of the drinker could also notify the authorities and request intervention, but this was to be determined in counsel with the clergy or medical officer.

In addition, although the laws from 1913 and 1930 emphasized the need to first utilize all means available to convince the problem drinker to voluntarily submit to treatment, a large space was reserved for those dangerous and unreasonable alcoholics who had to be taken into treatment through compulsory means. The dispersion of problem drinkers between dangerous and non-dangerous provided a space for police authorities to intervene. In the case of dangerous drinkers, who it appears also rejected treatment, the usual support from a doctor and clergyman could be foregone, and the police could intervene immediately. Medical and spiritual analysis could be provided at a later date (pp. 26–28).

Medical Discourse on Alcoholism

The notion that the 'drinker' was a burden, and hence responsible for his condition, was even maintained in the medical community at the time which was involved in the emerging debates around the temperance question. In response to the concerns raised by the poor relief committee and the claims of the temperance movement, the medical community established a working committee of its own in 1908. Its deliberations addressed the question of alcoholism, and considered possible solutions. The texts produced by the medical society were largely positive towards the proposal of the Governmental Committee on Poor Relief (Rosenqvist 1987). Compulsory treatment was regarded as necessary, although this was not so much with respect to the danger of the alcoholic, but as a possible deterrent of alcohol abuse by others. This seems to underscore the notion that heavy consumption was a willful act, rather than a compulsive one.

Moreover, it identifies the social community as a group from which others could be discouraged or encouraged to behave in a similar fashion.

As part of its contemplation, the committee also addressed the claim of teetotalers that alcohol brought forth a medical reaction in the body as a poison (see also Rothstein 1992: p. 136). This can be described as an attempt by non-medical experts to 'medicalize' the problem. Interestingly, the medical community did indeed assert authority on this question. It did so, however, by way of arguing that the effects of alcohol were *not* medically dangerous and declared that the propositions of the temperance community could not be supported by medical science.[13]

In addition to declaring that alcohol was not a poison, the committee considered the question of whether alcoholism was a disease, particularly a chronic disease. Interestingly, the committee came to a very different conclusion than their predecessors in medicine (see *Chapter 3*).[14] With respect to alcoholism, they stated in their lengthy report, *Alkoholen och Samhället* (1912) that:

> Alcoholism, which is not a disease, is a minor problem compared to alcohol abuse in general. Most abusers are not real alcoholics, but their abuse is an expression of bad or crude habits or customs. Even the worst alcoholics, those who are physically dependent on the drug, can overcome their need in a couple of sober days. Consequently, there are different forms of abuse which should be fought against by different, mostly non-medical means, such as advice, guidance, and supervision, and short stays in non-medical institutions. Initially, hospital care can sometimes be advocated. (Alkoholen och Samhället 1912; as translated and cited in Rosenqvist 1987: p. 511).

While a chronic condition related to alcohol consumption was not entirely rejected, it was described as a very rare incident. What concerned the society was a condition referred to as *alcohol abuse*. This condition, it was argued, was much more widespread and serious than the potential chronic illness of alcoholism.

A second interesting point that is illustrated in the above excerpt, concerns the causal dimension of the problem. As I shall illustrate in *Chapter 3*, latter-day medical professionals would relate alcohol abuse to other diseases such as tuberculosis and asthma, and regard the drinker as a victim. However, the medical society at this time regarded alcoholism as the result of "bad or crude habits or custom". In Bratt's words, the drinker was someone who drank too much and was of "weak character" (Nycander 1967: p. 122). As such, one could not regard the drinker as a patient or victim, but as a deviant who could

[13] I think we see here a shift taking place in assumptions concerning the distribution of authority more generally in Swedish society. Older hierarchies of knowledge and ways of knowing were being replaced by new hierarchies that placed science at the forefront. In the example of the medical community here, the physicians assumed the authority to define what was and was not poison, and hence assumed that poison was a part of their domain of objects to study.

[14] From approximately the mid 18th century through the middle of the 19th century a growing interest in a medical definition of 'drinking' can be detected. Among others, Magnus Huss coined the term alcoholismus chronicus, and defined alcoholism as a chronic illness. This point will be further discussed in *Chapter 3*.

in fact avoid his situation with better discipline. Bad habits were not strictly of consequence for the individual, but threatened society as the 'drinker' became dangerous. Hence, the medical community regarded alcohol issues as a "social phenomenon" and problem and not a medical question (see also Nycander 1967: p. 48).

While compulsory treatment was regarded as necessary, the medical society also proposed measures to "reduce the risks of injustice and unnecessary infringement on individual freedom". Taking their inspiration from already existing local health boards and boards on poor relief (Rosenqvist 1987: p. 512), they argued that temperance boards should be established in the local municipalities, and these should:

> be equipped with full-time employees and headed by physicians aided by other trained personnel. These boards, composed of lay persons, would represent the best local knowledge and wisdom on alcohol matters. Ideally the boards would not deal with alcoholics, but also general alcohol political matters on the local level (English quote from Rosenqvist 1987: p. 511).

A distribution of authority was proposed that involved several different groups. Although the society did not regard alcoholism as a medical condition, they did proscribe a role for medicine in dealing with it, as leaders within these temperance boards. At the same time, they did not assume full authority on the question. Boards were to include lay people who were familiar with the local environment. Moreover, treatment would be provided in various forms of non-medical institutions (sometimes run be temperance societies), and the temperance boards would consist of lay people and trained personnel.

Perhaps this proposed division of labor can also be detected in the fact that the medical community argued that the treatment of alcoholics should be looked upon as only one link in a chain of more general "individually oriented alcohol measures" (Rosenqvist 1987). The most outspoken among the medical community was the activist Ivan Bratt, who is today known as the father of the Swedish monopoly system. In a series of articles in the news media, in brochures and as a participant on the temperance commission that was appointed (see below), he argued for a more encompassing system of alcohol measures that aimed at individual control.[15] His suggestions, and those of the medical society, linked the treatment developed by the poor law committee to other public measures to deal with alcohol.

In particular, Bratt and the medical association argued for the introduction of an 'alcohol board' with two bureaus in each municipality. The first bureau, as largely outlined above, was concerned with those 'drinkers' who could not control their consumption, or who became a burden to the public. Such an authority would provide advice, but would largely operate as a board that

[15] Bratt's most cited works are "Kan nykterhetsfrågan lösas utan totalförbud?" from 1909 (Can the temperance question be solved without a prohibition?) and "Nykterhetspolitiska utvecklingslinjer" from 1911 (Development trends in temperance policy).

would receive complaints about drinkers and investigate whether such persons should be brought into custody and sent to an 'improvement facility' (förbättringsanstalt). At the improvement facility the individual 'drinker' would be taught discipline and formed as a useful citizen once again.

The second bureau, in cooperation with the first, would operate as a monopoly for the sale of spirits. This would accomplish two tasks. First, it would be possible to monitor 'drinkers' and, if necessary, refuse them service. Moreover, the local store could monitor its patrons, and identify potential 'drinkers' for the first bureau.[16] This is further described below.

Further Institutionalization of an Official Discourse on Alcohol

An official discourse on temperance (later alcohol) questions also became more clear with the appointment of a temperance committee in 1911, which presented its final report in 1920. Although the poor relief committee was considering treatment for alcoholism and compulsory incarceration at the same time, the establishment of a distinct committee to consider alcohol questions provided a further move towards the institutionalization of a distinct policy arena and discourse. Ivan Bratt was one of the more influential and well-known members of the committee, and the ideas and concepts he had begun to develop within the medical society were also expressed in this arena.

With the exception of temperance supporters, alcohol consumption was regarded as legitimate. Yet, 'drinking' was problematic. As Bruun has noted, the question for the temperance commission at this point in time was not whether alcohol consumption would be controlled, but how this would be accomplished (Bruun 1985: p. 87). Local monopolies and the registration of individual drinkers had been practiced in both Gothenburg and Stockholm. Local solutions to the problem of monitoring patrons had been resolved and different administrators vied to have their solution adopted as the 'official' practice.

What eventually emerged as the second bureau, was a combination ration and registration system known as the *motbok* system, which was instituted nationally in 1916. This involved limiting the amount of alcohol consumed by individuals and registering and monitoring all purchases. The maximum ration was determined centrally, but each independent shop was left the task of determining whether a person would receive a ration, and if so, in what amount. Individuals applied for the *motbok*, a small book that entitled him or her to purchase alcohol at the local monopoly. Earning this privilege often involved the completion of a lengthy application form that sought to collate information regarding the individual's private life, occupation and moral character (Bruun 1985).

[16] For a thorough discussion of the temperance boards, their role, and practices, see Rosenqvist (1985).

Formation 2: From Individual Control to Individual Responsibility

Questioning the Solution

The Bratt System, as outlined above, dominated the alcohol arena as a solution for nearly three decades. However, criticism emerged during the 1940s, and was aimed primarily at the rationing and registration system. This critique came from two different directions. First, temperance organizations were against the Bratt system and acted to bring an end to it (Uusitalo 1997). The movement introduced the concept of 'suggestion theory'. They argued that despite the administrative units of Bratt's system, the problem had not been solved. A fatal flaw in the system was that it legitimized alcohol consumption. Many more persons than expected had obtained a *motbok*; and, by introducing 'appropriate' levels of consumption, the rationing system actually encouraged individuals to drink more than they normally would. In this way the system "suggested" that people should drink 4 liters of spirits per month, per person (Nycander 1967: p. 124). While temperance organizations had originally regarded the system as a step towards a prohibition, it was clear that this was not the case, and that the problem remained.[17]

At the other end of the spectrum, the alternative critique pointed out that alcoholics, at whom the system was aimed, were still drinking large quantities of alcohol by purchasing it on the black market. This was achieved through bootlegging, among other means. Moreover, the system not only did not achieve its intended goal, but in the process it impinged upon the freedom of those individuals who were not the target of the system (Nycander 1967). In local newspapers and in other public arenas the bureaucracy of the *motbok* system was criticized for invading individual integrity. It was thus argued that the system should be abolished, and responsible persons should be allowed to drink and purchase alcohol. This position demanded 'freedom under personal responsibility' (frihet under ansvar) (Elmér 1983).

Also at this time, the medical discourse had increasingly moved towards adopting a disease-model for describing alcohol issues. This model suggested that alcohol was problematic for a group of individuals, only. Individuals in this group had a propensity to develop alcoholism that was independent of their free will to stop drinking. While this model did not strike directly at the former solution complex, it neither provided scientific support for the necessity of maintaining the system. This discourse is the object of analysis in *Chapter 3.*

In response to the growing debate, the government assigned a temperance commission in 1944 to evaluate the effects of the motbok system, and review

[17] Temperance members later came to criticize their own actions and support for breaking up the motbok system. Consumption drastically increased, and it is held that one of the groups to be most affected were those with more advanced drinking problems (Nycander 1967).

possible alternatives. This committee eventually suggested that the rationing system be discontinued, and in October of 1955 in an event now referred to as the "October Revolution", Swedish citizens could purchase as many bottles of alcohol as they pleased, although the state monopoly for the retail sale of alcohol remained in tact.

Towards a 'New' Surveillance System

Despite a more 'liberal' approach to alcohol distribution, some alcohol consumers continued to be regarded as problematic and in need of regulation. Given the parameters of this formation of the discourse, administrators appear to have adopted innovative solutions that sought to combine the new principles of sobriety policy with an interest in preventing unwanted drinking behavior. In a first step, alcohol retail shops were incorporated into a national retail monopoly for the sale of alcohol, *Systembolaget.* A second company was also established to act *as* the producer, importer, and exporter of wine and spirits. As a second component to this reconstruction, the *motbok* was abolished, and with it the rationing system. Moreover, individuals were no longer confined to making their purchases at their local shops, but they could purchase alcohol at any one of the new national retail stores. These moves were viewed as removing the individualized application of rules, which were viewed as defining personal integrity (Ragnarsson 1993).

At the same time more 'liberal' measures appeared to be imposed, one of the consequences of this institutional innovation was the ability to monitor individuals across a much broader space. The need to identify 'problem drinkers', now referred to as 'alcoholics', was still a major concern. Thus, the black lists that had been introduced under the new system's predecessor, and used to list those who were not allowed to purchase alcohol, were maintained. However, these lists now covered a much larger district, and increasingly so throughout the 1950s to 1970s (Ragnarsson 1993). The fact that this registration practice was maintained led to some interesting innovations in order to enforce the aims of the prohibition list (i.e. to ensure that those listed were not able to purchase alcohol). [18]

[18] An example of such a solution concerns the red light era, which is described by Ragnarsson (1993) in his history of the *Systembolag*. Although the 1944 commission and advisory committees following this provided guidelines for checking identification at the retail monopoly, it was soon discovered that personnel were not as conscientious as they were expected to be. One solution to this was the installation of a red lamp at each cash register, which would periodically light up as an indication that the customer's identification should be presented. The supervisor at each *Systembolag* store could control the rate at which each red light would go off. The random nature of the system was viewed as having removed the 'personal' indignation that was felt when a patron was pointed out as a potential member of the black list. It also eased the embarrassment of *Systembolag* staff, when asking to see identification.

Towards Individual Illness

Before the *motbok* system was abolished, an alcoholic treatment commission was appointed. In its report from 1948 (SOU 1948:23), the commission pointed out that one of the tensions in previous discussions of treatment laws was the extent to which one should consider society's interests in treating the alcoholic, or the alcoholic's own needs.[19] In a different twist on the question, the final report argued that the answer to this question depended upon why persons abused alcohol. Once again, the causes of alcoholism were on the agenda, and this time, what was considered was whether alcoholism was a disease or a bad habit. If alcoholics were simply deviant individuals, by which the causal story concerned personal choice to threaten society, then it was the protection of society that should be given the greatest weight. If, however, it could be successfully argued that the cause of alcoholism was beyond the control of the individual, then it was his interests that should be considered above all else.

As I shall further illustrate in *Chapter 3*, there was at this time a growing momentum among the medical community and the emerging alcoholics anonymous and links movement, to define alcohol abusers as sick or abnormal people. This seems to have been recognized by the commission, as one of the means of investigating this was to ask an expert in social psychiatry (Dr. Åmark) to examine a number of clients at a treatment facility. Dr. Åmark determined that the vast majority of them had physical deformities or abnormalities, that indicated that their condition should also be considered a medical phenomenon.[20]

What might be viewed as a further medicalization of the problem was demonstrated since the law adopted at this time suggested increased medical involvement in the 'treatment' of those who were already suffering from the condition of alcoholism (see also Elmér 1993, Abrahamson 1989). This was also indicated through the commission's move to change the name of the former 'alcoholic law' to 'temperance care law'. However, despite an increased interest in medical knowledge and authority in response to alcoholism, the commission sought a broader definition of the problem. For example, the aim of policy was to:

> Society's efforts to fight alcohol abuse should aim to affect both the states of illness and abnormality as well as the environmental factors that lead to or foster alcohol abuse (p. 53).

This excerpt illustrates that although the commission determined that the "suggestion theory" espoused by temperance organizations was without founding,

---

[19] This same concern is expressed today as well. However, it is found in the debates surrounding compulsory treatment. The individual's interest in 'getting better' is often not recognized by the patient himself, and it is argued that the state should step in and assist in such cases.

[20] Interestingly, Åmark took part in constructing the statement of the medical society in 1912, whereby the chronic disease of alcoholism was refuted. By this time, however, he was framing the issue as a medical phenomenon.

it was careful not to take a particular stance on the actual causes of alcoholism. This official stance, provided a space to discuss environmental factors in yet a 'new' way, as the discourse was transformed once again.

Formation 3: Alcoholism as Symptom

Questioning the Cause

As argued above, there was a growing regard of alcoholism as a disease, or medical condition throughout the 1940s and 1950s, and in turn, medical authority gained ground as an arena for defining the problem and producing knowledge about alcoholism. It was not long, however, before this definition was challenged. The protest came from social activists and the growing number of social scientists. As social scientific fields of research became more firmly institutionalized, alternative theories for understanding the alcohol problem (as well as other social problems) emerged. These theories can be traced to Sociology and Social Work in particular.

Although there were several types of empirical problems and theories, the theory with the most impact was probably, the "symptom theory". This theory posited that alcoholism was a symptom of other social, economic and political problems, not the problem itself (Elmér 1983). Consequently, alcoholics were not sick individuals or persons who suffered from an allergy or inherited trait. Rather, they were people who tended to be isolated from social and interpersonal networks. This dis-integration from a social network was the result of the current capitalist system, and inappropriate political and economic policies to offset these negative impacts. Hence, alcoholism was not a medical phenomenon, but a political or structural phenomenon.

This definition is not found distinctly in the official discourse, although it did have an impact on this. However, it was adopted by a number of groups involved in the discourse on alcohol. For example, Verdandi, which had acted as a temperance organization for members of the labor unions adopted this perspective. During the 1960s, Verdandi argued that an alcohol-free society was no longer its goal, and abstention from alcohol was no longer a prerequisite for membership. Rather, a commitment to providing support and a social network for those who were isolated was emphasized as recruitment criteria.[21]

This line of thinking was also legitimized in the leadership of the Social Democratic Party during the 1960s and 1970s (Strömbeck 1979: p. 13). Even the youth organization of the Social Democratic Party adopted a new policy line on alcohol in 1966, arguing that over the long run alcohol sales could take place under the same conditions as other goods; and, advertisements for alco-

[21] Verdandi has maintained this position today, despite shifts in the definition of the problem within the official discourse. This position can be contrasted with that of the other temperance organizations in Sweden that fully support the public health definition of the alcohol problem, and have adopted this within their organizational descriptions (Sutton & Olsson Hort 1996).

hol products should be allowed once again (Strömbeck 1973: p. 98). Moreover, both political organizations, like Verdandi, shifted their slogans from a demand for "an alcohol-free society" to a "society free from the risk of alcoholism", suggesting that the normative aspect of the problem was to rid society of the conditions that gave rise to alcohol problems, and not to control those who fell victim to the system (see also Arvidsson 1984).

There are two important consequences of this definition. The first concerns the distribution of authority. Framed as a socio-structural problem, rather than a medical question, the alcohol problem did not constitute an object of medical expertise, but became the object of political and social discourses. This meant that the medical community was granted a smaller playing field as an authoritative source. Additionally, the 'new' professional groups such as social workers, sociologists, psychologists and others assumed a more prominent position in solving the problem and helping unfortunate alcoholics (Elmér 1983, Abrahamson 1989). In particular, the growing core of professional social workers, who had previously consisted of voluntary and administrative workers, was critical of what they regarded as the 'repressive nature' of compulsory care. As Abrahamson has argued, social workers did not want to be associated with "the long arm of a repressive society, and contribute to a stigmatizing and socially rejecting process" (1989: p. 44). This organization of authority was further supported through the increasing visibility of social science discourse on alcohol issues for society, and in particular the rise of social work as an academic field that could intervene in social issues with the help of the growing public sector.[22]

In addition to questioning the cause, the 'socialization' of alcohol issues also opened up a space for posing different types of questions. For example, as pointed out above, sociologists took a greater interest in alcohol issues during the 1960s. It is not strange, then, that the structural-functional orientation of sociology at the time is seen reflected in approaches to describing alcohol issues in society. Moreover, the empirical interests of sociology during its period of institutionalization are also detected. For example, one of its major areas of interest was the sociology of work (Fridjonsdottir 1991: p. 258), and throughout the 1960s an interest in stress at the workplace in relation to alcoholism was formed as an object of scientific investigation.

In the context of what Svante Nycander (1967) has termed the "society of acceptance", several public commissions related to alcohol questions were convened. The first commission was established in 1965, and its members were asked to analyze alcohol policy since the most recent changes in 1954, when the last temperance commission had presented its reports. Several points in relation to this commission are important to note. First, the commission's investigation took over ten years to conduct. A final report was not presented until 1974, at which time it was heavily debated. Second, at the time the commission

[22] Abrahamson also notes that the organization of social assistence itself was cited as contributing to alcoholism and adjustment problems (p. 45).

was instated, it was assumed that the policy proposals emerging from it would lead to a more liberal approach to alcohol policy: However, by the time it presented a final report, the discourse had become more restrictive again.

Finally, the commission was called the "Alcohol policy commission". This was the first time that social policy in this area was referred to in this way. Earlier, terms such as 'temperance policy' or 'sobriety policy' were used. Framing the work of the commission in this way indicated a shift in the focus or object of policy from sobriety—located in the individual—to alcohol once again. This is also supported in the commission's task which was defined as , to "treat all those questions that are of importance for alcohol and temperance policy". The object of concern was further profiled as its field of interest was limited in relation to several other commissions that were engaged in related questions at the time. A 1963 investigation of public drunkenness and punishment (fylleristraffutredningen) was being conducted, and likewise an investigation of treatment and care. Moreover, a social policy commission was assembled to provide a general analysis of social assistance programs and legislation. Hence, this commission came to deal with what it termed *alcohol policy,* which it defined as that segment of social policy that dealt with preventive measures, and which was directed at alcohol consumption. Alcohol policy was distinguished from temperance policy which was defined as a broader term that also included treatment and care concerns. In addition to the introduction of a new policy arena, spirits, wine, strong beer and beer alcoholic beverages were now assembled into one category of "alcoholic beverages". The term "intoxicating beverages", (rusdryck) was no longer used.

Although this dissertation is primarily concerned with the discourse on alcohol as a public threat, a brief discussion of the treatment commission will shed additional light on the importance of distinguishing between two alcohol-related questions at this time. The treatment commission was rather broad in its analysis of the work to be done in the field, and rather than defining tasks, it identified basic principles for guiding social work related to addiction treatment. Interestingly these linked treatment to broader social concepts at the time, including democracy, solidarity, security and equality (see also Abrahamson 1989: p. 45). Alcohol addiction was also linked to other forms of addiction, particularly drug addiction. These means of organizing alcohol issues moved alcoholism from its relation to individual moral capacity to a political issue that is greater than the individual. The move to link alcohol to narcotics also emphasized that the problem or cause, was not located in the beverage, but elsewhere.

Questioning the Solution

Several practices emerged during the 1960s that contributed to less restrictive control policies. Several liberal experiments were undertaken, both before and as part of the commission work. Second, there was also a move to improve the surveillance techniques where alcohol was sold in order to more easily identify those in 'need of assistance'. One of the first examples of more liberal policy took place in 1963, when the Swedish parliament voted to abolish a distribution tax on alcohol and dropped former price controls for alcohol sold in restaurants (Hamberg 1986). A more well-known shift in practice took place in 1965, the same year the APU was assembled. A medium-strength beer, *mellanöl*, was introduced, and allowed to be sold at grocery stores. It was also largely argued that other beers and wine would soon follow. One of the arguments for this attempt was that it would encourage individuals to consume weaker alcoholic beverages. This seems to point to a distinction between types of beverages. The early years of debauchery in Sweden were associated with spirits drinking, and this beverage also appears to have become associated with abuse. Shifting consumption to the medium beer and to wine would encourage more moderate drinking practices, it was argued. This same logic and argument was realized in a shift in the taxation structure for alcoholic beverages. The tax on wines and beers was lowered during the 1970s. Moreover, the APU allowed strong beer to be sold in a limited number of grocery stores within two Swedish counties. Originally the commission had designated a 13 month trial period, but after public opinion and media attention raised concerns around increased drinking by young people and abuse by others the experiment was called off six months early.

During the 1960s it was assumed that through solving the structural problems alcohol problems would thereby be solved. By ridding society of those mechanisms by which individuals become isolated, and building stronger social networks throughout society, these individuals would no longer need to turn to alcohol to escape their problems (Elmér 1983). Such liberal measures can be explained by the fact that the mechanisms behind the problem were not located in the individual, and hence the problem would neither be regulated through measures directed at drinkers.

During the latter half of the 1970s and into the 1980s, the official discourse on alcohol turned once again towards arguments for more restrictive measures. These were justified as a means of protecting public health. The way in which alcohol was problematized in this formation forms a central point for my work in the forthcoming chapters.

CHAPTER 3

The Alcohol Problem in Medical Discourse

From Alcoholism to Public Health

In *Chapter 2* I introduced the reader to a number of different definitions of alcohol issues as a social problem that can be detected in contemporary Swedish history. In this chapter I want to hone in on two examples of definitions and how these have been shaped within one specific source of discourse, medicine. Methodologically, I extract two discursive formations in medicine from the broader social context in order to compare and contrast them. The purpose of comparing and analyzing the two formations, referred to as the *Alcoholism Formation* and the *Public Health Formation,* is twofold. First, I am interested in showing empirically the constitutive elements of the two definitions and the way in which these elements constituted objects for investigation. Second, I want to explore the extent to which the problem emerges as a social problem in medical discourse, rather than a strictly medical phenomenon. In order to investigate the latter, I shall also consider the relationship between medical and official discourse by way of identifying events that indicate the institutionalization of medical discourse and solutions in the official discourse. As a point of departure for these analyses, I present a brief genealogical context for medical discourse on alcohol.

Medical Expertise and the Swedish Alcohol Discourse

Although the discussion at hand concerns the very recent history of the Swedish medical discourse on alcohol, it should be kept in mind that regard for alcohol problems as 'medical' phenomena is not strictly a twentieth century phenomenon. If one were to conduct a full genealogy of medical knowledge on alcohol problems, or alcohol consumption as an object for investigation and research, such a project would extend much farther back in time. This is demonstrated by the growing historical and socio-historical work aimed at constructing the stories of medical knowledge and its relation to alcohol studies in other western countries (See e.g. Berridge 1996, Conrad & Schneider 1980,

Fahrenkrug 1991, Levine 1978, Mäkelä et al. 1981, Spournia 1990, Spode 1993).[1]

In Sweden, one of the earliest attempts to study alcohol and characterize its properties in relationship to the human body is found in the works of Carl von Linné who described spirits as, "a strong poison" in a 1748 almanac (cf. Elmér 1993).[2] Other biomedical attempts to deal with the problem included the German development of the so-called Schreiberian cure, a form of aversion therapy (Björ 1989).[3] This treatment was 'imported' to Sweden, by another important forerunner to the twentieth century debate surrounding alcoholism as disease, namely Magnus Huss[4]. Huss coined the term, "alcoholismus chronicus" which he defined as a the collective expression of a number of health problems related to the nerve , psychological, and motor systems. syndrome of the nervous system which resulted in behavioral changes and neurological complications (Björ 1988, p. 161).[5] The term was eventually adopted by later alcohol researchers both inside and outside the medical field, particularly after the adoption of the term by the World Health Organization during the 1950s. In Sweden, Huss's work on alcoholism led to the establishment of three different centers for treating the 'disease' towards the end of the 1800s and early 1900s, supported by temperance societies.[6]

---

[1] A list of sources for the Social History of Alcohol in English is presented by Jeffrey Verhey in a collection of pieces on drinking edited by Barrows and Room (1991). Among social constructionists studying alcohol and social problems a common argument has been that knowledge about the body and deviance has moved from a moral tone, whereby health and mental staiblity were linked to moral discourse, a to a more technocratic discourse that distinguished biology from morality. In general within social problems, it is pointed out that social problems have moved from being defined as moral problems, to legal issues, to medical issues. This is perhaps most fully developed by Conrad and Schneider (1980) but is also related to the welfare state by Manning (1985).

[2] The view that alcohol consumption led to a loss of control or loss of sanity is a much older notion than is often thought. Spode (1993, 1997) points out, for example, that there existed much classical knowledge from Greek and Roman views, e.g. Seneca is quoted as saying that, "Drunkenness is nothing but voluntary madness ...". This was 'rediscovered' during the Renaissance when it was referred to as "deliberate silliness" (Spode 1997: p. 3).

[3] The Schreiberian cure worked in the following way. A known 'drinker' was interned, often involuntarily, within an institute. During his stay, he was allowed to drink as much alcohol as he wished. Additionally, alcohol was mixed with all food and drink. Eventually just the smell of alcohol made the patient vomit, and hence he quit drinking (Elmér 1993). The effectiveness of this treatment was debatable. Although Huss argued for its benefits, others argued that the break in drinking pattern was only temporary and that the cure did not have a long-lasting effect (Björ 1989).

[4] For an extensive English discussion of Huss's work and contribution to alcohol studies, see Spournia (1990).

[5] Huss's work was recognized internationally. For example, Huss received an award by the French Academy of Science in 1854.

[6] These clinics were based on Huss's medical theories and therapies, but were coordinated and administered largely by temperance societies. This could be interpreted as another example of the distribution of authority surrounding the 'alcohol question'. Even at this early point in time, one can detect the 'social' aspect of solutions, whereby we do not find a single group in control of the question and solution. This is also supported by Stenius (1996) whose examination of treatment centers over time demonstrates that neither medical nor state agencies have monopolized the treatment arena. This can be compared with the United States, for example, where medical solutions and therapy largely competed for authority over providing care.

A characteristic of modern discourses on alcohol and other social problems has been a belief in the material-technological discourse of rationality, which placed scientific reason and progress at the forefront of identifying the problem and determining its related series (Sulkunen 1991: p. 211). In the Swedish case, the move in this direction can be detected in such practices as the Schreiberian cure, which was founded on the belief that the medical community could in fact intervene and 'treat' those prone to such drinking, and hence that nature and its effects could be conquered through the rational and enlightened intervention of medicine.[7] In addition to the authority of science in society, it has also been noted that in modern discourses on alcohol problems there is a recognition of the will as something distinct from desires. For example, Levine argues that Benjamin Rush's work in the United States during the mid 1700s referred to the "ardent spirits upon the human body", in which he argued that drunkenness was a "disease of the will" (Levine 1978, Cf. Schneider 1978: p. 362). This formulation indicated these objects as independent from one another (the former becoming debilitated by drink in some people).

Among the political discourse can be detected definitions of alcohol as a disease-like condition. For example, an extensive debate took place during the mid 1700s, within which the status of the condition as a disease, and hence the need for an introduction of hospitalization and treatment with government funds was discussed. The debate did not lead to a breakthrough for the disease concept in public discourse, as the parliamentary committee examining the proposal suggested that 'drinkers' should be considered under criminal legislation, rather than a specific policy area devoted to alcohol (Elmér 1993).[8] Again, the problems related to alcohol were regarded as an extension of deviant behavior in general, and not specifically due to alcohol. [9] Alcohol remained predominantly a moral and religious question and not a scientific endeavor during the last century. Indeed, the consumption of small doses of alcohol was generally regarded as a healthy practice, and 'spirits' were often prescribed as treatment for other ailments. It was heavy consumption that was regarded as problematic, and as a "burden that the individual had the ability to abstain from" (Elmér 1993, p. 5). As such, the causal story did not blame the alcohol, but rather the deviant 'nature' of an individual.

[7] This opinion was shared by the *Sundhets Kollegium* (the runner-up to today's Swedish National Board of Health and Welfare), which introduced experimental use of the cure within the military in the mid 1800s (Björ 1988). This points to an increasing regard for alcohol issues as collective concerns rather than individual concerns.

[8] It is intersting that at this point in time the alcohol question could not be disengaged from other social concerns. Later, as Stenius (1996) has noted, and later Tigerstedt (1998), alcohol policy could be characterized as occupying an arena of social policy that was more independent from broader social and welfare policy in Sweden and the other Nordic countries.

[9] This is interesting, because in a later discussion I shall be noting that the current discourse treats criminal activity and behavior as one potential consequence of alcohol consumption. Hence, according to the discourse described here, the deviant or criminal framework was primary, but in later formations of the discourse the alcohol framework was superordinate to the criminal frame.

A renewed interest and belief in science and its ability to logically intervene and treat problems, as well as a regard for the state and administrative practices as a means of directing such endeavors emerged around the turn of the century in Sweden. Among other factors this shift was supported by the process of industrialization and urbanization, which hastened the 'discovery' of a number of social conditions that came to be regarded as public problems and the object of legislation to deal with them.[10] An important aspect of the politicization of public and alcohol issues and the role of science in dealing with these was that the new definition linked the strictly 'moral' or behavioral definition of alcohol abuse, formerly associated with drinking, to an administrative question that could be dealt with in rational ways. Following from this, the evolution of public problems and a public alcohol problem involved not only the transformation of formerly private troubles to a status of public problems, but also a shift from moral and religious issues solved through the clergy, to the growth of professional groups to deal with various problematic groups (see also Gusfield 1993, Abrahamson 1989: p. 39). Although medical professionals were initially reluctant to define alcohol problems as strictly a medical condition (Rosenqvist 1987), modern definitions of alcohol problems have supported and indicated medical professionals as one of the most influential and visible professional groups. This became particularly true with the introduction of a new concept of 'drinking', namely, alcoholism as disease. However, as I shall show, medical expertise and professional authority has never attained an autonomous role in discussing alcohol problems. One of the aims of this chapter is to investigate medical discourse in an effort to identify in what ways medical knowledge constructs physicians as an expert.[11]

[10] In Sweden, the initial discourse on what came to be social policy issues took place even before the tweentieth century. Olsson (1990) show s that from approximately the 1880s various social issues were the topic of discourse, and increasingly so through the 1890s and into the twentieth century. The two most common themes in texts published during this time were the workers question and the temperance question, but other subjects included such things as: hygiene, education, housing, poor relief, crime, etc. (p. 51).

[11] Bryan S. Turner (1987) has referred to diseases such as alcoholism as 'modern diseases'. Turner exemplifies this with the condition known as repetitive strain injury, RSI and notes AIDS, anorexia nervosa, the hyperactive child syndrome and Muchausen's syndrome as additional examples. 'Modern' diseases, he argues, are characterized as chronic, difficult to diagnose and to treat, have a complex and uncertain aetiology, and are the focus of professional and political controversy (pp. 14–15). One of the key controversies concerns whether or not the condition in question indeed exists. An example found in current debate is the recently detected allergy to electricity (also oversensitivity to electricity) that an increasing number of persons are complaining of. In Sweden the status of this condition as either a disease or imagined condition has consequences for whether or not one will receive health benefits, be allowed time off from work, is entitled to special equipment, etc.

The Alcoholism Formation[12]

A Brief Context

In Sweden, the notion that chronic heavy drinking constituted a medical phenomenon known as alcoholism, and not strictly a moral issue as Bratt had suggested, gained a position in medical discourse during the 1940s but had been evident as early as the 1920s and 1930s despite legislation that discounted this view (cf. Kristenson 1993), as well as medical statements that claimed otherwise. Although it is beyond the parameters of the current discussion to explain why this medicalized view emerged when it did, a few factors are worth mentioning. As noted in *Chapter 2,* medical practitioners played important roles in the local temperance boards that were established throughout Sweden during the latter part of the 1910s and 1920s, both as gatekeepers to rehabilitation services and as leaders of these boards. This position provided medical professionals with an institutionalized location for coming into contact with problem drinkers and the problem of drinking to a greater extent than previously. In turn, such regular contact provided an opportunity to begin generating specific knowledge about this 'condition', which could be contrasted with other psychiatric and health problems. Evidence of this can be detected in the articles submitted to *Läkartidningen*, which drew upon the authors' experience gained through their work with the temperance boards. Medical professionals increasingly described their role in the treatment of alcohol abuse as a more effective alternative to forced incarceration by local authorities and the police. This provided an additional point of contact for the medical profession, although physicians were largely involved in sobering up the drinker, rather than long-term treatment, which was carried out by temperance societies (Stenius 1996).

After two decades of dealing with 'drinkers', medical professionals began to generate a definition of alcohol issues during the 1930s and 1940s that can be distinguished from the moral definition constructed by their predecessors (Kristenson 1993). Although legislation was passed in 1948 that supported medical views of disease, it was not until the 1950s that this view permeated the contributions to *Läkartidningen.* The definition that emerged in the sanctioned discourse of the medical community as well as in the official discourse was reminiscent of some of the claims put forth before the turn of the century. It centered upon the classification of alcoholism—sometimes referred to as "drinking" or "alcohol abuse"—as a medical condition to be studied and rectified by the medical community with support from other institutions and groups in society.

[12] Others have referred to this as the 'medical model'. However, I want to abstain from this label since what I seek to illustrate is the introduction of yet a second type of medical model to describe and define the alcohol problem. As Johannisson's (1997) essay on "Medicinens grammatik" (the grammar of medicine) points out, medical models take very different forms, and can even compete within the same space.

Although there was agreement within the medical core that treatment of the condition could and should be delivered by medicine to a greater extent than previously, there was disagreement that this condition indeed should be regarded as a disease. A line of thinking that shared similarities with the ' symptom theory' presented by social workers during the 1960s (see *Chapter 2*) was presented in medical discourse from the 1950s. This position challenged the notion that alcoholism was a disease of the body. One physician argued, for example, against colleagues who supported the medical notion, and posited instead that people drank due to "life's trivialities, cruelty, general shabbiness and injustices" (Thullberg 1956: p. 296). People needed alcohol because they were not offered anything better. Industrialization and increased secularization were responsible for the isolation and despair experienced by so many people. Alcoholism was not the disease, but a symptom of something else, either in the alcoholic himself, or society. For this physician, it was not only medical rehabilitation that would help, but also support by religious organizations.[13]

Basic Propositions

As a point of departure, and as a means of providing a quick overview of the alcoholism formation in medical discourse, I want to pierce the discourse by way of introducing a dissertation written in medicine, on the alcohol problem in 1951, titled *A Study in Alcoholism, Clinical, Social-Psychiatric and Genetic Investigations*[14]. The aims of the studies it contained, as defined by the author of the dissertation, illustrate both the major questions and debates surrounding alcoholism at the time. The aims were as follows:

- To examine the siblings and parents of an as far as possible representative material of alcoholics, and to try to determine the morbidity risks for psychoses and psychiatric abnormalities among them.
- To endeavor, taking the material thus obtained as my point of departure, to answer the question as to the role played by hereditary and environmental factors in the origin of alcoholism.
- To endeavor through analysis of the personality types found among alcoholics and in available comparative materials to ascertain whether certain personality types may conceivably have significance for the origin and development of alcoholism.
- To try through a clinical analysis of the material to show whether any special factors affect the clinical picture of alcoholism.

[13] This is another example of the way in which discourses are not wholly 'new', but contain fragments of logic and concepts from previous formations. Thullberg's statement is reminnescent of the moral definition of alcohol issues proposed by Bratt and others during the early decades of the 20th century.

[14] I take Åmark's work as a point of departure since it was the first dissertation to be mentioned in the materials I have examined. It was also critiqued within *Läkartidningen*. Based on a search of titles in Libris-STAIRS for dissertations and theses related to alcohol, it appears that one other medical dissertation on alcohol appeared before Åmarks. This was by Curt Gyllenswärd, titled *Bidrag till frågan om alkoholverkningar* (A contribution to discussions concerning the effects of alcohol) from 1923.

- To try through a comparison of the environmental conditions of the alcoholics with those of the general population to show whether any special environmental situations may conceivably affect the development of alcoholism.

The goals outlined above suggest an interest in several questions. One of these concerned the identification of causal mechanisms, or etiology for the disease. Both the environment as well as genetic factors were identified as locations for investigation. Second, these points also reflected a need to identify different types of problem drinking and develop a matrix, or series of related conditions. This task contributed to the construction of boundaries for the problem; it identified what would be included as part of the same problem. Finally, the questions posed inherently pointed to observation of cases as a primary method for investigation.

This dissertation is similar to a growing claim by a number of medical professionals who compared alcoholism or alcohol abuse to other detrimental and epidemic diseases at the time. It was argued for instance that:

> It would not be an exaggeration to claim that alcoholism, with respect to both its prevalence and its social consequences is fully comparable to tuberculosis, cancer and rheumatism. Alcoholism should be regarded as a doctor's concern and as a problem we cannot ignore in our day to day work. (Myhrmman 1955: p. 1520).

The claim that alcoholism was a disease was based on the further claim that structural changes within the organism could be detected. S:son Frey argued, for example, that:

> It seems that Thullberg is blind to the correlation between alcohol and liver cirrhosis, alcohol polyneuritis, Korsakows Syndrome and the extensive pathalogical-anatomical research, which has revealed serious lesions in the central nervous system with deaths from delirium tremens and Wernickes 'hämmorhagiska encephalitis'. It is also clear that he has not had the opportunity to witness the detrimental dementia condition due to alcohol abuse, which we psychiatrists see on our chronic wards daily. (S:son Frey 1957: p. 816).
>
> The alcohol consumer's behavior in this situation, that is, since the first glass, is no longer correlated with moral character. A biochemical process is induced that proceeds independent of the person's will (S:son Frey 1957: p. 818).

For Frey and others, "all alcohol abusers are seriously ill physically with structural changes and therewith in their spirit" (ibid.). This was evidenced in the many physiological conditions that could be detected in persons with a long history of heavy consumption. By the 1960s, the addictive state that followed after a long period of heavy drinking was also deemed to be "fully comparable to a state of illness" (Alström 1965: p. 208).

Locating the Disease

Regardless of whether one agreed that alcoholism was a disease or not, physicians groups recognized the same persons as displaying alcohol abuse, and as having developed problems due to their drinking that fell within the jurisdiction of medical authority. The alcoholism formation concerned a particular group of 'patients' or potential patients only. As one doctor put it, "What one wants to get at, is that the alcoholic, in relation to alcohol, deviates from the average person" (Åmark 1955: p. 2297). That is, some persons demonstrated deviant traits through their drinking behavior, and this trait—if it could be 'known'—distinguished them from 'average' citizens. It was the abnormal citizen that the alcohol doctor was concerned with describing, analyzing, and treating. As I shall later point out, this forms a key point of transformation.[15]

Health and disease were distributed over two classes of persons that were constructed through the discourse: the ill (the haves), and the healthy (the have-nots).The fact that medicine was concerned with a specific type of deviant, and not an entire population, raised the question of how could one distinguish this group. Which signs indicated a person was an alcoholic? How could the disease be detected? In response to this, it was suggested that:

> The important factor is the uncontrollable need for alcohol, as a means of distinguishing alcoholism (Åmark 1955: p. 2298).

The alcoholic was described as possessing an 'alcohol hunger' that could not be satisfied. His behavior was out-of-control (for whatever reason), to the extent that this hunger became the primary driving force in his life:

> ... the alcoholic cannot control his consumption. He takes a hair of the dog (återställare) and he is ready to do almost anything to get a hold of spirits, once he has begun drinking. This response in relation to alcohol is characteristic also for the alcoholic who has been abstinent for several years. (Åmark 1955: p. 2298).
>
> The most extreme form of this abnormal reaction to alcohol is the classic pathological intoxication. By this is meant that a person, with a minimal quantity of alcohol, enters into a state of confusion, which intensifies emotional sensations and violent behavior can result (Dimberg 1949: p. 757).
>
> ... the alcoholic is forced to continue drinking against his will as long spirits are within his reach and he still has the capacity to stretch his hand to take hold of a glass or the bottle, according to his usual habit (Kindstrand 1956, p. 2275).

This link between control and illness, and the loss of this, supported the notion that although alcoholism was a distinct condition, it was not entirely separate from the broader family of mental disorders. In Sweden as well as elsewhere, the disease was often located in the mind, as a psychosomatic condition or psychiatric disorder. The drinker's condition was due to "an inherent psychiatric abnormality" (Petrén 1948, p. 2315).[16] It was deduced by some, that since

[15] This conceptualization of alcoholism seems to be in line with the disease model generally applied in medicine from approximately the turn of the century until at least the late 1950s. According to the discourse at the time, the world of health fell into two categories: those who have it, and those who do not (Rose 1992, p. 6); or as Pickering stated in 1968, "Medicine in its present state can count up to two but not beyond." (Pickering 1968, cited in Rose 1992: p. 6).

[16] This account was adopted by the WHO's Alcoholism Subcommittee, for example, which first considered alcoholism in the early 1950s with an interest in developing a plan of action for studying and treating the disease as a mental illness.

psycho-pathology was particularly evident in the majority of cases it must also be an important causal factor (see e.g. Åmark 1950).

Locating the illness in the mind is likely linked to the fact that suspicion of illness was raised due to the observation of behaviors that were otherwise associated with 'known' psychiatric conditions. It is evident from the data that alcoholics were often sent to psychiatric hospitals for treatment during the early decades of this century, and psychiatrists at both these hospitals and those working with the temperance boards were therefore the most common medical specialty to deal with alcoholism, and begin to study and treat the condition. In this context, abuse would have been compared and contrasted with 'other' cases of psychiatric and mental disorders, and in some cases distinguished from them as a 'new' condition.

Symptoms and Signs of Disease

In addition to the 'alcohol hunger' that distinguished the alcoholic, other signs were discovered that allowed boundaries to be drawn for which cases should be counted as alcoholism. The identification of these symptoms allowed others to identify the alcoholic and link him[17] to the 'correct' form of rehabilitation. Among Swedish medical researchers, there was a focus on identifying symptoms that related to the progression of the disease and indicators of alcoholism[18]. An example of this effort is Dimberg and Salum's (1955) contribution, in which they identified the following symptoms in the cases they had observed:

- Poor or reduced financial stability during drinking bouts.
- More or less reduced financial stability irrespective of alcohol (parasitic types, vagabonds, etc.).
- Clear reduction in working capacity due to abuse.
- Working capacity reduced more or less continuously.
- Criminal tendencies during drinking bouts.
- Criminal tendencies even without direct correlation with alcohol abuse.
- Uncharacteristic violent tendencies (abuse or threats to wife, children, parents, etc.)
- Organic brain damage resulting from abuse (escalation of psychiatric problems or varying degrees of dementia, epilepsy, Korsakow, alcohol psychoses).
- Psychiatric disorders without direct correlation with alcoholism (psycho-neuroses, psychopaths, psychiatric-symptoms, etc.).

[17] I use the pronoun 'him' since the alcohol abuser was conceptualized at the time as a male. It was not until the 1960s and 1970s that chronic consumption by women was 'discovered'.

[18] In addition to the drinking, there were a number of other sings. Jellinek's work, for example, identified not less than 43 different symptoms. These include such things as memory loss, avid drinking, guilt, an increase in memory loss, a loss of control over drinking, rationalizing one's drinking, termination of employment, change in family relations and how one behaved within the family, a dampened sexual drive, and even a type of jealous paranoia. During the critical phase (see below) Jellinek noted that one begins to drink continuously over longer periods of time, alcohol psychosis can become a problem, one might consume technical alcohol when other products are unavailable, strong tremors, impaired motor skills.

Looking at the list above, a couple of comments are in order. First, it is interesting to note that the symptoms are not strictly of a physiological nature. Criminality, financial capacity, family life and labor market potential, which today are largely related to social issues, are here presented as symptoms of something known as a disease. These social consequences of alcoholism drew upon earlier definitions of the problem, and could be found in later texts. Indeed, throughout the 1950s, the social consequences of alcohol abuse were emphasized as one of the reasons temperance boards and physicians were needed. 'Prevention was mentioned in numerous texts, by which was meant intervention before the social consequences were too great.

A second point of interest is that the symptoms were derived based upon the primary method at the time: observation of cases by physicians. This was particularly noteworthy in the many contributions by Alfred Petrén, which contained detailed excerpts out of the author's case logs for different patients (often referred through the temperance boards). These contained few accounts of the patients' physical condition—although often of their psychological or psychiatric state—but detailed accounts of the patients' family life, social life, alcohol career, history of contact with authorities, treatment proscribed, etc. It is through these case accounts that symptoms were identified and linked to other 'known cases' so that the accumulation of indicators for identifying alcohol abusers in the future could be constructed.

The search for symptoms of the disease continued to be a challenge for medicine throughout the twentieth century; and the detection of both social and physiological or psychological consequences was discussed in the contributions to *Läkartidningen.* In one piece from 1969, psychological dependence was presented as an early symptom. Later symptoms included memory loss after alcohol use, i.e. "black outs", but also attempts to rationalize use after a bout with alcohol, or guilt after drinking. Physical symptoms included being more quickly influenced, and the 'dangerous alcoholic' who is described as easily irritated. Moreover, other outward signs to indicate the condition included complaints about stomach issues and heart problems such as heart palpitation. Practical symptoms were also identified, which included: poor nutrition, general nervousness, fatigue and depression, difficulty with swallowing, stomach and intestinal discomfort and glandular pain, jaundice as well as numbness and a prickly sensation in the extremities. Other medical conditions of a serious nature included: delirium tremens, acute hallucinations, Korsakows syndrome, Wernickes enceafalopathy, and dementia (Bergsman 1969: p. 13).

A final symptom, or effect of alcoholism should also be noted. This concerns damage to the liver.[19] Liver cirrhosis had become identified as one of the effects of long-term drinking, which could be used as an indicator of alcoholism. Liver cirrhosis also provided a stepping stone for other types of research.

[19] Liver cirrhosis was both an indicator of the disease as well as one of its consequences.

In particular, research into other effects of alcohol on both chronic heavy drinkers and those who drank large amounts within shorter periods of time were studied, in an attempt to map out the relationship between alcohol and the human body. Many of these studies provided the basic 'facts' to support future medical models (see below).

Phases of Illness

One of the modes by which the problem of alcohol takes on meaning as a certain type of problem is through the construction of series and related objects through the discourse. The problem is broken-down into manageable pieces, or sub-problems. Several examples of dispersion principles or rules can be detected in the alcoholism formation.

One such mode of dispersion relates to the perception of alcoholism as a progressive condition. Medicine at this time sought to establish and identify different phases, or stages, of illness that followed an identifiable order. For example, Åmark identified three phases in his dissertation: 1) chronic alcoholism, 2) alcohol addiction, and 3) alcohol abuse. Chronic alcoholism was defined as cases in which acute poisoning took place and as a consequence of this, distinct pathological symptoms of a somatic or psychiatric nature were evident. Alcohol addiction referred to cases where an acute 'craving' after alcohol was described, while alcohol abuse provided a catchall category for other symptoms. It is not quite clear how these phases were associated with one another.

Another example of this means of dispersion is found in Myhrman (1955). Like Åmark, Myhrman identified three stages of the disease. In the beginning stage (begynnelsestadiet), patients were described as assuming the ties to alcohol abuse that alcoholism is known for. The 'alcohol hunger' or dependence was exhibited and expressed by the persons themselves in many cases. Myhrman stated that the condition was usually known to the drinker himself and maybe even to others in his company, but it had not led to any social complications of a serious nature, which is why these cases "often [went] undetected for a long period of time" (p. 1521). The sick person did not present any signs of alcohol damage of a somatic or psychiatric nature. However, the subtle signs of this first stage of the illness, became more evident at the second stage. Social disorder in the person's life was detected as abuse and became more apparent through controversies in the family, with employers, authorities and marriages were destroyed. At this stage, "intervention by society [was] necessary". The person also began to develop alcohol damage of a somatic and psychiatric nature. In the final stage of the illness, "the patient reflect(ed) the traditional image of the drinker", and he was characterized by "a more or less advanced physiological, spiritual and social decline".[20] It was at this last stage that the social consequences of alcohol abuse were particularly clear.

[20] See next page.

Some variations in the illness were regarded as existing with respect to different 'types' of alcoholics or alcohol abusers. One type of alcohol abuser was the drinker with *svårt alkoholhumör* (a severe temperament when intoxicated). This type of drinker was especially dangerous to his family, as it was noted that the children's and wife's nerve systems could often be damaged by their experiences with the alcohol abuser. Some of the documented cases presented by psychiatrists and medical examiners at the temperance boards involved suicide attempts by spouses of drinkers (see e.g. Petrén 1950). Another type of drinker was the paranoid alcohol abuser. Again, this type of drinker could be dangerous to his family, particularly his wife whom he accused of engaging in extramarital affairs, etc.[21] There were also those alcoholics who were criminal and posed problems for cooperating with police authorities (e.g. Petrén 1953: p. 775), those with alcohol depression (e.g. Petrén 1952: p. 3182), and those with a more general problem of being "psychologically abnormal alcoholics" (e.g. Petrén 1950: p. 2709).

The Role of the Physician

I have already noted above that one of the roles of the physician in cooperation with other authorities was to intervene in order to 'prevent' the social consequences of drinking from playing themselves out. While this was one issue, physicians were also concerned with how to treat those afflicted with the disease, or diseases resulting from alcoholism, and cure them. During the 1950s there was an optimism that medicine could indeed intervene successfully.

> The medical treatment of alcoholism has made so many major advances during recent years that one could almost call it a revolution within this branch of therapy (Knöös & Johnson 1954, p. 1338).
>
> The acute alcohol poisoning is ... something doctors can treat, especially if they have support from the alcoholic's support network and not least from the Links (Grönberg 1956, p. 1669).

In the texts I examined, two phases or types of cure-related practices were referred to. First, physicians who worked with the temperance boards were

[20] These works can be compared with the internationally renowned work of Jellinek, particularly his 1960 work, *The Disease Concept of Alcoholism* in which he identifies a very general outline of the stages of alcoholism. According to Jellinek, four phases constituted the disease process: the prealcoholic phase, a prodromal phase, a crucial phase and the chronic phase. Each stage was described in terms of a combination of behavioral and physiological attributes that indicated a stage in the development of the disease.

[21] Petrén cites one case that was so out of control that "During 1949 [the husband's] jealous ideas became increasingly apparent even in a sober state, such that his fiancée was subjected to unpleasant control measures—he called her place of employment relentlessly to ensure that she was there, and locked up her better undergarments and forced her to wear old discarded garments so she would make a worse impression upon any potential admirers. This became even more grave with his second wife, as he sewed together her undergarments so that she could not take them off until he came home and helped her out of them." (Petrén 1950: p. 2355).

charged with recommending appropriate care. Their first order of business was often the 'sobering up' of the alcoholic either at the temperance board offices, which sometimes had special rooms for this, or in acute cases by sending the alcoholic to a hospital ward. Second, the physician could then apply for psychiatric treatment or longer-term treatment at a special treatment facility. Apparently, many alcoholics were sobered up, sent to a psychiatric ward and then for longer term care at a non-medical institution. Responses varied depending upon the 'type' of alcoholic one was dealing with.

Before the 1940s, insulin treatments, electric shock therapy and various forms of aversion therapy were utilized. By the 1950s, this arsenal was complimented with a treatment form that was strictly medical: the introduction of pharmaceuticals, antabus and abstinyl in 1948. These were used as a means of dealing with the 'alcohol hunger', as they suppressed the craving for alcohol. As early as 1949, Dimberg presented an overview of some of the early experiences with this treatment as a means of dealing with the "behavioral problems" related to alcohol and the "physical suffering" that the alcohol-sick person and his family experienced (pp. 756–768); and in 1950 Forssman presented an overview of experiences with these drugs at psychiatric clinics, and reported that despite some side effects, the drugs were so clearly useful that they should be included in other treatment regimens (p. 2817). The use of these drugs continued and was expanded throughout the 1950s and 1960s (see e.g. Alsén & S:son Frey 1959; pp. 2244–3351; Danielsson 1954: p. 565; Dimberg 1960; pp. 1112–1144; Knöös 1954: p. 1337; Scherstén 1954: p. 341, Tillgren 1959; pp. 2791–2795). In addition to these drugs, vitamins, insulin, and cortisone were also combined in various ways to both sober up the alcoholic, and help him return to health.

This initial period of treatment was seen as an important stage in preparing the way for additional forms of treatment.

> The greatest benefit of this method, in our view, lies in its effectiveness in breaking a period of drinking, thereby creating the possibility to work with the patient in psycho-therapy. The strong subjective improvement he experiences also makes him more inclined to return for further treatment (Knöss & Johnson 1954: p. 1341).

Following sobriety, or in less acute cases preceding sobriety, it was emphasized that treatment success was dependent upon patients themselves 'realizing' their need for treatment and developing a desire to return to a 'normal' life. To meet this challenge, the second strategy developed in treatment involved psychotherapy. Dimberg and Salum (1955), for example, writing on their experiences from treatment programs saw psychotherapy as a necessary means to enlighten the patient so that he adopted an illness perspective, through learning about his condition[22]:

[22] Although this is the overwhelming view expressed in the articles in *Läkartidningen,* there was also discent. Mårtens (1955), for example, described this as a "misunderstanding", that assumed that with medical enlightenment followed rationality.

> By systematically penetrating the patient's own symptoms, it is easy to exemplify alcoholism's symptomatology in a simple way for him; he should be especially informed of the change in response associated with alcohol, which is, practically speaking, relevant in all cases... The pathological alcohol hunger is also an easily understood concept for the patient with an alcohol sickness and helps him to adopt a better illness perspective. (p. 585).

It was the physician who had the appropriate status and power to bring forth the rationality of the drinker. It was suggested that medical doctors, who possessed 'facts', could enlighten the alcohol abuser with correct 'knowledge' that would help him realize the nature of his uncontrollable impulses and thereafter seek to gain control once more. Psychotherapy appears to have played an important role in constructing treatment as a voluntary procedure, and hence as an alternative to other forms of compulsory control performed by other groups in society. In addition, the medical discourse emphasized that this approach was more effective than involuntary care, since the patient became engaged and desired treatment for himself.

During the 1950s, arguments for a more humane approach to alcohol abuse and intoxication was a common theme in the medical discourse. The 'patient' was to be treated with humility and respect:

> It is useful that the sick person is able to visit a physician's private practice. Rigid, austere forms must be avoided unconditionally. The physician must be familiar with, and make use of, the entire scale of available social assistance. Determination and kindness must be combined in an informed way. The alcohol-sick is often sensitive, fragile and he quickly recognizes and internalizes the slightest devaluation of his dignity (Danielsson 1954: p. 569)

Advances in both psychotherapy and drug treatment were cited as support for an increased involvement of medicine in defining and treating cases of alcohol abuse,

> The official temperance care has largely been in the hands of the social authorities, where medical expertise has been greatly underrepresented. The new possibilities to practically intervene in alcohol problems demands a greater influence from medicine, even in public temperance care (Knöös & Johnson 1954: p. 1342).

In some cases, medical attention was proposed as an alternative to forcing persons into care, which had been practiced in preceding decades before medical approaches were incorporated into treatment (e.g. Dimberg & Salum 1955: p. 582). In fact, the medical discourse largely emphasized that the patient was a victim of abnormal impulses over which he had no control (see also Nycander 1967: p. 152). For this reason, it was important to emphasize the patient's need for care, rather than society's need for him to be rehabilitated. This could be best achieved by medical practitioners since animosity and control was associated with other groups (e.g. temperance boards and the police). In contrast, the physician could provide friendly support and assistance.

> The sense of discrimination that they naturally feel when the temperance board intervenes, is foregone; instead the more adequate view that they are being treated for an illness is conveyed. All measures must be used to give the patient insight into his illness... Treatment results are dependent upon whether or not this is successfully conveyed (Dimberg & Salum 1955: p. 583).
>
> It is of utmost importance that the alcohol patient is approached like any other patient... their condition and problems should be discussed in the same way and with the same discretion as one approaches any other sick person (Lublin 1957: p. 824)

At the same time, medical discourse pointed to the illness concept as a means of introducing a more sympathetic approach to abuse, physicians did not see themselves as the autonomous caretakers of rehabilitation and treatment. Rather, they consistently pointed to the importance of cooperation between the various institutions in the alcohol policy arena.

> Intimate cooperation is necessary between police authorities and public physicians, particularly in "complicated" cases of intoxication, e.g. with respect to 'svårt alkoholskade' (severely damaged) and intoxicated young people (Norell 1949: p. 726).

A new emphasis upon medical expertise was not aimed to replace all other measures, but it was emphasized that these needed to be organized in cooperation with a physician (see e.g. Dimberg & Salum 1955: pp. 582–584).

In addition to their strictly medical role, physicians were also engaged in debating alcohol policy. When the rationing system practiced in Swedish alcohol policy was abolished in 1955 physicians saw an increase in the number of cases of acute alcoholism and the data I examined shows an active reflection upon this (e.g. Ask-Upmark 1956; pp. 3206–3207; Boström 1956; p. 2961–2962; Petrén 1956; pp. 3503–3506, S:son Frey 1957; pp. 814–820). Sudden freedom from restrictions was viewed as having let loose "an alcohol flood" that brought with it "suffering and criminality that must be 'damned up'" (Ask-Upmark 1956; pp. 3206). In this context, physicians argued both for more general policy measures in order to deal with the problem, as well as the need for greater support for their own enterprises.

The Disease Model in Official Discourse

The actual sanctioning of the disease turn in medical practice was not encoded in official discourse until the late 1940s and early 1950s. Until then, policy largely encoded the moralistic view of physicians and others from the 1910s and 1920s. One of the conditions that supported the introduction of a 'medicalized' view of the problem in public discourse was a growing criticism of the current internment practices and demand for treatment that 'cured' the disease (Stenius 1996). It was pointed out that the practice of incarcerating alcoholics at facilities served to remove them from society, and prevented them from causing further damage. However, repeat offenders were common (Abrahamson 1989). Current practices were viewed as ineffective, and in this space medical discourse offered an alternative. An investigation into care took place in 1946, and it was with this event that the psychiatric and medical dimensions of alcoholism as a disease gained greater support in official discourse (see also Rosenqvist & Kurube 1992, Stenius 1996).

Like the medical discourse, the official discourse was also undecided with respect to the status of alcoholism as a disease (see also Abrahamson 1989: p. 41), although conditions around the problem were seen as linked with illness.

> ... [A]lcohol abusers are often sick or abnormal persons, their alcohol abuse is brought about by psychiatric or physical underdevelopment, deformity, or disease of some sort, or through abusing alcohol they become sick or develop improperly. (SOU 1948:23: p. 40)

Also in line with the medical discourse, the official discourse acknowledged, and drew attention to the fact that alcohol abuse had social consequences. In the commission's report, theses consequences were recognized, and in addition, the environment was also noted as a potential cause. It was stated, for instance, that an unsatisfactory environment could impact an already weak person (by medical standards) negatively (SOU 1948:23, pp. 38–39). However, such social factors were largely subordinated to more psychiatric and somatic factors.

There was also a strong support and implementation of more medically-oriented solutions to the problem. The proposal suggested the creation of four state alcoholism hospitals,[23] and provided an overview of specific forms of medical intervention, including insulin injections, electrical shock therapy, hormone treatment and aversion therapy. Additionally, economic resources and qualified personnel were increased in the area of medical treatment of alcoholism at this time (Stenius 1996: p. 9), leading to a strengthened medical involvement and the professionalization of alcoholism treatment, built up to cure, rather than control, drinkers. [24] At the same time, voluntary organizations that had previously run treatment centers were increasingly regarded as lacking professionalism, or scientific knowledge, and more as sources of enthusiastic citizens who could be mobilized for public education purposes (Stenius 1996: p. 10)[25]. Medical professionals, in contrast, were regarded as a means of introducing professional expertise. At a time when treatment was emphasized

[23] The report went as far as to present blueprints for how the state hospitals should be structured and organized, where beds should be placed, and where different wards would be located in relation to one another.

[24] Treatment provision in Sweden has, with the exception of this short period of time, been provided by a pot pourri of providers, including temperance organizations, philanthropic groups, self-help organizations, municipal social services, etc. For a summary of care providers and their relationship to the state, see Stenius (1996).

[25] The increased medicalization of the question also led to further central regulation and involvement by the state, which provided medical care through the welfare state structure.

over education, this approach constructed a hierarchy in which scientific expertise was granted an dominant position in relation to other types of interest groups.

The move towards adopting a stronger medical perspective in official discourse lagged the advancements of medicine. For example, the 1948 proposition was criticized by the medical community for not defending the 'health of the alcoholic' as a reason for taking him into care. More importantly, the medical community argued that the medical procedures outlined in the 1948 report were largely outdated. In particular, advancements made in pharmaceutical use were not be included (*Svenska Läkarnas nykterhetsförening* 1949: pp. 397–399).

The events summarized in Table 1, in combination with how the role of medicine was defined within the context of medical discourse indicate that the medical profession did not achieve a position of autonomous expertise and control over alcoholism as a disease, or the treatment of it. Legislation of the period points to both increased medicalization, e.g. in the form of developing alcohol studies as a formal discipline within medicine, and a retreat from this. In the official discourse, for example, an alcohol clinic was established. However, the authors of the law that created this clinic were careful not to take a stance on the debate of whether alcoholism was a disease or not. As a symbolic gesture in this direction, they adopted the terms 'abuse' and 'alcohol abuse' to replace alcoholism in the text, and titled the law 'temperance care law' rather than 'alcoholic law' (See also Elmér 1993: p. 9).

Bergmark and Oscarsson (1994) in their analysis of Swedish alcohol treatment note that the medical community, and hence medical facilities run by the state, have generally been assigned the task of treating acute medical and psychiatric problems and detoxification, but not treatment in general. This argument is supported by the analysis in this chapter. What appears in the Swedish case is a 'socialization' or de-medicalization of treatment, but a continued medicalization of acute care.

The Public Health Formation

Having outlined above the alcoholism formation of medical discourse, I want to turn now to providing a similar analysis of a second formation in discourse, which I refer to as the *public health formation*. In order to identify this construct I will be moving away from statements about heavy drinking, although it should be emphasized that the public health formation emerged alongside a continued interest in alcohol abuse within medicine. Within the context of this second formation empirical findings related to alcohol and the human body were reorganized. My discussion of this formation will be somewhat sparse in this chapter since this formation merged with the official discourse, which will be discussed in detail in *Chapter 4*. Moreover, this formation evolved slowly in

Table 1. *Events related to the disease formation*

Year	Action	Significance
1946	Alcoholic Care Commission (Alkoholist vårdsutredningen) was appointed (presented report in 1948, SOU 1948:23).	Focused on drinker as problem, and location of problem. Also pointed to continued need for support from temperance boards.
1948	New Alcoholic Care Law proposed. (SOU 1948, 23)	Argued for improved medical significance in alcohol arena through increased funding, and establishment of medical facilities.
1948–1950s	Use of disulfiram (Antabus) and calcium carbimide (Dipsan) introduced.	Throughout 1950s the use of these drugs for treating alcohol increased. Prescription drugs were controlled through the medical profession and therefore brought authority to this arena.
1954	Temperance Act passed.	Supported the development of medical care and authority, in part by establishing the alcohol clinic at Karolinska Hospital. But also stated that all care facilities should have access to a medical doctor and if possible one with psychiatric background.
1955	Rationing system abolished.	Increase in cases of alcoholism, medical community concerned.
1955	The 'Links' (Länkarna) were established in Sweden.	Adopted alcohol as disease concept, but did not view medical care as the proper form of treatment. Social support was the key to recovery.
1956	New alcohol institute established (Prop. 83), with approx. 60 care places, and institute for theoretical alcohol research.	Institutionalized theoretical and clinical work by the medical profession in relation to alcoholism by contributing to the disciplining of alcohol studies as a field of formal knowledge.
1957	Propositions for establishing alcohol disease clinics at Lund, Uppsala and Gothenburg University Hospitals were voted down in Parliament.	Could be viewed as step against further institutionalizing alcoholism as a medical problem.
1960	Proposition to investigate reasons for alcohol abuse among young people presented (FK 232, AK 294).	Reflected a continued interest in the causes, or reasons behind abuse. Also drew attention to young people as a specific target group within alcohol consumers, and likewise drew attention to notions of prevention rather than strictly treatment.
1961	Commission on Care of Alcoholics presented report (SOU 1961:58).	The focus of investigation was on treatment and care, rather than general policy measures. Distinguished alcoholism from other forms of alcohol consumption.
1961	A special care ward was instituted for treating young people with alcohol problems.	Institutionalization of special care needs of distinct groups. Could be viewed as a move away from a universal conception of alcoholism.
1964	A professorship in Psychiatry for alcohol diseases at Uppsala Academic Hospital, Psychiatry ward, was created and mandated by parliament.	Support for a medicalized alcohol problem, and in this case one that was related to mental illness or disorders.

Table 1 *(cont.)*

1964	A legislative proposal (FK 296, AK 357) to create health insurance for alcoholics is voted down by parliament.	
1968	Commission on public drunkenness presented report (SOU 1968:55,56).	Proposed decriminalization of public drunkenness.
1968	Proposed position in social medicine (assistant researcher) at Karolina Hospital, clinic for alcohol diseases voted down in parliament.	
1969	Motions turned down for introduction of a research assistant in social medicine at a proposed clinic for alcohol addiction research.	
1969	Proposals voted down (prop. FK 561, AK 354, 660) for creation of medical research clinic for substance abuse (addiction research?).	
1969	First graduate degree awarded in alcohol studies at Karolinska Institute.	Alcohol studies became further institutionalized as a field of knowledge within the medical community.
1974	New commission reports presented from Alcohol Policy Commission (APU).	Separation between treatment for alcohol dependence and reasons for abuse made. Treatment is considered in a separate commission. Reports recognize physiological as well as environmental factors contributing to alcohol problems.
1980s	Those with an alcohol were allowed sick leave, sick pay, and receive early retirement for complications related to alcoholism, for time spent at a treatment center.	Official recognition of alcohol dependency as a medical condition of illness, of equal status to other disabilities.
1982	Social Assistance Law	Brought an end to the temperance boards, and introduced professional knowledge rather than 'local' knowledge. Social work and medicine became important authorities.

the medical discourse, and was not fully articulated until the 1990s. In this section I will therefore concentrate on locating traces of this formation in medical discourse and outlining some of the major claims within this framework.

Transformation of Discourse

Although my interest in this section is not on alcohol abuse and treatment, but on public health, there were some shifts in the alcoholism formation, which likely shaped the terrain upon which the public health formation emerged. First, the social consequences of drinking, as argued above, were cited in medical discourse as a reason for intervening in the lives of individuals. Throughout the 1960s and 1970s, the social consequences of drinking continued to receive attention, a trend that gained further support with the entrance of social science to the field. In relationship to this, problematic drinking, although initially assigned to those with excessive consumption practices, also became applied to other forms of drinking that were experienced as problematic, but which did not appear to result in dependence upon alcohol. Moreover, conditions such as accidents, head injuries, and a greater risk of death were identified. These conditions became linked to alcohol abuse, but were also seen as conditions to be treated. This diffusion of the boundaries between alcoholics and other forms of drinking contributed to opening up a space of considering a broader range of consumption practices.

The terms for alcohol abuse or alcoholism were also reconsidered, both in Sweden and internationally. 'Alcohol abuse', 'alcohol disease', 'alcoholism' with several sub-categories, and 'alcohol problems', were deemed confusing, if not "useless" (Rydberg 1986: p. 16). They were used in varying contexts with varying meanings, such that confusion rather than clarity was created (see e.g. *Sveriges Läkarförbund* 1982: p. 11). One attempt to bring order to the field internationally was conducted by the WHO, which published a series of reports were after the 1950s that aimed to clarify and specify the use of these terms.

One result of the discussion around terminology was a shift in some of the more common concepts and how they were related to one another. For example, the concept of an 'alcohol hunger' was reconceptualized in medical terms as signs of abstinence, which indicated a dependence on alcohol. Dependence itself was regarded not as a sign, but as part of a medical condition.

> ... alcohol dependence can be seen as a medical concept and is wholly comparable with other forms of narcotics and drug dependencies (Isaksson 1982: p. 2519)

This condition was referred to in Sweden and internationally as *alcohol dependence syndrome.*[26] Conceptualizing dependence not only as a condition but as a *syndrome* was considered a useful tactic since :

> Defining alcohol dependence as a syndrome means that all enumerated criteria do not need to be present at the same time (*Sveriges Läkarförbund*: 1982: p. 12).

An important step in shifting terminology was a report by the Swedish Medical Society in 1982. In this report, a small, yet revealing, discursive change was that the syndrome of alcohol dependence was compared to asthma. These

[26] The concept of alcohol dependence was not entirely new. Myhrman in 1955, for example, refers to a *state of dependence*, which was associated with alcohol consumption, and which he and others regarded as the key element to the alcoholism as disease concept.

Table 2. *Symptoms : Alcohol dependence syndrome*

Behavioral changes	Change in subjective state	Change in psycho-biological state
Increased consumption (against accepted social norms and earlier behavior) Continued consumption despite harmful effects (illness, family problems, economic concerns, sanctions imposed by social milieu)	Impaired control craving (and inner need for alcohol) Psychiatric fixation Occupation with alcohol	Abstinence Consumption to rectify absti-nent state Increased tolerance for alcohol Need for greater quantities of al-cohol to achieve same effect

conditions likened one another since, "... recovery from an attack should be distinguished from the disposition to develop asthma." (*Svergies Läkarförbund* 1982: p. 12). That is to say that, once asthmatic, always asthmatic; once dependent, always dependent. Recovery from one bout or attack, does not imply a freedom from the condition all together. This equation can be compared with the earlier formation whereby alcoholism was likened to tuberculosis and other epidemic illnesses that could breakout in a population, but which could be cured. Although it was not explicitly stated, it could be deduced that relapses no longer implied failure, but became 'a part of the problem'.

Like alcoholism as disease, the syndrome was identifiable through a number of symptoms that were categorized along three dimensions: change in behavior, change in subjective state and change in psycho-biological state (Rydberg 1986). Each of these states were associated and described through specific symptoms (see Table 2).

In addition to considering known terms, a new concept was presented by the working group of the WHO, *alcohol related harm* (alkoholrelaterade störningar), which was slowly adopted in Sweden. This was defined in a very broad way as, "disturbances in the individual's daily environment that affect his ability to take care of himself, social relations and economic activity that should be expected in relation to the individual's age, gender and expected social roles" (as cited in Jonsson 1971: p. 42). One of the consequences of introducing this concept was that it opened up a means of conceptualizing any of life difficulties as alcohol-related (Levine 1984). As I shall also emphasize in *Chapter 4*, by expanding the boundaries of alcohol abuse, it appears that the medical discourse itself supplied the terrain upon which social science entered the field.

The Public Health Formation and Strategies

At the same time alcohol dependency continued to be discussed in medical discourse, it appears that the broadening of problematic drinking contributed to a more fertile ground for the emergence of a second formation of medical discourse, and with it a different means of problematizing alcohol. This conceptualization of the problem slowly emerged as a framework that incorporated the two approaches. I want to first present some of the major statements made in the context of this formation, and then look at how this emerged.

Rose (1992) in his discussion of public health as strategy notes that the most important difference between public health and disease approaches is the fact that the public health framework moves medical inquiry away from such questions as "Has he got it?" towards "How much of it has he got, and why?" (Rose, p. 9). Public health presents health, and indeed disease, as a continuum along which each one of us finds him or herself.[27] In addition, public health and preventive medicine focuses on the community as problematic, i.e. populations, rather than on individuals. As Rose (1992)[28] further points out:

> The essential determinants of the health of society are thus to be found in its mass characteristics: the deviant minority can only be understood when seen in its societal context, and effective prevention requires changes which involve the population as a whole. (Preface)

The problem, no longer a disease, has moved from inside the individual's body, to somewhere outside it, 'out there', among populations and their statistical relations. Health is complicated since the world is constituted by different series of activities and elements that combine in different ways, leading to potential problems. The challenge to individuals is to avoid contact with risk situations or behaviors which could open the pathway for the development of health problems.

The collective target of medical gaze can be detected in the Swedish medical discourse in the form of an increasing number of arguments for preventing rather than attempting to treat problems. It was furthermore argued that prevention involved a different target group since one could never know in advance which individuals would actually develop problems:

> An improvement in current treatment methods, which are unsatisfactory, is not enough to affect alcohol abuse. It is therefore necessary to combine care measures with prevention measures. Such preventive measures must be made general, since it is not possible to identify the majority of risk individuals in advance. (*Sveriges Läkarförbund* 1982: p. 6)
>
> Comprehensive experience from several countries, among others Sweden, on various occasions, have shown clearly that restrictive measures that lead to a reduction in average alcohol consumption even bring about a reduction in many known alcohol-related injuries and problems. Not least of which, heavy consumers who have not yet developed alcohol dependence should gain from [this approach] (Romelsjö 1982: p. 592).

[27] It is precisely this aspect that also distinguishes the public health of the last two decades or so, from that which was practiced in previous centuries and even during the early decades of the twentieth century.

[28] Rose's book presents an argument for public health as an important strategy for dealing with a number of health conditions. This is a Brittish text, and not directly related to alcohol questions, and might therefore seem to be a strange text to cite. It has been used in courses related to alcohol studies, among them, one that I have particiapated in, and is cited in alcohol papers from time to time.

A consequence of this formulation is that all persons were viewed as potential sites for the development of various conditions correlated with alcohol consumption.

The strategy suggested above also involved a shift in research interests. Since all persons were considered potential sights of problems, public health approached the study of the problem through examining populations, and locating observable statistical patterns of unwanted conditions that are correlated with alcohol therein. This 'counting of cases' is based on the methods of epidemiological research. Epidemiology is by no means a new field of medicine, but it is a quickly growing one that has gained in influence and visibility with the emergence of the new public health discourse (Petersen and Lupton 1996). The legitimacy of this narrative was, as Bergmark and Oscarsson point out, "dependent upon the extent to which other types of harm are regarded as indicators of ill health" (1989, p. 214). The language of the narrative describes various conditions as "related to", "correlated with" or "caused by" alcohol use (ibid.). Within medicine this took the form of identifying a growing number of long and short term physiological conditions, social, economic and psychological problems that share a statistical relationship with alcohol consumption. While these were once referred to as symptoms of alcoholism, they were now regarded as part of the problem, i.e. they were the thing to be explained and treated. Perhaps the most important theoretical support for this transformation was the adoption and rediscovery of the Total Consumption Model, as will be outlined in *Chapter 4*.

Given this approach, alcohol dependence syndrome, formerly *alcoholism*, was still problematic, but it was no longer the problem *par excellence.* It was transformed into one of many statistically observable patterns (see *Chapter 4*). Indeed there was very little difference between normal and heavy consumption since both could give rise to health risks and harm:

> Thus there is no sharp boundary between normal consumption and consumption that gives rise to alcohol-related disorders or harm, or alcohol dependence (*Sveriges Läkarförbund* 1982: p. 12).

In addition to a shift in the position of alcohol dependence in relation to other forms of alcohol problems, the framework of public health as an organizing logic, contributed to shaping how the syndrome itself was conceptualized. The condition was no longer an epidemic illness that was spreading through the social body, but was a syndrome with varying degrees of symptoms. Like health in general, the syndrome and the symptoms were described as points along a scale. This meant that the symptoms were not specific in terms of their intensity:

> Each of the respective symptoms can vary continuously along a scale. Among the population there are people with different degrees of the condition (*Sveriges Läkarförbund* 1982: p. 12).

Even in a more general sense, the discourse pointed out that in some cases the syndrome involved little effect upon the individual's behavior, while in other cases a person's entire life existence could be affected.

Thus, the conception of the alcohol problem shifted from one of alcoholism as disease, to focusing on so-called alcohol-related problems or alcohol-related harm, which were caused not only be alcoholics, but predominantly by consumers whose drinking was well below the levels associated with alcoholism (Leifman 1996: p. 4). Thus, those conditions that could be associated as part of the problem expanded from the 'inability to abstain from drink' to a broad range of various social, physiological and economic conditions.

An important text in the public health formation is a 1982 position piece by the Swedish Medical Society, *Sveriges Läkarförbund,* in which the medical profession officially adopted the total consumption model. The report signaled an important turning point in medical discourse, as it laid out a new program for research and political engagement that was based on a new framework. Around the same time the medical community participated in a number of seminars and conferences aimed at discussing alcohol issues. Fragments of the emerging public health or epidemiological approach to alcohol problems can be detected in these. For example, the *Riksbankens Jubileum Fund* organized a symposium in September of 1981, bringing together many different types of researchers and experts, under the title *Risken att bli alkoholist* (Risk of becoming an alcoholic). Although much of the discussion was focused upon why some persons become alcoholics and others not, the dispersion of alcohol consumers, the risks of so-called "normal consumption", as well as a discussion of the relation between the total consumption of alcohol within a society and the level of medical and social harm in that same society received attention. It was this concern for the population and for drinking in general, rather than the specific consumption of problem drinkers, that was later transformed as the primary framework within which problems were discussed within medicine.

Initially, the total consumption model was not related to the relationship between alcohol consumption and the rate of other medical problems. Rather, it was argued to be an important basis for understanding the relationship between total aggregate consumption and the number of persons with alcohol abuse problems. It was further argued that if total consumption could be decreased, alcohol abuse could be minimized.

> The entire modern international alcohol research community points unequivocally in this direction. Alcoholism and alcohol harm are directly related to the total consumption among a population. If one wants to fight alcoholism and alcohol harm, one must therefore decrease total consumption. And all research and experience shows that this can only be accomplished by making alcohol expensive and hard to attain, i.e. through restrictions (Söderquist 1980: p. 2307)

However, as other empirical evidence emerged that identified a correlation between alcohol consumption and other medical problems, the regulation of total consumption was also linked to these forms of 'risk'.

> The total consumption of alcohol within a population can be compared with exposure to other poisonous substances. The frequency of lasting medical problems—e.g. liver cirrhosis—within a population has also been shown to have a strong correlation with total consumption of alcohol within the same population. The logical consequence of this is that the most important preventive measure should be to reduce total alcohol consumption. (Cronholm 1984: p. 108).

An important discursive factor for the adoption of a public health perspective seems to be the differentiation of different levels of prevention. This implied a need for multiple strategies (Rydberg 1982); and thereby integrated individually-centered measures with population based restrictions. In the discourse, three levels of treatment or prevention were identified: primary, secondary and tertiary. These levels were based on the notion that health was a continuous variable. Following from this, strategies for the problem were not dispersed according to the 'type' of problem drinker one was dealing with, but in relation to where along the scale of health and illness a person found him or herself.

Different types of alcohol harm were related to the different positions on the scale of health as well as to the different levels of prevention. Among other problems were: acute medical alcohol damage (e.g. accidents while intoxicated, alcohol intoxication) acute psychiatric alcohol damage (e.g. pathological intoxication, delirium tremens) acute social alcohol damage (e.g. fights, drunk-driving, abuse) chronic medical alcohol damage(e.g. alcohol dependence, damage to the liver, nerve system, digestive tract, etc.) chronic psychiatric alcohol damage, e.g. memory loss, sleep problems, Wernicke-Korsakows Syndrome, alcohol dementia) (Rydberg 1986: p. 13), as well as acute and chronic social problems (Rydberg 1982: p. 171).

The identification of positions along the scale allowed different types of strategies to be applied and also introduced different professional and expert groups to deal with them. With respect to primary prevention, which was aimed at the general population, the medical community argued for basically the same principles as were identified in the official discourse (see *Chapter 4).*

> The correlation between the degree of poor health in a society and total consumption of alcohol has also been clearly demonstrated in successive WHO reports in 1980 and 1985. A decrease in total consumption leads to a decrease in complications (Almersjö 1989, p. 26).
>
> a large Swedish social project where information and legislation aim to successively reduce the level of toxins in the form of ethyl alcohol that the population are supplied with (Almersjö 1989, p. 31)
>
> A national ambition to reduce alcohol problems in Sweden most therefore aim primarily at the large group of moderately increasing consumption levels. This follows the total consumption model, but constitutes a further development of it (Andréasson 1992, p. 1854).
>
> To summarize, there is thus a convincing documentation that shows that decreased amounts of alcohol in a society, through restrictions and high prices for example, also reduces the number of alcohol-related problems. Clear corrugations have also been shown between increased consumption due to relaxed restrictions and increased levels of alcohol harm (Allebeck & Andréasson 1991, p. 831)

What the total consumption model demonstrates, on the other hand, is that in order to achieve an optimal effect we must also work for a general decrease in consumption for the entire population. This is an example of the so-called prevention paradox, which even concerns other risk factors such as high blood pressure, cholesterol and smoking: The greatest health effects are achieved in groups with moderately raised risk levels, since these are so much greater in number than the high risk group (Allebeck & Andréasson 1991, p. 831).

These types of prevention measures are generally difficult for the clinical practitioner to engage in. The task of educating the public is a large one, and one which medical professionals have deferred to other groups in society. Boström and Allebeck (1989), reflecting upon how the medical community could go forward with alcohol as a public health problem, argued that:

Health care measures are not enough if one wants to achieve a substantial decrease in alcohol's medical and social harm. Measures taken at the population level are necessary for this (p. 3388).

Those tasks that the medical community could engage in at the level of primary prevention were summarized by Boström and Allebeck as the following: 1) to collate information and knowledge; 2) to spread information; 3) to constitute a pressure group for influencing public officials; and 4) to work for a scientific evaluation of various test programs for limiting the availability of alcohol.

At the levels of secondary and tertiary prevention medicine argued that there was a need for treating acute medical problems and those with advanced abuse problems or with more or less hidden abuse (see e.g. Kristensson 1984).These practices were aimed at subgroups who were targeted as so-called 'risk groups'. These groups included pregnant women, for example, and suspected heavy consumers whom the medical community came into contact with and could refer to treatment.

Public Health and Official Discourse

As indicated in *Chapter 2,* a public health approach to the alcohol problem was implemented through legislation and institutionalized following the presentation of the 1975 report by Bruun and his colleagues. The table below identifies a number of important events in the evolution of this narrative both within the public arena and medicine.

An important point to keep in mind is that the medical community lagged public policy and legislation with respect to the adoption of the public health formation. Thus, although the total consumption model was adopted in a 1977 law on alcohol, and active measures to decrease total aggregate consumption of alcohol by the population became key strategies, the medical community continued to consider the disease of alcoholism. As medicine entered the

Table 3. *The public health formation in official discourse*

Year	Event	Importance
1977	New alcohol law adopted in Sweden.	Argued for the total consumption model as a guideline, and for limiting availability and demand for alcoholic beverages.
1981	Article series in *Läkartidningen* on alcohol.	The public health approach had not yet been adopted in these articles.
1982	Medical Society presented *Läkare om alkohol,* an alcohol policy program, and argued that there was a common interest in more powerful policy measures to reduce alcohol's harmful effects by decreasing alcohol consumption. The authors were careful not to make specific policy suggestions, however.	Encoded a shift in the medical definition of alcohol issues and introduced public health in a professionally sanctioned text.
1984/1985	Sweden officially adopted the WHO organization, European Region, resolution *Health for All in 2000,* which included a commitment to decrease alcohol consumption by 25% in each European country by the year 2000.	Was later interpreted in Sweden as an international sanctioning of public health as strategy and discourse.
1987	Board of Health and Welfare prepared a report on health care and alcohol, and outlined how medical professionals in primary care could help detect and prevent alcohol problems.	Had earlier been concern that emergency ward staff and others knew little about signs of alcohol dependence, and hence only 'obvious' cases came to the attention of health authorities.
1989	Alcohol committee established within Läkarsällskapet. It was to work with alcohol problem, and do so emphasizing a public health perspective. A similar committee's work was to be a model, that which worked on tobacco questions.[a]	The public health perspective officially adopted within the medical discourse.
1990	The alcohol committee organized a symposium on alcohol prevention, and how to achieve a 25% drop in consumption before the year 2000, as Sweden had agreed to at the WHO European Action Plan in 1985.	Engagement with political discourse.
1991	Public Health Institute (Folkhälsoinstitut) established	Institute was primarily administrative, and engaged in public opinion formation, but did include doctors from social medicine as part of advisory council.
1995	Plan for harmful use	A second position piece, that strengthened the public health approach.

[a] The committee consisted of the following members: Harry Boström (chair), Peter Allebeck (secretary), Christer Alling, Lena Dahlgren, Sven Dahlgren, Hans O Hallander, Birgitta Hovelius, Hans Kristensen, Nils Brage Nordlander, Ulf Rydberg.

Table 4. *Alcoholism formation vs. public health formation*

Formation approach	Alcoholism	Public health
Strategy	Cure/ Treat	Primary prevention
Target	Patient-centered	Population based
Causal models	Simple (e.g. genetic)	Complex, over time
Methods	Experimental, Genetic	Epidemiology, Medical statistics, Social medicine
Expertise	Medical hegemony Shared expertise with respect to treatment	Shared with other scientific experts such as sociology, economics, etc.
Medical field of expertise	Psychiatry, Biology, Bio-Psychology	Social medicine Epidemiology
Medical emphasis	Clinical & Theoretical	Theoretical

1980s a great deal of the basic research on alcohol centered on etiology and biochemical effects such as epidemiology, treatment research and attempts to ascertain early signs of abuse problems and intervene (Boström and Allebeck 1989, p. 3388). In 1981 a series of articles dedicated to alcohol in *Läkartidningen* gave a greater space to biochemistry, drug pharmaceuticals, acute care and hospital treatment than to social medical issues. Throughout the 1980s, however, a greater interest developed in Social Medicine (samhällsmedicin), and primary care for alcohol and other health problems. Thus, when a similar series of articles was presented during 1989, the emphasis also included epidemiology and discussions concerning how such results could be used to support public policy aimed at preventing alcohol disabilities, lowering overall consumption, and preserving public health.

The emergence of a more integrated discourse was not evident until the 1990s. At that time, the articulation of different levels of prevention provided a means of linking the claims of those arguing in favor of the total consumption theory and primary prevention to those who were concerned with alcohol abuse. In the following chapter I will show how, in addition to providing a basis for integrating medical discourse, the public health perspective also offered a platform for inter-disciplinary cooperation.

Medical Discourse and the Social Problem of Alcohol

To recapitulate the foregoing discussions, a quick overview of the main components of the two formations is in order. A summary of the major points of contrast is provided in Table 4 above.

The table illustrates that there are some differences between a public health approach to the study of health and illness and the traditional disease approach. One of the most important differences concerns the object of control and regulation. The disease approach has often resulted in an interest in controlling and managing alcoholics in an effort to rehabilitate them and return them once again to society as useful citizens. In contrast, the public health formation suggested measures that aimed to manage the risks and risk situations that can lead to a degeneration of health. Within medicine, perhaps to a greater extent than the public discourse, these two approaches have existed simultaneously during recent years. Despite its high profile within official discourse, it is not the case that the public health formation altogether replaced the alcoholism as disease formation.[29] Rather, links were constructed between abusive consumption habits and moderate drinking, as I shall further point out in *Chapter 4.*

The disease formation as expressed in medical discourse is similar to that identified in a number of western countries, particularly in North America. This is not surprising, given that the Swedish discourse refers to texts by the World Health Organization as a point of departure for discussions of this. However, medicine did not gain autonomous authority within the field. Pia Rosenqvist's (1987) work on the Swedish physicians during the 1920s, points out that even at this time, medical professionals sought to share the field with other players. Medical professionals at the time explicitly stated that they wished to move away from medical terms such as 'disease' (see also *Chapter 2,* this volume). Although the doctor was granted a role, it was in the capacity of an administrator and authoritarian, rather than a diagnostician. One might argue, that alcohol at this time had yet to be medicalized; after all, medicalization is generally regarded as having definitively taken place during the 1950s, with the widespread acceptance of Jellinek's work on the *Disease of Alcoholism.* Yet, during the 1950s in Sweden, at which time we do indeed see the adoption of a disease approach, the data for this study revealed that the role of the physician was related to the broader apparatus of controlling and regulating alcohol consumption and abuse in society. Contributors to *Läkartidningen* explicitly stated that they had a contribution to make, but that this would be little use without the larger apparatus that could only be operated by the state and local authorities.

[29] As evidence of the fact that the disease narrative never really disappeared, it can be noted that the Alcoholics Anonymous movement—a strong supporter of the illness notion in the US—gained in following throughout the mid to late 1980s after three slow decades in Sweden (Helmersson Bergmark 1995). Moreover, the 'Minnesota Model', which holds strong ties to the AA movement, for treatment of alcohol addiction was introduced during this same period with strong support from the medical community (p. 70).

CHAPTER 4

Total Consumption, Public Health and the Official Discourse

In the foregoing chapter, I described and analyzed two discursive formations in medical discourse on alcohol issues. In this chapter I will continue to investigate the social aspects of the alcohol problem. Here the focus is primarily on the total consumption and public health formation as it has been constituted in legislative, administrative and public information texts. Strategically, this chapter investigates a single formation in the alcohol discourse, in an effort to better understand how alcohol is constructed and built up as a social issue and object of legislation. Some context for this analysis is provided by way of considering the formation from which the public health approach emerged, beginning with the Alcohol Policy Commission (APU) reports presented on alcohol in 1974. Analysis provided in this chapter provides a further backdrop for a consideration of current changes in the discourse that are presented in *Chapter 5*.

Transformation of Discourse

The Social Context

The total consumption and public health formation in the alcohol discourse appears to have emerged in the public arena within the context of several decisive factors. First, throughout the 1960s and 70s there was a public demand for more "technocratic" and less "moralizing" discourse (Mäkelä 1983). This called for a shift in emphasis from 'deviance', which in Swedish society was regarded as moralizing as it was linked to those types of explanations that indicated individuals as 'different' rather than 'equal to' others in society.[1] Recalling some of the claims regarding the role of medicine that were presented in *Chapter 3*, the need for technocratic-based discourse was also identi-

[1] Equality and solidarity arose as two central ideas in the social arena during the 1960s, in part, due to the leftist social movement in Sweden. This movement was felt in Sociology, which came to play an increasingly important role in formulating the collective trouble of alcohol.

fied by doctors who favored disease descriptions of the problem. Disease was said to be less stigmatizing and persons with problems would be more likely to seek help and treatment. However, the medical model was quickly challenged by the emerging professions of Social Work and Sociology.

This shift in the scientific terrain forms a second factor that contributed to a shift in discourse. A further institutionalization of Social Work and Sociology during the 1970s brought new concepts and theories to the field. Although the first professorship in alcohol research was not created in the social sciences until the early 1980s, researchers such as Kettil Bruun drew attention to a problem that medicine had been unable to solve; namely, the distinction between those who use alcohol in excess and become alcoholics and those who drink excessively but do not develop an addiction. For Bruun, the boundaries between excessive and problem drinkers was a sociological question related to norms and our understanding of when these norms were broken (not a medical one) (e.g. Bruun 1968). Social scientific interest in alcohol questions continued to grow throughout the 1970s and 1980s as did official support of it. By 1983, Kettil Bruun argued that it was time for "alcohol research rather than alcoholism research" (Bruun 1983). Bruun's position and an increasing body like it, firmly delimited a new field where alcohol and not strictly alcoholism was the object of analysis, and where social scientists came to play a role on equal footing with medical researchers.

Also highly noted in the Swedish discourse is the adoption of the public health approach by the World Health Organization in 1975 by the twenty-eighth World Health Assembly (WHA 28.81). This resolution shifted discourse about alcohol issues from mental health to levels of alcohol consumption and their health implications for populations. A WHO resolution was adopted by the European Region and endorsed by the Swedish state. This resolution called for attempts by all countries of Europe to reduce total alcohol consumption in respective states by 25% by the year 2000. For Sweden this meant a drop in aggregate consumption from 6 liters pure alcohol per person per year, to just 4 liters.[2] As a further step in this direction, a European Action Plan was adopted in 1992, which led to the adoption of a European Charter on Alcohol at a European Conference on Health, Society and Alcohol in December of 1995.

Finally, a number of failed experiments in alcohol liberalism, among them the "medium beer crisis" (Lenke 1975 1989) ushered in support for more restrictive measures in the face of increased alcohol consumption by youths and public drunkenness in general during the late 1970s. These incidents continue to be cited as 'evidence' for the need to restrict availability of alcohol.

[2] As I shall point out in *Chapter 5*, this resolution is often cited in discussions concerning the maintenance of Swedish alcohol policy in light of potential integration with Europe.

Emergence of the Total Consumption/Public Health Formation

Discursive transformation does not occur as a 'rupture' in the conceptualization of an object (Foucault 1992). Rather, what is detectable within the space of a new formation is a reconfiguration of concepts, assumptions and formulations of the problem which have previously been utilized in discourse but which assume a unique logic within the current context. Following from this, it is difficult, if not futile to search for the 'roots' or 'origins' of the new formation (Best & Kellner 1991). In contrast to this analytic formulation of how transformation takes place, discourses often refer to their 'origins' and 'roots'.[3] With regard to the total consumption model and public health, the adoption of legislation in 1977 and reports from a public commission that preceded this policy are commonly regarded as the point of adoption of a better understanding of the problem. My investigation of the official public health formation begins, then, with the reports from this earlier commission. I will attempt to detect fragments of the current discourse; in particular, references to total consumption or the total consumption model are sought. Additionally, I will look for deviations in these from the public health formulation of the problem that is currently put forth.

As noted in *Chapter 2*, the APU commission was originally established under the auspices of 'liberalizing' alcohol policy. However, following a number of experiments in this direction during the 1960s, the discourse shifted back towards what are currently referred to as control-oriented policies during the latter half of the commission's work period.[4]In its report, the commission was primarily concerned with questions and issues addressed in the previous formation of alcohol issues, in particular: "Why do people abuse alcohol?" Among the key concepts that were defined and utilized in the commission's work and texts were: alcohol harm, alcohol abuse, alcohol abuser, and alcoholism, indicating that what was regarded as problematic within the context of the report, was the fact that some people become alcoholics, or alcohol abusers, however this condition might be defined. A large segment of the reports was dedicated to understanding how alcoholism should be defined, identifying its symptoms, and the causes of alcoholism, and the effects of alcohol on the human body (SOU 1974:99: pp. 57).

[3] This contributes to the construction of the object of current discourse as continuous, and progressively developing.

[4] The current discourse commonly refers to 'liberal' and 'control-oriented' policy periods. This seems to suggest that at some points in time there has been control, and at others points none, or very little. Although it is not my aim to explore power relations through the case studies in the dissertation, it is interesting to note that so-called 'liberal' formations are also characterized by administrative and regulative control practices by the government. However, what distinguishes these practices is that they are aimed at specific members of the community, or particular groups, while 'alcohol control' measures involve attempts to control the entire society. Hence, I would also distinguish between different historical periods, but would do so based upon the mode of control employed, and in particular, the target of policies, as opposed to the categories of 'liberal policy' or 'alcohol control policy'.

The causal story related to alcohol abuse contained fragments of earlier alcohol discourse, but also incorporated some of the 'new' knowledge supplied by social scientists. In a three point model the individual, the environment, and the substance were identified as locations of factors that contributed to the condition. Biological inheritance and acquired personal traits were related to the individual, while one's environment was described as influencing how one drank, and how the effects of alcohol were expressed. It was noted, for instance, that "There is a strong correlation between alcohol abuse and social misfortune" (pp. 20–21). Additional factors as competition and efficiency, tempo of life, and alienation, mechanization and automation at the work place were attributed a causal relationship with alcohol problems and alcohol abuse.[5] Alcohol itself was said to contribute to shaping problems based on the type of alcoholic beverage, how different alcoholic beverages were combined, and how different beverages were metabolized in different ways. An innovation that this model contributed to was an expansion of alcohol issues to include both the social and medical debates at the time; and hence, as well as both alcoholic drinking and other forms of consumption practices. This is also interesting since medical discourse had referred to the social consequences of alcohol abuse, but at this time there was a move to looking at the social causes of abuse.

At the same time the report pointed back to the heretofore concepts of alcohol issues, there some shifts can also be detected. In particular, the definition of abuse moved the discourse towards a broader category of drinking practices than previously associated with alcoholism. Abuse was defined by the committee as "use (of) alcohol in such a manner that of experience is known to give rise to clear risks for alcohol damage" (p. 91). At the time, damage was largely related to an increasing number of conditions that had been found to result from extensive alcohol consumption. These conditions were no longer simply symptoms of disease that could be used to identify problematic drinkers, but increasingly became a part of the problem itself, i.e. the thing to be explained and dealt with.

A second point of departure from earlier discourse, although subtle, was a recognition of a recent WHO report that pointed to the relation between the total aggregate consumption of alcohol in a society and the number of heavy consumers (see below). The new information was incorporated into what at the time was the essence of the problem, but the commission did not fully succumb to the collective problem of alcohol and the problem of availability as a 'cause' of alcohol problems, and stated that, "Availability is obviously never the primary reason. It contributes only together with other factors." (p. 96).

[5] The emphasis upon working life as a source of agitation contributing to alcohol abuse, as well as the identification of the workplace as a sight for detecting alcohol abusers, and collectively assisting them through solidarity, reflects a broader turn in Sociology at the time. During the 1960s and 1970s, and the expansion of the welfare state, sociologists were expected to, and did, study the problems of working life and contribute to legislation for social policy (Fridjonsdottir 1991: p. 254; Allardt, Lysgaard, Bottger, Sorensen 1988).

The major concern was still on alcohol abuse, rather than a more general notion of harm to the general population, which is currently associated with the same WHO report.

The APU formulated the aims and messages of policy as that of moderation, or in the words of the report: "the aim of alcohol policy shall be to bring about moderate drinking practices" (SOU 1974:93, p. 32). As a number of sub-aims the committee defined policy measures as a means to:

- achieve moderate drinking practices
- de-glorify alcohol
- inform young people and adults, about alcohol through the latest knowledge and keep them informed
- increase the non-drinking sector
- support abstinence in situations that demand particular reaction and judgment
- shift consumption to weaker alcoholic beverages
- support consumption of alcohol-free drinks as an alternative to alcoholic beverages
- create a drinking pattern where alcohol consumption primarily takes place in connection with meals
- work towards an alcohol-free childhood and teenage years
- limit access to alcohol
- raise consciousness about the impact of alcohol in the planning and development of the environment we live in
- work for alcohol-free environments and forms of social interaction

In the list of policy aims, moderation and moderate drinking were presented as an alternative to heavy consumption which was regarded as problematic. Particularly, the fourth through ninth aim, focused on this shift.[6] A distinction between the two types of drinking was encouraged by propaganda from the *Systembolag* following a later proposition, which aimed to shift consumption from spirits to beer and wine.[7] Moderation was also encouraged through information to young people and their teachers, in particular. In general, information became constructed as an important mode for regulating drinking behavior through attitudes (Rothstein 1992).

In legislation adopted in 1977 (Prop. 1976/77:108), there was a further shift in the discourse. Abuse was still the focus, but general use was also included in the formulation of policy, and the goal of limiting alcohol consumption was formulated more clearly in the introduction to the legislation:

[6] These goals seem to reflect what Olsson (1990) and Room (1991) have referred to as the 'dream of a better social order'; i.e. the notion that a population can be taught, and learn, to drink in a rational, controlled manner, rather than drinking that leads to inebriation. Olsson's work refers to how this dream has been used as argumentation in Swedish mass media as support for a reorientation of policy. This example of legislation demonstrates that this dream has also been encoded in official discourse.

[7] One of the points for which the report was criticized, by among others Kettil Bruun (1975), was that it did not define what constituted moderate drinking. There was no attempt to determine where the line between moderate and immoderate consumption practices could be drawn.

> ... includes suggestions for social policy measures of various kinds that aim to remove the causes of abuse and hinder use of alcohol that leads to harm. It is further suggested that measures should be taken that focus on limiting total alcohol consumption (Prop. 1976/77:108, p. 1).

Fragments of an emerging formation in discourse can be detected here. Alcohol issues were described in the passage above as both more expansive and more diffuse than they were identified in previous discourse. The proposition referred to "causes of abuse" as well as "use of alcohol that leads to harm". The latter phrase is quite broad. Harm caused by alcohol consumption could include the drinking of alcoholics or alcohol abusers as well as other types of drinking that were related to forms of harm, but with which, addiction could not be detected. Thus reference to *harm* opened up the discourse, so that other forms of drinking could be defined as problematic without openly challenging the alcoholism as disease formulation.

In broadening the boundaries to alcohol harm, new boundaries were also introduced. Of particular interest here is that questions related to care and treatment of alcoholism became disentangled from broader alcohol concerns and policy during the 1960s and 1970s. During the 1970s a commission to investigate treatment and social services related to several conditions was introduced and alcohol abuse treatment was shifted over to this arena.[8] The 1974 APU report emphasized that its primary concern was not with the treatment of alcoholism, but with understanding what caused people to drink too much. Policy suggestions focused strictly on the latter. This introduced a distinction between measures taken before alcohol abuse had occurred and those taken afterwards, and placed a greater emphasis upon prevention than at any time previously.[9]

Still, it is clear that the APU report largely focused on the need for individuals to maintain responsible drinking habits, and defined the problem as one of the individual (see also Bruun 1975, p. 10–11). Even with the 1977 legislation

[8] A social services commission was established in 1968; legislation, however, was not adopted until 1982. One of the major issues dealt with in the commission was the question of compulsory treatment. During the early years of the commission, there was support for compulsory care in at least some cases. However, by the end of the 70s the commission turned against such measures (cf. Gould 1988: pp. 42–43). While it is beyond the parameters of the dissertation to consider shifts in treatment issues, it is interesting to note that in the 1970s a law was passed that developed a unified committee for considering cases related to child care, temperance and social assistance. This replaced the formerly separate committees for each of these social issue arenas. One of the results of this, may have been a further integration of alcohol questions within the broader project of the advanced welfare stat. Ironically, it also linked alcohol abuse once again to social assistance from which it emerged in the 1910s. Two new laws were initially constructed, the SoL (a social services law) and LVU (compulsory care of young popel) in 1980. A second commission was initiated to investigate compulsory care of adults, resulting in LVM (compulsory care of alcoholics and drug abusers) in 1981. In this case, alcohol abuse was associated with drug abuse and addiction in general.

[9] As Svante Nycander has pointed out (1967/1996), the unique character of the motbok system was that it integrated these two aspects of alcohol issues. This means that the legislation emerging during the late 1960s and 1970s was a turning point since it introduced a distinction here.

that followed, the total consumption and public health definition of alcohol issues was not fully articulated. It was not until 1980 that total consumption and the protection of public health became key concepts in the formulation of policy goals. In 1980, a coordinating body for alcohol concerns, *Samordningsorganet för alkoholfrågor,* SAMO, was established by the Board of Health and Welfare following the suggestion of the APU in 1974.[10] Members of the committee included a broad array of policy arenas including representatives from several ministries—social, justice, communication, budget, education—and from the labor market, leaders from municipal levels of government, customs officials, and the minister of health and welfare. The inclusion of such a broad array of voices followed the more social orientation of the alcohol discourse after the 1960s.

Policy was to be based on research, particularly "international alcohol research" that had "shown that when the average consumption level of alcohol increases, there is also a tendency for the number of heavy consumers (storförbrukare) to increase and therewith for medical alcohol harm to increase" (DsS 1980:10, p. 63). Additionally, strategies for dealing with alcohol issues and limiting consumption were to take the form of limiting availability, through price policy and the closing of the retail monopoly on Saturdays, among other means. Population-based regulation methods were emphasized.

The SAMO report also briefly considered treatment for alcohol abuse. Such discussions were coupled with overviews of additional health care costs associated with drinking, but which were the result of non-alcoholic forms of drinking. This was also an interesting shift in the discourse, since the relationship between alcohol harm and alcohol abuse could be logically described, as it could not have been during earlier discursive formations. This will be more fully discussed below.

Major Tenets of the Total Consumption/ Public Health Formation

The total consumption of alcohol and public health were fully articulated in discourse by the 1980s, and in the remainder of the chapter I will examine this. As an initial example, one can consider the following quote from 1993, which provides a point of departure for further exploring the form of discourse. The problem is stated as follows:

> Alcohol problems affect everyone, not only a small group of alcoholics. Research demonstrates that increased availability of alcohol leads to greater total consump-

[10] In the 1977 legislation, primary responsibility for overseeing alcohol policy was transferred from the Department of Finance to the Board of Health and Welfare, as per the suggestion of the APU.

tion levels in society. As this takes place, more persons find themselves in the risk zone, and more people become alcoholics. Experience from Sweden as well as other countries demonstrates that the more alcohol is available, the higher the average alcohol consumption level and therewith the more we find alcohol problems including: diseases, mortality, violence and social isolation (Systembolag brochure, "Varför ska vi behöva lida...", fråga ett).

Within this text is a repetition of the claims detected in the medical discourse presented in the last chapter. Indeed, the excerpt refers to 'research' that 'demonstrates' certain 'facts'. These 'facts' concern the relation between the total consumption level of a society and the incidence of conditions defined as 'alcohol problems'. The text draws attention to some additional information as well. First, the problems associated with alcohol belong to everyone since they "affect everyone". There is, here, a collective threat at stake. This is not just the problem of "a few unfortunate alcoholics", i.e. some individuals. Indeed, the consumption practices of one individual are linked to those of all others in society since the more alcohol is consumed by a society in total, the more we find people "in the risk zone". This statement also implies that the total consumption of a society is an indicator of harm or alcohol problems. Finally, there is a key relationship between availability of alcohol and the amount of alcohol people drink. The more alcohol people *can drink*, the more they *likely will drink.*

The excerpt above was selected from a public information brochure. However, as I shall further demonstrate in this chapter, similar concepts, arguments, assumptions and narratives are found in reports and texts throughout the 1980s and into the 1990s. In particular, the importance of the total aggregate consumption of a society and its relation to the 'problem' is the most cited 'fact' of the discourse. This 'fact' was promoted through the adoption of a scientific model to describe this relation, and several theories that were developed in relation to it. These theories were also coupled with what has been referred to as a 'public health perspective' or approach, to form the basic parameters for defining alcohol as a public problem during this formation.

Basic Parameters of the Formation

The Total Consumption Model[11]

In 1983, Leif Lenke observed that "A thesis that has begun to pervade more and more of the Swedish alcohol debate, is that total- or per capita consumption is the factor with the greatest bearing upon alcohol-related harm in society." (Lenke 1983: p. 45). Indeed, from 1975 onward, total consumption be-

[11] As others have duly noted, it is difficult to find an English equivalent to the Swedish term, "totalkonsumtionsmodellen". While many studies utilize the term 'single distribution model', I have chosen here to use a direct translation of the Swedish term, 'total consumption model'.

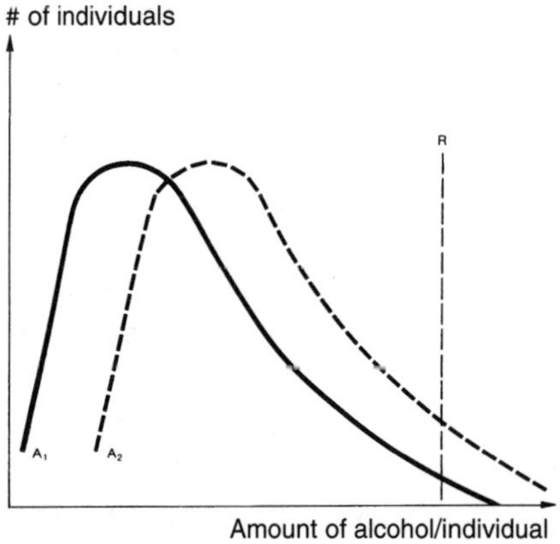

Fig. 3. The correlation between total consumption and alcohol abuse in a populatin according to the total consumption model, from. Arvidsson, O. (Ed.) (1984) *Alkohol-politiken och forskningen* (Alcohol Policy and Research), Riksbankens Jubileums Fond, p. 109. Line R indicates the boundary, above which, individulas are regarded as having an alcolhol abuse problem.

came a key concept in the alcohol discourse.[12] References were made to the model and key texts that are regarded as developing it[13], in all public documents concerning the alcohol problem as a social problem between 1977 and the present. In these, emphasis is given to the link between the total aggregate level of alcohol consumption and the rate of unwanted medical, social and economic conditions in society.[14]

Although the total consumption model appeared as a 'new' fact within the texts from the late 1970s to the present, the model was in fact 'discovered' by the French demographer, Sully Ledermann. In 1956, Ledermann's work, titled *Alcool, alcoolism, alcoolisation.* received little if any attention in Sweden.[15] However, it was rediscovered by a group of international scholars in 1975 and linked to public health and prevention strategies; and by the mid 1980s, Ledermann's doctoral dissertation was one of the most cited texts within the discourse.[16]

As a short summary, Ledermann's work suggested a universal distribution

[12] Although there are references to aggregate alcohol consumption in the official discourse prior to the 1970s, it was not until the late 1970s that this formed a major premise of discourse. For example, the temperance commisison which presented its reports during 1944 contains reference to "totalkonsumtion" of alcohol, and presents aggregate statistics.

[13] These key texts include Ledermann's 1956 dissertation, which is discussed below, several works by Ole Jørgen Skog, who tested the model's validity and adapted the model to better reflect the Scandinavian reality, and the Bruun et al. work from 1975, as well as other texts.

[14] See Ds S 1977:1, Prop. 1976/77:108; Ds S 1980:10, Dir. 1980:47, Ds S 1981:23, Ds S1981:25, SOU 1981:1, Prop. 1984/85:181, Socialstyrelsen redovisar 1987:5, Socialstyrelsen 1987, Socialstyrelsen 1990, SOU 1993:50, SOU 1994:24–29, Ds S 1994:92.

[15] Berridge and Thom (1996) have also noted that in Great Britain, where the total consumption model/theory has also been adopted in public documents, Ledermann's initial work and report received no attention. It was 'rediscovered' during the 1970s.

[16] The total consumption model was named in the organizational platform of IOGT-NTO in1961, although it did not have a strong pull at the time (Gustafsson 1984).

curve for alcohol consumption across societies. In particular, he argued that alcohol consumption was log-normally distributed in homogeneous populations, i.e. consumption followed regular patterns. Following from this, he also suggested that the total average consumption of a society could be used as an indicator of the number of heavy alcohol consumers (alcoholics) in that same society. Keeping in mind that the scientific discourse during the 1950s was largely concerned with alcoholism, the model developed by Ledermann was proposed as an instrument for locating and studying the *disease*.

Initial verification of the total consumption model was carried out by two Dutch epidemiologists, Jan de Lint and Wolfgang Schmidt (working in Canada), and in a series of studies from the end of 1960s to 1970s they demonstrated that the the general distribution of heavy consumers of alcohol tended to rise and fall in concert with the average alcohol consumption level for a population. During the 1970s, de Lint visited Sweden to attend a temperance conference, attended by additional social scientists to present these results (Bromme 1996).

The breakthrough for the total consumption model in Sweden came with a WHO seminar in Toronto in 1975. Alcohol researchers and health administrators tested Ledermann's basic thesis and theories through cross-national data. This seminar resulted in the publication of the WHO report, *Alcohol Control Policies in Public Health Perspective* (see below), which came to have a tremendous impact upon future policy formulations.

Further testing of Ledermann's thesis was conducted by Ole Jørgen Skog, (1982) a Norwegian statistician and sociologist who confirmed the log normality of distribution. Skog also provided some explanation of why the distribution of consumption moves in concert up and down the chart with average consumption level in a theory of collectivity of drinking cultures, or social network model of alcohol consumption (Skog 1985, 1991a, 1991b). Following Skog's work, the most recent alcohol policy commission summed up the "message behind the model" in the following way:

> The message behind the model is that alcohol habits are transferred from group to group until nearly the entire population has been affected. Use gives rise to abuse, thus total consumption must be restricted, this is the message (SOU 1994:24, p. 52)

Theoretical and conceptual compliments to the total consumption model included the 'availability theory of alcohol'. At the WHO meeting in Toronto, it was stated that the empirical data collated, pointed to price level and availability as having an effect upon consumption levels. Availability was particularly an important factor for the general consumption level (Bruun et al. 1975). It was also noted that there was a complicated interplay between availability and distribution on the one hand, and price levels of alcohol on the other.[17]

[17] This theory provided an opportunity for economists to also join in research practices around alcohol later on.

Introducing Public Health

In 1975, a group of researchers, in cooperation with the World Health Organization, presented a position pieced titled *Alcohol Control Policies in Public Health Perspective* (Bruun et al. 1975). The report built on epidemiological methods and a public health model that emphasized the broader implications of Ledermann's findings (the total consumption model) for alcohol-related disabilities and problems at an aggregate level. These were linked to a conception of health rather than to a 'disease'. In defining public health, the report stated that it:

> ... refers to all matters related to the physical, mental and social health of populations. The concern of public health is for this report seen as speaking to the broad concerns of the community, with the ready admission that any statement in terms of population means (or even means and distributions), will not necessarily illuminate consideration of the individual case. (Bruun et al. 1975: p. 12).

As this excerpt reveals, the work introduced not only a new concept, that shifted research and legislative attention to a broader group, but also proposed a shift in strategy for dealing with alcohol problems. The evidence accumulated was used to argue for the development of alcohol "control policies" that were aimed at populations and decreasing total consumption, rather than upon individuals.

The Definition of the Problem

The Cause of Alcohol-related Problems

Although Ledermann's model and the 1975 position piece discussed above (Bruun et al. 1975) presented total consumption as a concept related to the distribution of drinkers, the link to public health strategy and availability theory contributed to a transformation of the model to a causal framework within discourse. This was particularly true as the model became linked to the availability theory. In particular, the causal relationship between alcohol consumption and other putative conditions provided guidelines for using research and interpreting findings in official discourse. It appears to be have been assumed that there was not only a correlation between rates of alcohol consumption and other putative conditions in society, but that it was the role of science to uncover these conditions. The model, being scientific, provided support in the legislative texts.:

> Behind the alcohol policy goal of reducing the total consumption of alcohol is the knowledge that there is a close correlation between the extent of alcohol consumption and the extent of alcohol harm. The conviction that this correlation is true, has been confirmed during recent years. International alcohol research has shown that when the average rate of alcohol consumption increases, the number

of heavy consumers does as well, and therewith medical harm increases. (DsS 1980:10, p. 63).

As the above citation suggests, the cause of alcohol issues was formulated somewhat differently according to the public health formation. The causal agent was not the person, his or her morality, or the social or political structure that had let her down. Rather, alcohol was presented as the active agent. For example, the foreword to the 1975 report by Bruun et al. stated that it should be recognized that:

> ... alcoholism or alcohol dependence is only a part of alcohol-related problems and that alcohol problems and alcoholism cannot be tackled without a policy towards the agent, alcohol. (Kaprio 1975, p. 9)

This statement, and regard for alcohol as the "active agent", was repeated in future research reports, policy statements and public information materials. The relation between alcohol consumption as correlated with, and often assumed as the cause, of other negative phenomena became a part of the common stock of knowledge (Berger and Luckmann 1966):

> [T]he problems caused by alcohol are an obvious reality (Systembolag 1988, p. 23).
>
> It is a well-known fact that alcohol is an important causal factor behind far too many accidents. (Romanus, Uppdraget 1989 p. 4).

The shift in the causal story also had consequences for the configuration of the social context (environment) and its importance for alcohol issues. A report from SAMO in 1980 stated, for example:

> That the alcohol question should be placed within a social context does not mean that it is just an expression for dissatisfying social conditions. *Alcohol plays therewith an independent role in creating and exacerbating problems.* Heavy consumption of alcohol is far from always a symptom of poor social integration. (DsS 1980:10: p. 29; emphasis my own).

Although this is not a direct challenge to the previous formation, there was a shift from presenting the social environment as a contributory factor, to placing a greater emphasis upon the destruction of one's social environment as a result of drinking.

As the causal agent, the substance of alcohol, was transformed from a substance that *was "abused" by alcoholics* or by troubled and isolated persons, to a dangerous substance that *would abuse people's bodies and minds.* Its mere presence became increasingly worrisome. This is particularly clear in relation to young people's consumption, where any amount of consumption was described as dangerous. Exposure to alcohol was said to lead young people inevitably along a destructive path because young people were especially vulnerable to addiction, due to their immaturity.

This dependence means that they miss their elementary education and therewith lose their chance at making it on the labor market.

Youths who drink often have financial problems. Beer and wine cost money and since intoxication goes before morals, many young people end up in criminal activity and prostitution. (Systembolag brochure, "Vad gör alkoholen i ditt barn", unknown year, p. 2).

The Threat Posed by the Alcohol Problem

Although alcohol had previously been formulated in many different ways, as posing various sorts of threats (Mäkelä 1983), health concerns came to occupy center stage. This followed demands for a non-moralizing discourse. As Bergmark and Oscarsson (1990) have remarked in their observations of the current discourse, "The alcohol question is no longer a public health problem only; it is *undeniably* a public health problem" (p. 214). The centrality of public health was seen as a new consciousness and the basis for restructuring policy:

> Alcohol harm has thus developed to a major public health problem. The rising consciousness of this fact has led to increasing demands for a new orientation in alcohol policy. (DsS 1980:10:p. 64).

Conditions that were caused by alcohol were presented as something most of us have experienced, and thus as something we all share an interest in resolving.

> But at the same time, one cannot be indifferent to the fact that children are born every year in our country with significant disabilities that are the result of their mothers' drinking. No parent wants to pick-up their intoxicated teenager from a hospital or the police station. Almost everyone has a relative or workmate who has a problem with spirits or knows someone who has been battered by a drunk person.
>
> Alcohol harm is a tangible reality for most people—not some unrealistic 'invention' of the mass media or authorities. The last few years have provided frightening and to some extent new knowledge about alcohol. This has to do with fetal damage, violent crimes, rape and battering of women. New medical techniques have made it possible to detect liver damage and provided new knowledge on brain damage. (Systembolag, brochure, "Bakgrund", 1989: p. 9)
>
> Alcohol harm affects individuals, as well as groups and society as a whole (Folkhälsorapport 1991, SoS rapport 1991:11, p. 180)
>
> The problems that alcohol causes, affect not only alcoholics, but have to do with all of us.
>
> The more alcohol that is sold, the more the Swedish people lose... (Systembolag brochure, "Det svenska Systemet", p. 5).
>
> The alcohol question has to do with each and every one of us. It is really about taking responsibility for oneself and standing up for one's 'fellowman' (medmänniska) (p. 14).

The collective aspect of the problem, constructed through phrases such as 'most people', 'almost everyone', and by identifying parents, linked each individual to a broader issue. This is further emphasized since alcohol-related harm was presented as a consensus issue among the general public and even among political parties.[18]

> Decisions concerning the focus of alcohol policy are made by the parliament, where opinions often cut across party lines. Everyone is in agreement that as we face the future, one of our most important tasks is to limit alcohol harm. (Folkhälsoinstitut et al. 1993, p. 13).

It was not only the fact that anyone might come into contact with problems that provided a basis for arguing that alcohol was a problem. An important aspect of how alcohol consumption was elaborated as a collective problem, was through reference to the links between moderate consumers and heavy consumers, and to the potential for any person to suffer harmful effects from their drinking. One of these claims was that moderate consumers contributed to the existence of heavy consumers. In the official discourse, Skog's observation that alcohol consumers moved up and down the scale of consumption, was transformed to something of a causal relationship between these two groups. Moderate consumers contributed, together with heavy consumers, to an aggregate of consumption that then determined how many heavy consumers and problems there would be in society.

> That the risk for medical and social harm increases together with alcohol consumption is something that everyone agrees upon. The correlation between harm and consumption holds for both each individual person and for the population as a whole. The more a person drinks, the greater the risk for harm, and the greater number of heavy consumers of alcohol there are in a society, the more alcohol harm (Folkhälsoinstitut et al. 1993, p. 40).
>
> This has to do with the empirically demonstrated relationship, that the more alcohol that is drunk in total in a society, the greater the number of heavy consumers will be and even more will be harmed by their drinking (SOU 1987:11, p. 91).

Intertwined with this claim, was the introduction of a more subtle boundary between these two types of drinkers; these were no longer two distinct groups, but the one merged into the other.

> There is no sharply defined boundary between abusive and normal drinking levels. Rather, there is an even transition from moderate consumption to excessive consumption. If total consumption increases, a larger proportion of the population will therewith assume consumption levels that lead to problems (Systembolag brochure, Bakgrund, 1988: p. 41).
>
> When total consumption increases, it is thought that moderate as well as heavy consumers increase their alcohol consumption (SOU 1987:11, p. 91).

---

[18] This point reminds me of a telling anecdote. I presented a paper titled, "Many Problems, Many Experts, One Model" at a NAD research meeting in 1995. My point was that Swedish discourse on alcohol could be characterized as highly hegemonic and lacking a critical or reflexive voice. One of the participants of the seminar, from CAN, recalled that she had been involved in organizing a political debate before the 1993 election. A representative from each of the parties in parliament were invited to discuss their position on alcohol policy. The first member of the panel described his party platform, and thereafter all other members of the panel stated that their views were the same, and there was no debate.

Through these claims, the drinking practices of one individual were linked to those of all others. All drinkers were constructed as potentially threatening for the good of society as well as themselves, and in turn were accountable for the level of social, medical and economic problems related to alcohol.

With this equalization of moderate and heavy consumers, all persons were regarded as potential sites for the emergence of alcohol-related harm and disabilities. It was no longer the independent and deviant consumer, or the person already displaying signs of alcoholism who were problematic, but all persons' drinking was potentially problematic. In this sense, the threat as well as the resulting harm was collective. Perhaps ironically, most alcohol harm was viewed as something caused by moderate drinkers since they represented a much larger percentage of the population than heavy consumers.

> It is not only chronic alcohol consumers who are harmed by alcohol. These stand a greater personal risk of being harmed, but since normal consumers comprise a large proportion of the population the account for a substantial share of alcohol harm. This concerns, in particular, injuries related to intoxication associated with accidents and violence (SOU 1987:11, p. 91).

Although the emphasis was on the health threat of alcohol as the primary threat, other types of threats were also linked to alcohol problems. Among the most visible was an economic threat. Economic concerns related to alcohol surfaced during the latter half of the 1960s and the 1970s. These focused primarily upon alcoholism as a threat to worker productivity. This concerned individual companies, of course, but it also threatened the Swedish economy at large. Programs aimed to assist workers with alcohol problems at job sites were introduced during these decades with government support. Although these programs have not disappeared, the emphasis during the 1980s and 1990s shifted somewhat. The economic threat of alcohol was posed by the cost of society for dealing with and resolving alcohol-related problems not to the productivity per se. This is to say that the arena of economic difficulties related to alcohol was expanded to encompass not only loss of productivity due to individual drinking problems, but also the cost of hospital care for those injured in an alcohol-related road accident, incidences of violence, battering, child abuse and long-term care. In one information brochure consumers were informed of the "real costs" of alcohol to society:

> What many do not know, is that the state's costs for alcohol due to sick days, accidents, care, etc. amounts to 33 billion crowns per year. The state's 'profit' from alcohol is calculated at 22 billion crowns per year if one includes the revenues from taxes, profits generated by the monopoly and a certain decrease in among other things, the cost for state pensions... The state's 'loss' is, then, approximately 11 billion crowns per year... It is, therefore, more cost effective for society to limit alcohol consumption, which is the whole idea behind the Systembolag and around which there is a broad political consensus. (Systembolaget brochure "Vad gör alkohol i ditt barn", unknown year, p. 18).

Not only was alcohol costing the tax payer and the state more money than one might think, but it was also draining resources from other areas where there is a collective interest. If consumption could be decreased:

> Then we can use a great deal of these tax revenues for things other than rehabilitation and care-taking of forsaken (utslagna) youths. Everyone benefits if we can limit alcohol harm. (Systembolaget brochure, "Varför ska vi behöva lida för några få alkoholisters skull? och sjutton andra frågor", unknown year, fråga tre).
>
> If we succeed in lowering alcohol consumption... it would imply tremendous welfare and health-related benefits at the same time health care could reduce care measures currently necessary to care for those suffering from alcohol-related illnesses (Prop. 1984/85:191: p. 69).

The economic threat that alcohol posed was further supported with the presentation of a text by Anders Johnson, an economist, in 1983, *titled 50 miljarder kostar supen (*Booze costs 50 billion crowns).[19] A follow-up to this book was also presented in 1991, at which time it was argued that alcohol cost society 100 billion crowns (and the title of the book was consequently updated). The figures and arguments Johnson presented, appear often in the median and in informational materials, and even legislative statements although his work is not formally cited as the source of such figures.

The Dispersion of Alcohol-related Problems

As already indicated, the total consumption model together with the public health perspective suggested that alcohol was not merely a problem of consumption, but led to the contraction or development of numerous other conditions that were experienced as putative. Already during the 1950s liver cirrhosis was identified as an indicator of alcoholism since there was a correlation between the condition and chronic alcohol consumption. As additional forms of harm to the body were discovered this began to provide evidence that damage occurred not only as the result of chronic consumption, but also through heavy consumption on single occasions. Moreover, these empirical findings were imbued with a somewhat different meaning in the public health/total consumption context. While the existence of liver damage and other medical and social problems was once regarded as a means of identifying alcoholics, it now became the thing to be explained and prevented.

Alcohol-related conditions included both physiological ailments—including disease, acute illnesses, and psychiatric problems—as well as social problems (e.g. domestic violence, child abuse and neglect, isolation of the drinker, unemployment, etc.). Although Swedish texts concerning the alcohol problem generally stressed that there was no clear boundary between moderate consumers and heavy consumers, there was still reference to a group of persons with chronic heavy drinking. However, alcohol-dependency was not *the* problem,

[19] As of September 1997, this amounts to approximately 6.3 million U.S. dollars.

Table 5. *Discursive objects—Alcohol harm*

Alcohol harm			
Alcohol-related disabilities and mortality			
Physical-acute	Physical-chronic	Psychological	Social disabilities
Overdose/ alcohol poisoning	Liver cirrhosis	Impairment of emotional control leading to violence	Failed work performance
Trauma from road accidents	Other liver damage	Short-term memory loss	Absenteeism
Injury (from alcohol-induced violence)	Damaged nervous system	Dementia	Dismissal
Acute pancreatitis	Brain damage	Delirium tremens	Unemployment
Head injuries	Peripheral neuritis	Alcoholic hallucinosis	Workplace accidents
Acute hepatitis	High blood pressure	Withdrawal fits	Debt
Fatal alcohol syndrome	Bood vessel damage	Poor sexual performance	Housing problems
Birth defects	Heart disease	Disinterest and loss of initiative	Destitution
Drownings	Anemia		Child abuse
Boating accidents	Stroke		Domestic violence
	Gout		Drink-driving
	Abdominal complications, e.g. chronic pancreatitis		Violence
	Stomach ulcers		Theft
	Heartburn		Fires
	Cancer of oropharynx, larynx, esophagus, stomach, liver, rectum, female breast		
	Skin disease		
	Blood disorders		
	Muscle disease		
	Bone disease		
	Disorders of the immune system		
	Low blood sugar level		
	Skeletal deterioration		
	Gangrene		
	Balance problems		
	Poor muscle coordination		
	Blackouts		

but one of many alcohol-related problems, an important shift from previous formations. Physiological problems related to alcohol consumption were generally detected in relation to mortality and alcohol consumption was therefore considered a contributing factor in numerous forms of death (from the victim of a drunk-driving accident, to the heavy consumer who contracted a fatal liver disease).[20]

A good example of the 'official list' of alcohol-related problems (conditions to which alcohol is viewed as contributing to in some way) is provided in the book *Vid dina sinnens fulla bruk* (With the full use of your mind) (Dahlgren et al. 1991), which is distributed to consumers by the state alcohol retail monopoly, *Systembolaget.* Table 5 summarizes the conditions identified in this publication, with the addition of conditions also named in the various public

[20] A regularly cited figure for the number of alcohol related deaths per year is somewhere between 5000 to 6000.

reports examined in this study (SOU 1974:90, SOU 1980:1, SOU 1994:24), and research reports related to them (e.g. Norström 1994).[21] The sheer volume of the empirical work that had been conducted by the 1980s and into the 1990s, and the conditions that were discovered no doubt constituted an important building block for constructing alcohol as problematic, and as something that any of us could come into contact with. As more conditions are discovered, the greater the likelihood that someone we know has experienced an alcohol-related problem.

This list of conditions is both broad and extensive. As Hauge (1991) points out, given this interpretation pretty much any form of social policy or social steering could be based on the public health perspective. Indeed, the lines between alcohol as a public health problem and other phenomena is rather unclear, as the newly established *Folkhälsoinstitut* demonstrated[22]. Conditions appeared to belong to the alcohol problem series if a correlation could be located between consumption and the condition. Such conditions become public health problems—even if they are also recognized as social problems—indirectly, as alcohol is a category within a series of public health problems.

The dispersion of the problem also involved a categorization of what 'type' of drinking caused what 'types' of problems. I detect here two additional rules for organizing the problem. Drinking 'types' were often considered the basis for defining drinking culture or drinking habits, and concerned how much and how often alcohol was consumed.[23] Generally speaking, a distinction was made between high levels of consumption on single occasions, daily or chronic heavy consumption over very long periods of time, as well as illnesses developed slowly in relation to daily moderate consumption.With regard to the types of alcohol problems that were constructed, the discourse referred to those that were immediate in their consequence, and those that develop over longer periods of time. Among the former category were traffic and boating accidents, violent acts against women or among two intoxicated persons. Among the latter are such problems as liver cirrhosis and various forms of cancer.

[21] Such conditions are also summarized or further explored in international collections of research on alcohol from a public health perspective, including publications by the Oxford Medical Group, in which Scandinavian alcohol researchers have contributed (e.g. Edwards et al. 1994, Holder & Edwards 1995). Both the Swedish and international research findings provide the basis for public reports and informational materials. For example, the policy guidelines for a new Alcohol Control Board (Ds 1994:92) point to Edwards et al. (1994) and Holder and Edwards (1995).

[22] During its first years of operation the new public health institute was to focus on alcohol, narcotics and sexuality as public health arenas.

[23] These are generally the two dimensions that are used when comparative analyses are carried out. Thus, drinking culture, particularly in Sweden, is largely considered in quantititative terms rather than, for example, interpretative or symbolic terms. The study of alcohol consumption as symbolic practice would involve an investigation into how those persons who consume alcohol define what they are doing, and its meaning. Examples of this type of approach are Sulkunen's (1992, 1994) studies of the new middle class and why they are opposed to alcohol control, Sulkunen, Alasuutari, Nätkin, Kinnunen (1997) of the urban pub, and a similar study by Abrahamson in Sweden (forthcoming), among others.

Table 6. *Damage effects due to alcohol consumption*

Damage effects from alcohol consumption	Direct	Indirect
Chronic effects, long-term use	Liver cirrhosis Cancer Ulcer High blood pressure Other organ damage	Psycho-social and economic problems
Excessive consumption, single occasional	Acute poisoning with different related harm Cases of death Intoxication	Accidents Violence Problems of public order Criminality

> (Harm) can be direct or indirectly a consequence of alcohol consumption. Harm can arise immediately following consumption that led to intoxication, e.g. accidents, poisoning and violence, or after long-term or periodic bouts of heavy consumption, e.g. organ damage (Folkhälsorapport SoS rapport 1991:11: p. 180).

In a public health report from 1987 (Socialstyrelsen 1987:15), this division and dispersion is clarified in a typology of health issues related to different forms of alcohol consumption. This table is reproduced above (table 6). Different solutions could be adopted according to the different 'types' and conditions identified.

The Distribution of Authority

Since alcohol was constructed as a scientific problem, research communities provided an important function within the alcohol discourse as they were distributed authority for generating knowledge about the problem. Typically, public information such as the brochures cited earlier and policy proposals and reports pointed to expert authorities as they quoted statistics and other 'facts' about the alcohol problem. Additionally, the two public commissions that dealt with the alcohol problem after 1974 relied upon research by social and medical scientists. The two reports by the special research committee established in 1980 both cited researchers' work concerning links between the state of public health and alcohol consumption, and argued for an expansion of support to the research sector dealing with alcohol (DsS 1980:23, DsS 1980:25). The 1994 commission report on alcohol offers a clear example of a dependence upon the research community, and included several appendices of studies carried out by social scientists (see Olsson, Kühlhorn, Norström, Hibell).[24]

Reference to the scientific community does not necessarily imply the predominance of one group over another. As Schneider (1978) points out, the more specific definition of the alcohol problem is decisive for what scientific community will be indicated to treat or provide information about alcohol; if alcohol is defined as a disease, medical practitioners, because they have a monopoly over the use of labels such as 'sickness', 'illness' and 'disease' will be indicated. However, the distribution of authority concerning social problems is more than simply the application of a label. If, for example, we strictly focused our attention on the label of the current problem as one of 'public health' one might be led to believe that medical professionals are the foremost or only experts. Yet, the discipline of alcohol studies is constituted by a multi-disciplinary field of scientists. Among the literature one finds contributions by medical doctors (including psychiatrists, micro-biologists, neurologists, etc.), sociologists, social workers, and criminologists, and economists among others.[25]

Based on the extensive list of alcohol-related problems examined above, it would seem that alcohol problems can be found all around us. The public health concept included all types of injury—both medical and non-medical (Hauge 1991), which provided an opportunity for different types of scientific experts to contribute to the advancement of knowledge about alcohol problems. Moreover, as I argued in *Chapter 3*, once prevention was described as a multi-level strategy, a further basis for multi-disciplinary cooperation was created.

The extensive list of empirical findings also implies that the field of alcohol research had become highly diversified by the 1980s. Rather than a single field of alcohol studies, numerous specialty areas in medicine and social science had emerged. It can probably be deduced that research findings were not only the result of a shift in the framework for conceptualizing alcohol problems, but also fueled this shift. New discoveries provided the basis for developing new specialties, and in turn, additional discoveries were made from within these areas. The total consumption model and in particular, the concept of prevention, offered a means of integrating these within a social order.

The Solution Complex

Statements made in the context of the public health/total consumption formation reflected a strong belief in the ability of science to predict the occurrence of problems and in the state to intervene in order to bring about social order. While this can also be said of other formations, in this context the solution complex was based on a theoretically formulated logic of prevention, and a

[24] The studies requested by the alcohol policy commission concerned: the effects of alcohol policy restrictions, the total consumption model, prevention strategies, projections of alcohol harm development in Sweden, unregistered consumption, statistical and non-statistical alcohol, and methods for determing the extent of alcohol abuse.

[25] Psychologists are not absent from Swedish discourse either, although their work seems to be primarily focused upon treatment concerns, and does not figure prominently in the current discussion.

distribution of this logic in relationship to an imagined continuum of health. Following from this, intervention was viewed to be possible at different stages along this continuum. Three levels in particular were addressed in the official discourse, which were borrowed from medicine: primary, secondary and tertiary (SOU 1994:24). Each level of prevention was associated with a strategy focused on a more specific group within the population:

primary prevention—population strategy
secondary prevention—high risk strategy
tertiary prevention—care and treatment strategy

The continuum of health and prevention moved from measures that aimed to provide a universal means of prevention on the one hand, and on the other, policy aimed at specific target groups, that were shaped in relation to the concept of 'risk'.

It is important to note, that in the discourse itself, it was argued that there tended to be two ways policy was constructed. Policy could either aim at "high risk groups", i.e. those with a likelihood of contracting alcohol-related illnesses, etc. through individually-oriented measures, or through universal measures of prevention that were aimed at the entire population (see for example SOU 1994:24: p. 56). An interesting feature of Swedish policy and discourse at this time was that it consciously combined both, something that became possible due to the identification of the different levels of prevention. Combining individually-centered and universal measures was presented as an "integrated strategy" (SOU 1994:26), rather than as an alternative or competing strategy.

Primary prevention spoke to the broad concerns of society, through public health that was regarded as a public good (Sulkunen 1991). The Bruun et al. report from 1975 provided the basis for formulating public health in future documents, by defining it in its working statement:

> The concern of public health is for this report seen as speaking the broad concerns of the community, with the ready admission that any statement in terms of population (or even means and distributions), will not necessarily illuminate consideration of the individual case. (p. 12).

The strategy of primary prevention in the form of universal policy tied together with the threat that was constructed in the context of this formation. At the level of primary prevention, the official discourse pointed to universal policy measures that were logical given the "prevention paradox".[26] This paradox stated that:

[26] From what I was able to observe in my data, the prevention paradox was first discussed internationally by Kreitman (1986), and was accepted in Swedish discourse without further testing of the argument until 1994, when Norström (1994) was asked to review prevention strategies by the alcohol policy commission.

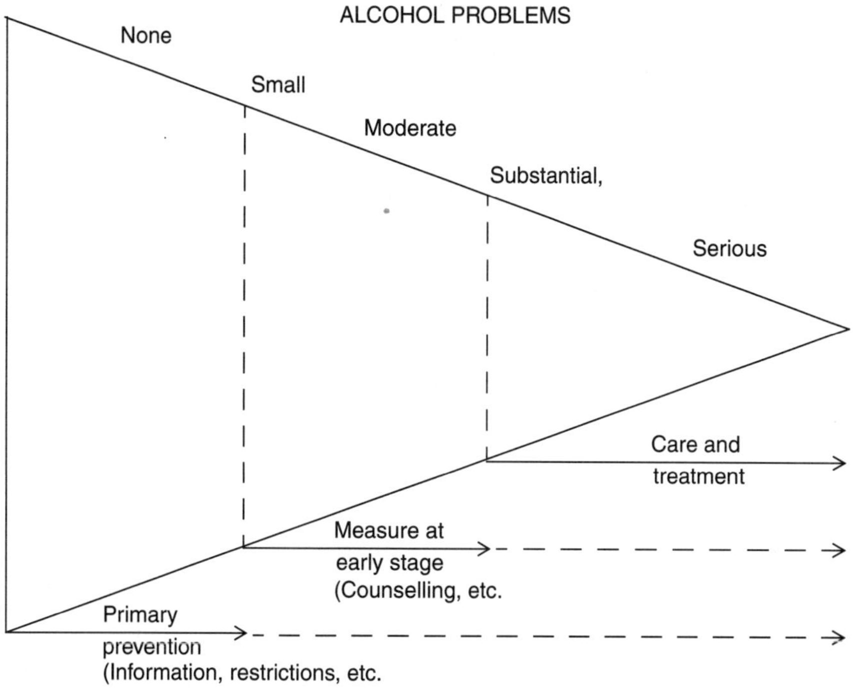

Fig. 4. The dispersion of alcohol problems and prevention measures according to the total consumption/public health formation. The figure is adapted from SOU 1994:26, p. 24.

> Research results have shown that a population strategy has a great potential for preventing a number of health problems. One explanation for this is the so-called prevention paradox which states the following. Even of the risk for injury and illness is greatest in a smaller group of high risk individuals who are very vulnerable to risks, this group is nonetheless so small that only a minor portion of injuries will occur here. The reason is that the rest of the population is likely exposed to a smaller risk, but nonetheless contributes to a greater number of injuries due to its size (SOU 1994:24: p. 56; see also discussion in SOU 1994:26, pp. 28–29).

What is interesting here is that since all drinkers were to be submitted to prevention techniques, such measures needed to be coordinated at a macro level. Thus, while science was charged with identifying the types of harm that needed to be prevented, the provision of such measures fell largely upon the state. This was further supported since alcohol harm prevention was linked to a general welfare policy:

> Prevention work must be carried out in several arenas. The basis for this is a general welfare policy that relates to e.g. the labor market, housing and free time as well as a good social policy, all aimed at providing people with a solid social environment (levnadsförhållande). In addition, special measures are necessary in order to change attitudes and behavior with respect to the consumption of alcohol. (Folkhälsorapport 1987, Socialstyrelsen redovisar 1987:15: p. 139).

The specific goal adopted in relation to primary prevention was based on the Bruun et al. report from 1975, and aimed to reduce consumption levels, which was to be achieved through two modes: controlling supply and demands.

> [C]hanges in the overall consumption of alcoholic beverages have a bearing on the health of the people in any society. Alcohol control measures can be used to limit consumption: thus, control of alcohol availability becomes a public health issue (Bruun et al. 1975: pp. 12–13).

Supply was regulated through limiting the availability of alcohol. This was based on the notion that, "the less alcohol is placed on the table, the less people drink". In this respect, the state retail monopoly for alcohol sales, *Systembolaget,* became a protector of public health, and was regarded as a tool for achieving a 25% decrease in alcohol consumption as dictated in the WHO resolution.

> Today, the close correlation between the availability of alcohol and the measure of alcohol consumption is viewed as clearly documented. While alcoholic beverages are made more available alcohol consumption tends to increase. Inversely, restricting availability tends to have an inhibiting effect upon consumption...
>
> If Saturday closings in Sweden would lead to a decrease in alcohol consumption—albeit limited—this is in and of itself given the alcohol policy goal of reducing total consumption (DsS 1980: 10: p. 74).
>
> All measures that can lead to a decrease in alcohol harm should be therewith, according to the committee, considered, both measures that limit availability of alcohol and those that reduce demand (DsS 1980:10, p. 94).

Such a measure resulted not only in lower levels of alcohol consumption, but also fewer problems and harm. For example, violence was used in the case above as one measure of the success of limitations.

Demand was regulated through prices levels, which were identified as a particularly useful means of protecting health, if not the "most important instrument". Additionally, it was also posited that consumption rates were correlated with economic growth and personal income:

> Regulation of price levels on alcohol beverages is perhaps the most important instrument for hindering consumption of alcohol drinks. As a policy, prices on these beverages must be set relatively high and be continuously adjusted to the general fluctuation in price levels (DsS 1980:10: p. 67).
>
> Fluctuations in income also determine to what degree individuals can afford to purchase alcoholic beverages. Disposable income, in real measures, has seen a sharp increase in recent decades. This has provided a means for a substantial increase in alcohol consumption despite what have been basically unchanged prices on alcoholic beverages in real terms (ibid. p. 67).

These measures are summarized in a public health report where two lists of practices are identified and presented in table 7 below.

It was also argued that the prevention paradox did not hold for some forms

Table 7. *To limit demand and availability*

Measures to limit demand aim to	Measures to limit availability are exemplified by
Influence attitudes and knowledge to create favorable public opinion for decreasing alcohol consumption	Age requirements for purchases
Limit advertising and marketing	Restrictive approach to the establishment of sales locations and limiting business hours.
Maintain a high price level	Ban on boot-legging (for minors), moonshining, and limiting traveler's' quotas.
Support activities of organizations and associations (as alternatives to drinking)	Alcohol sales are allowed only under specified conditions
	Creation of alcohol-free environments

of injury such as liver cirrhosis (e.g. SOU 1994:26, p. 30, Norström 1994). It was therefore necessary to also adopt measures aimed at those who were heavy drinkers, in order to:

> prevent both acute and long-term alcohol-related injuries. Measures should be taken whether or not it is thought that the person is especially likely to development a more serious abuse problem (SOU 1994:26, p. 30).

Secondary prevention strategies concerned 'risks' and 'risk groups'.[27] [28] In general, risk dealt with the *possibility* that danger and putative conditions could arise, not on their actual existence (Petersen & Lupton 1996: p. 19). It was calculated using epidemiological methods and bio-statistics that provided an assessment of the probability that ill health would develop under certain conditions, e.g. alcohol consumption at different rates. In the Swedish discourse, the concept of a risk group appears to have replaced the former notion of the 'deviant'. Rather than moral problems, "risk group strategies" were referred to in the discourse.

> The logic behind risk group strategies is that heavy consumers run the greatest risk of developing alcohol harm and that it is therefore particularly useful to reduce their consumption in particular (SOU 1994:24: p. 56).

Although alcohol consumption could be a risk activity for any drinker, some groups were particularly identified as vulnerable to developing problems. The public health discourse defined a risk group as:

[27] Texts from earlier formations of the discourse also touched upon risks and risk groups. However, risk groups were generally regarded as those collectives that were more likely to develop alcoholism or alcohol abuse, and not the broad range of conditions related to alcohol harm according to the public health. An example of the 1970s discourse on risk is found in SOU 1974:93: pp. 71–73 concerning the medium beer crisis and abuse of this beverage by young people.

[28] Although there is a substantial literature on 'risk', I am here concerned with how risk is constructed in the discourse at hand, and not within the Sociology of Risk. For an introduction to the Sociology of Risk, see Beck (1992). For applications of risk sociology in the area of social problems and health see e.g. Gabe (1995).

> groups that are vulnerable to more or more frequent health problems than other groups. (Prop. 1984/85:181: p. 25).

Two common risk groups that were identified in the discourse were women and young people or children. Both of these groups were regarded as possessing one or several unique attributes that meant they had a greater probability of experiencing harm than other groups. With respect to young people and children, the concern was that young people had not developed self-control and maturity that would allow them to handle the choice of what to drink, when, in what quantity and how to handle situations with alcohol in their bodies.

> There are, of course, differences between different people when it comes to sensitivity to alcohol. Children and young adults are particularly vulnerable; for example, they can suffer serious brain damage since their brain cells are still developing. Neither are they psychologically mature to use alcohol
> (Systembolag brochure, Bakgrunden 1988: pp. 23–34).

As the second risk group in the discourse, women were targeted as a consumer group whose total aggregate consumption had been on the rise, and was therefore of concern. Moreover, women's bodies were viewed as more susceptible to the effects of alcohol due to their status as potential mothers, and due to the composition of their bodies. [29]

> (T)he same amount of alcohol has a much greater effect upon women than men. This is not only because women generally weigh less than men, but also because women differ with respect to body fat, hormones, and burn alcohol at a slower rate than men. (Systembolaget 1988, pp. 23–24).
>
> There are few today who would raise their eyebrows to see a woman 'having a glass'. But there are always two sides to the coin and when it comes to alcohol there are big differences between men and women. Biologically women are more sensitive to alcohol than men. Put plainly, women can't handle as much. Furthermore, when a woman is pregnant it is also dangerous for the child if the mother drinks alcohol. (Systembolaget, Kvinnor & alkohol, p. 1).

In addition to public health campaigns, the most recent public commission to investigate alcohol prepared a special report to specifically address women and alcohol (SOU 1994:28). Of specific concern was that:

---

[29] Additional risks were associated with women's alcohol consumption. One campaign in 1993 by the public health institute took the form of a television advertisement. In the ad, an 'obviously' intoxicated woman is raped at a party by a man. The ad then states, "A 'no' always means 'no', but the fact is that women who are drunk stand a much greater chance of being raped than those who are sober". In this example, a woman's safety from men is correlated with her level of consumption. Contact with alcohol is contact with problems and harm. Although the dissertation does not deal with the issue of power and modes of power in relation to the 'modern' problem of alcohol, I think this advertisement could be interpreted as an example of the ways in which alcohol, as a public health problem, is linked to other elements constituting a lifestyle and practice of the self. Women are targeted in the ad as sexual beings who must control themselves by controlling their bodies in order to avoid the negative consequences that can follow from carelessness.

> alcohol consumption among women has increased, that women's drinking patterns have changed and that our knowledge of support, care an treatment needs to be developed to meet women's special needs. There is also a need, according to the directive, to pay particular attention to the damaging effects of alcohol on fetuses (p. 9).

The Alcohol Problem as a *Social* Problem

In this final section I want to answer the question: What is it that is social about the social problem of alcohol in Sweden? I will not discuss the ways in which the problem is constructed through a social process; rather, I take this as a given since others have already analyzed the social process of constructing legislation in Sweden (see e.g. Bruun & Frånberg 1985; Johansson 1995, 1996; Rothstein 1992). What I will consider here are the kinds of social implications that can be detected through the discursive formation discussed in this chapter; the 'social-ness' of the problem, if one will. There are three implications that are important: 1) the link established between moderate drinking and heavy consumption, 2) the construction of the collective as both a perpetrator and object of threat, and 3) an inclusive distribution of authority.

In the analysis above, I indicated that in the context of the total consumption/public health formation it was emphasized that there were no "sharply defined boundar(ies) between abusive and normal drinking levels." Moderate drinking was linked to abusive drinking in three ways. First, abusive drinkers were seen to be recruited from moderate drinkers. This took place as the mechanisms behind the propensity to drink (e.g. availability and price) were loosened up, and all drinkers increased their drinking in concert so that more individuals ended up in the 'risk zone'. Second, the 'prevention paradox' suggested that moderate drinkers, because they were greater in number, actually accounted for a greater proportion of harm related to alcohol. This group shared something in common with immoderate drinkers, and in this way they could not be strictly distinguished from them as non-deviants. Finally, research practices that contributed facts to this formation, identified conditions that were not only related to long-term chronic drinking, but also to single occasions of drinking and other drinking practices. This again, distributed the problem over a larger group of persons in society, and suggested that all persons potentially constituted a site for the emergence of harm.

Alcoholism, or alcohol abuse, is typically regarded as a social problem in a number of western countries. In these countries, the problem is indeed social because a group of deviant individuals are regarded as posing a threat to or cost burden on the social community in various ways. In these cases, we can say that the social aspect of the problem is related to those who can potentially be objects of threat. As I show in this chapter, the alcohol problem in Sweden is not restricted to the problematic behavior of a specific group, but drinking as such has also been problematized. In the context of the public health/ total consumption formation, the story of threat proposes that individuals contribute to a collective amount of alcohol consumption, and thereby collectively contribute to the level of harm in society. So, in this case, all individuals can potentially pose a collective threat. At the same time, all individuals are also regarded as potential objects of this threat, since different forms of alcohol consumption can lead to various forms of alcohol harm in themselves, or in others who could in turn harm them. In short, it can be said that the social impact of alcohol problems is found on both sides of the threat equation.

Finally, the concept of alcohol harm, as opposed to alcohol abuse or alcohol-dependence syndrome, opened up the field of phenomena that could be related to alcohol. Physical disabilities, mortality, social disabilities as well as alcohol dependency syndrome/alcohol abuse, were related to the problem. This in turn, opened up a space for cooperation among a broad range of experts. Rather than competition between the medical and social scientific communities, as is sometimes the case outside Sweden, the total consumption model and public health perspective provided a common point of departure for research in all these disciplines.

Having outlined the ways in which the public health/total consumption formation has constituted alcohol as a social problem, the following chapter, *Chapter 5*, will look at current challenges to this social order. I shall show that, among other things, the integrative hegemony described in this chapter is currently being threatened by the introduction of additional actors in the arena bearing concepts and statements that adhered to other discursive formations.

CHAPTER 5

Swedish Public Health and the European Free Market

In this final empirical chapter I investigate some very recent shifts that can be detected in the alcohol discourse as well as consider some of the implications of these. Although the previous three chapters focused upon the official and medical discourses, this chapter will consider a range of voices, including the medical and official but also pay attention to previously suppressed sources of discourse. My reasons for presenting a broader range of voices are in part due to the fact that the discourse is in motion, so-to-speak, and official statements are in the process of being formed. In addition, I will be arguing that the confrontation between the Swedish alcohol discourse and the EU discourse has resulted in the opening up of an alternative framework for discussing the alcohol problem, and particularly its solutions. One of the characteristics of this space is its openness to a different grouping of discursive participants.

Paving the Way Towards 'Liberalism'

In *Chapter 2,* I noted that during the 1960s and early 1970s a unique discursive formation could be detected. The notion that alcohol problems were individual problems was questioned. Causal mechanisms for alcohol problems were located in social and economic structures. In response, the necessity of *Systembolag* and other control measures were brought into question as these aimed to shape individuals rather than systems. A reversal of this formation, particularly the causal formulation, was then detected during the mid 1970s and well into the 1980s. However, the 1980s is described as a paradoxical period during which time, state rhetoric emphasized restriction, while actual practices shifted towards more liberal forms (Reuter & Tigerstedt 1992).

One of the contingent factors that supported this move towards a restrictive approach to alcohol was that existing institutions, such as the retail monopoly and other control measures, were linked to scientific theories and 'facts'. It was argued that the availability theory and the total consumption model indicated that alcohol was indeed a social problem, and that limiting availability for all persons was a key to solving the problem. Moreover, the scientific model provided a bridge between alcoholism and other forms of alcohol consumption; and established the necessity of universal control measures. One of the key features of the discourse that emerged with EU integration was a questioning of this normative position.

Despite a move towards more restrictive alcohol measures a second momentum in the official and scientific discourses was a recognition that the legitimacy of control measures rested upon their acceptance as reasonable practices by the population. This is to say that the legitimacy of state intervention was no longer taken-for-granted as it had been before the 1960s.[1] The critical discourse of the structural definition of alcohol appears to have left behind a residue. Hence, in all the Nordic countries, a more 'liberal' and less restrictive approach in practice developed throughout the 1980s (Reuter and Tigerstedt 1992). One expression of this was a turn towards a more customer-oriented and service-minded approach at the state retail monopolies. In the Swedish case, one can note that while Gould observed in 1980 that the displays in the windows at *Systembolag* encouraged patrons to 'flush it down the loo' (Gould 1980), these same windows present attractive exhibits of the latest products in the monopoly's assortment today. There is an acceptance within the official discourse that persons do find alcohol consumption a positive activity since this is a part of Swedish culture. However, this consumption should be kept at a minimum.[2] One can increasingly read about the positive sides of wine and spirits consumption in the customer magazine *Uppdraget*; and the homepage for Systembolaget boasts Europe's largest selection of wine.[3] In a very general way it has been accepted that persons do and will consume alcohol. With the emerging discourse around the EU, this 'liberalism' as it has been called, continued to be institutionalized.

[1] This is likely due to the legacy of the critical discourse of the 1960s, which specifically questioned the problem and solutions.

[2] Robin Room (1991) has described this as a move from a 'dry' to a 'wet' alcohol policy. A dry policy would aim at encouraging less consumption with an eventual aim to wipe out alcohol completely. In contrast, 'wet' policies accept that persons do drink and take this as a starting point in constructing policy. The wet policy approach can be likened to the 'harm reduction' ideology practiced in the area of narcotics control in many Western European countries. These programs assume that persons will and do engage in narcotics consumption, but that the role of intervention is to reduce harm as much as possible, rather than stamp out use altogether since this is an unrealistic goal.

[3] *Systembolag's* advertising campaigns have also shifted over the last two decades. In particular, campaigns tend to be less moralizing, and attempt to provide 'information' rather than judgement (Pogacar 1994). This appears to follow a shift in the 1954 legislation adopted and again reiterated in the 1970s to an emphasis upon the need for information.

Is There a European Alcohol Discourse?

Against the backdrop presented above, and the analyses of *Chapters 3 and 4,* I want to consider the emergence of an official European alcohol discourse.[4] This presents an immediate problem since an established arena for alcohol policy does not exist at the EU level (Ugland 1995). Even at the national level, an 'alcohol problem' such as that institutionalized in Sweden and the other Nordic[5] countries is not found in the policy discourses of other European countries (Fahrenkrug 1993).[6] Neither is alcohol an institutionalized segment of social or welfare policy, as in the Nordic countries. Rather, policies relating to, and influencing, alcohol-related practices are scattered throughout various policy arenas such as agriculture, fiscal, or economic.

With respect to the scientific or expert discourse, there are also several hurdles. Indeed, a prerequisite for discussing the 'facts' of alcohol problems as defined according to the Swedish discourse of the public health problem of alcohol, is access to statistical records and other data for measuring the problem. Yet, these are incomplete or unavailable in most countries, making international comparison very difficult.[7] Since statistics are only kept when there is an interest in such information (Kitsuse & Cicourel 1964, Simpura 1987), this further indicates a very different perspective on alcohol than that found in the Nordic countries. Not surprisingly, there are few research reports and other texts produced in continental European countries on alcohol and alcohol problems (Fahrenkrug 1990: p. 59).[8]

---

[4] In addition to different discourses, one could also consider the different symbolic meanings associated with drinking between Sweden and Europe. As Mäkelä (1983) has pointed out, while alcohol consumption—particularly wine—has historically been integrated with mealtimes in Southern Europe, it has been disassociated from food consumption to a great extent in the Nordic countries. Alcohol in Sweden—generally in the form of strong spirits—has signalled festivity and the symbolic transition from the Lutheran work week characterized by the suppression of pleasure to a the celebration of pleasure. See also Gustavsson (1991) for a cultural analysis of Sweden's alcohol consumption from pre-industrial to industrial society; and Ambjörnsson (1991) for working culture.

[5] By Nordic countries, I am referring primarily to Norway, Sweden, Finland, and Iceland. Denmark is also a Nordic country, but has followed a different course with respect to alcohol policy, as well as EU membership. Norway is a member of the EES, but not the EU, while Finland and Sweden both became members of the EU in 1995. There are many similarities, but also differences among the Nordic countries. Currently a Nordic project, Sammanligninger av Nordiska Alkohol Politiska Systemer (SNAPS) supported by the Nordic Council for Alcohol and Drug Research (NAD) is considering the impact of European integration upon the control systems of Norway, Sweden and Finland, as well as the modern history of these systems. A forthcoming book is planned for January 1999.

[6] In his study of alcohol policy in EC-member states, Fahrenkrug discovered that in 1989 before Sweden and Finland joined, only four EC countries had what could be likened to alcohol policy programs (Denmark, France, UK, and West Germany).

[7] In Germany, for example, Bloomfield (1996) has sought data and statistics on drinking patterns and consumption levels. At this point in time national surveys have not been conducted, and data must be drawn from national health surveys that contain questions concerning alcohol.

[8] These types of documents are readily available in the Nordic countries. Additionally, statistics have been easy to keep since all sales of alcohol are regulated through state monopolies. In Norway and Finland alcohol research centers exist, and Sweden boasts Europe's largest library for alcohol and narcotics (at CAN).

In the absence of a specific EU alcohol discourse or control policy, I turn now to a consideration of what might be regarded as a counterpoint to such policy: policy to support the alcohol trade. The alcohol and spirits industry constitutes a substantial economic sector within the EU, and in world markets. European producers account for 58% of all wine on world markets, and the EU is the biggest malt producer in the world (EC 1997: p. 3–119,134). Various spirits are produced as well, notably brandy and whiskey. Among some of the issues concerning Europe at the present time, is an imbalance in supply and demand in the wine market.[9] A second policy issue has been a reduction of barley cultivated area and a simultaneous growth in the demand of malt from non-EU countries. This has led to a restriction of supply on the EU market and generated a rise in prices (EC 1997).

In light of the economic significance of the alcohol industry, the institutions developed in the European countries have very different aims than those of their Nordic neighbors. An example of one of the institutions created in the EU is a common agricultural policy, CAP.[10] One of the aims of this policy was to construct special organizations to market agricultural products, including wine and spirits (see Sulkunen 1978 and Kortteinen 1990). Following these intentions, a wine board was established in 1970 specifically for the marketing of wine. Its purpose is to secure incomes in the agricultural sector and to stabilize prices in order to achieve a balance between supply and demand within the union, and regulate price levels. Additionally, the wine board seeks to coordinate trade with third parties outside the EU and support structural changes in the market. The EU has also adopted action plans from time to time as a means of intervening in the market. Actions have aimed both at decreasing production, as well as increasing demand within the EU, especially in countries that are not traditional wine-drinking cultures, and in this way, reduce surpluses and maintain price levels (see Kortteinen 1990 for further discussion).

It should also be noted that discussion of alcohol and problems that are associated with its consumption are not completely absent. In several European countries efforts to develop what are referred to as "point sobriety programs", such as legislation and campaigns aimed at drunk-driving, have been introduced by the state or local activists.[11] At least some of these were initiated in response to the adoption of the health for all goal by the European Regional

[9] Wine production has increased by approximately 1% per year while demand for has been decreasing in Europe. This has led to an overproduction through the 1980s and to what has been referred to as Europe's "wine lake". This condition has been regarded as a problem to be dealt with through common policy.

[10] An important part of the backdrop to this policy is that in 1958, when the common market was created, two of the world's largest wine producing countries—France and Italy, were forced to provide equal access to one another's markets. This was not without its problems. Although France had a history of interventionist policy related to control of overproduction, Italy's market was far more liberal (Kortteinen 1990).

[11] Notable here is France, where alcohol consumption rates are the highest for Europe, yet have been steadily declining since the 1950s (Moser 1992). France is likely to be the only country to acheive a 25% decrease in consumption to the year 2000.

Council of the World Health Organization in 1992.[12] This plan included a cut in alcohol consumption by 25% in all European countries by the year 2000. A recent meeting in 1995 resulted in the adoption of the message "alcohol—less is better" by the delegates of the conference (WHO 1996).[13] Also in this direction, the adoption of the International Classification of Diseases system, ICD-9, by the WHO in 1977, and its attention to clarifying and further identifying several alcohol-related health conditions and death classifications, has raised some awareness among the medical communities in different countries (see also Helmersson Bergmark 1995: pp. 48–53).

Several resolutions have been taken by the EU-Parliament, which center on organizing European-wide efforts to combat specific problems related to alcohol (See also Fahrenkrug 1989; European Community Resolution 1982, 1986a, 1986b). These efforts do not constitute a specific policy arena at this time, however. Rather, alcohol concerns have found entry into EU policy at a more general level of health and particularly public health issues, which have gained more attention within the EU in recent years. The Maastricht Treaty[14], included a commitment to developing EU-wide policies aimed at improving the health of all its citizens (Articles 3(0) and 129 note explicit provisions on public health). The only health issue that was specifically named as an arena for action is drug dependence. As a priority issue, several resolutions have been adopted throughout the 1980s and 1990s. At this time, however, alcohol has not been classified as a drug, neither has alcohol dependence been linked with drug dependence.

On the heels of the Maastricht Treaty, a commission communication from 1993 (COM (93)559 final 1/11) investigated the "common issues" facing all European nations. These issues were identified as: aging population, increasing population mobility, rising expectations concerning health, socio-economic problems. Of the diseases and health threats that are identified, alcohol does not figure prominently. It is mentioned only briefly in relation to lifestyle changes necessary to bring about a reduction in those health problems that are highlighted.[15] For example, it is stated in relation to forms of cancer related to the respiratory system that, "In recent decades there has been an increase in cancers related to tobacco and alcohol" (p. 3). In contrast, drugs and drug dependence is mentioned as a specific concern, and related to the increase in

---

[12] Representatives from all countries in theWHO European Region met in 1991 to develop a European strategy for health for all. As part of this, they endorsed a European Alcohol Action Plan in 1992, and made a commitment to develop a positive set of guidelines at a later time. This action plan was adopted by the Swedish government during the same year. A third meeting took place in 1995, the WHO European Conference on Health, Society and Alcohol, held in Paris.

[13] In the charter, five ethical principles and ten strategies for alcohol action are laid out. See WHO 1996.

[14] The Maastricht Treaty came into force in 1993 and essentially established the European Union (formerly European Community). With the Treaty, the Treaty of Rome was replaced.

[15] The diseases identified are cancer, cardio-vascular diseases, accidentes, suicides, AIDS and other communicable diseases, and a catchall category that includes:mental illness, musculo-skeletal conditions, and respiratory conditions.

population mobility which translates to "the potential for increased drug abuse" (COM (93) 559, Part A, p. 1).

Cross-nationally, efforts to combat alcohol issues in Europe have found support among different professional groups, especially researchers, activists and pressure groups. One outlet that brings many alcohol activists together is Eurocare, a pressure group supported by Nordic alliances (e.g. temperance organizations and medical professionals), among others. Even in this cooperative effort, discrepancies with respect to the definition of the alcohol problem are evident. The group has found common ground primarily in relation to point sobriety programs and support for alcohol-dependent persons. More radical measures, such as support for national retail monopolies across Europe, have not been regarded as feasible. Interest in alcohol issues has also grown among researchers, particularly within the growing field of social medicine. Perhaps a stronger platform is the fact that epidemiology is gaining in importance internationally, and with it the 'new public health' (Petersen & Lupton 1997). This potentially provides a common language – based on risk and potential harm— and a framework for producing knowledge on alcohol in much the same terms as epidemiologists and social medicine in Sweden. For example, a group of researchers was appointed in 1983 to write a report that would include future policy recommendations concerning the EU (Davies and Walsh 1985; see also Fahrenkrug 1993).

Despite the efforts and initiatives identified above, several hurdles remain. An explicit authority or institution has not been created in order to construct and implement policies in this direction. Moreover, the Commission's involvement in health-related issues is generally "justified in terms of its relevance to economic, employment and commercial considerations" (Randall 1997: p. 278). One expression of this is that all the public health issues now identified by the EU can be related to the economic sphere. For example, the over-proportional aging population is a concern since "the burden of paying for them will fall on a relatively smaller working population"; economic and technological developments in the workplace are said to affect people's health as they become more mobile; rising expectations from employment will lead to greater costs; and socio-economic problems concern high levels of unemployment that "are leading Member States to apply tight constraints on public spending" (Randall 1997: p. 278).

This situation points out that despite the programs, initiatives, and measures noted above, one can expect that alcohol is generally defined in relation to its use as a product within an economic market on continental Europe. Its position in relation to health, has only recently begun to receive more attention at a European level. As shall be illustrated below, the economic and legal framework for EU discourse poses problems for Nordic official and medical discourses where social policy goals, until only recently, have taken precedence over fiscal and economic goals. Economic policy was constructed in order to support the aims of the welfare state discourse and associated practices. For alcohol, this has meant that although alcohol policy has important impacts on fiscal arenas, it is defined foremost as an arena within social and welfare policy in general.

EU Discourse on Swedish Alcohol Policy

The Road to EU Membership

Before delving into the EU discourse, a brief synopsis of the process behind Sweden's membership is useful. Sweden, together with other EFTA (European Free Trade Association) countries, entered into negotiations with the European Community to join what would become the European Economic Space in 1989. Due to set-backs in reaching an agreement between Sweden and the European Commission, a final agreement was not ratified until the spring of 1992. At this time, it was decided that Sweden would join the EES on 1 January 1994. During the Fall and Winter of 1992, harmonization and integration of many policy areas took place such that Sweden came into compliance with the EU constitution following a proposition in the parliament (Prop. 1991/92:170).

During the EES negotiations, the Swedish government argued that its discussions with the EC were focused on economic issues; alcohol policy was a social policy issue, and as such was not a current theme. The government further argued that alcohol policy would be discussed when the time came to negotiate membership in the EC. However, a number of decisions were made during this time that affected Swedish policy.

In 1990, before the EES negotiations were completed, Sweden's then Prime Minister Ingvar Carlsson announced that Sweden would submit an application for membership in the European Community. The application itself was submitted by the Prime Minister on 30 June 1991, only a few months before the 1991 general election, but before Sweden joined the EES. Negotiations concerning membership in the EU began during 1993 and continued until the spring of 1994, only a few months before a general election.[16]

In addition to the negotiation process, the fate of Swedish membership in the EU was also to be determined through a public referendum held in November of 1994, only six months after the negotiations concerning the terms of membership were completed. Some groups, e.g. temperance associations, argued that their decision to vote 'yes' or 'no' to the EU would depend upon the outcome of these negotiations (Sutton & Olsson Hort 1995).[17] Two major mo-

[16] For a discussion of the Swedish negotiation strategies, and a comparison of these with the other Nordic countries in relation to alcohol policy, see Ugland (1996).

[17] Elsewhere, myself and Sven Olsson Hort have investigated the response of Swedish temperance associations to potential EU membership. Although these organizations initially threatened to vote in a collective 'no' if alcohol policy were compromised through negotiations, all but the youth section of IOGT-NTO and Verdandi, backed away from this in the end. Organization leaders argued that this decision was for each individual member to decide since the EU involved many issues and concerns.

vements emerged in the period prior to the referendum: Nej till EG/EU and Ja till Europa. The 'no' campaign incorporated the EU threat to alcohol policy as an argument against membership.[18] However, it is interesting to note that the 'yes' campaign did not argue that a good reason to vote yes was that alcohol would be more readily available or cheaper. Rather, EU enthusiasts merely pointed out that membership did not necessarily imply that sovereignty on alcohol regulation policy would be foregone; there were strong indications that Sweden could maintain its monopoly system[19].

The EU Challenge

From its inception, the EU has sought to support free commerce within the Community through the development of a common legal structure for regulating trade (Godfrey & Powell 1989). The goals of the EU are framed first and foremost according to an economic discourse, and second, according to a legal discourse that takes its point of departure from the Treaty of Rome and later, the Maastricht Treaty. This has meant that economic concerns have been given precedence over social policy issues. This priority structure was apparent in the official texts produced in the name of EU in response to Sweden's membership application. Swedish practices were judged in the first instance for their compatibility with the economic goals established in the EU, and second for their legal compatibility.

Already in 1988, before Sweden applied for EU membership, discussions in the EC concerning a harmonization of tax levels within the Community raised questions concerning Swedish practices related to alcohol (Ugland 1996: p. 7).[20] The Commission suggested a common point tax on goods that would be regulated centrally (COM 1987). This would have had a tremendous impact in Sweden, where taxes at the time were based on a highly progressive tax schedule in relation to volume percent of alcohol (Lag om Dryckesskatt 1977:306). After much criticism, a second tax plan was presented in 1989 that established

[18] Much of the critique began with the EES negotiations. Among others, "Kritiska Europa Fakta", printed by Nej till EG,argued that "EC membership would worsen the pain" since "An increased flow of alcohol and narcotics will be the result if Sweden takes a full step and becomes a member of the EC-union. Namely, border controls will disappear" (EES special).

[19] For example, in an informational brochure from December 1992, Ja till Europa answered some "common questions about the EC". In answer to the question, "Will *Systembolag* disappear if we join the EC?", Ja till Europa answered, "Systembolag will be around as long as we ourselves want it to be." (Ja till Europa 1992: p. 26). I requested information from Ja till Europa in 1993 on its alcohol policy stance. I received a photo-copy of a document on LUF:s EG-handledning. This piece was interesting because the dominant discourse on alcohol is the major framework. It is pointed out, for example, that:

We continue to maintain that sales of alcohol should only take place via Systembolaget. The risk for large private purchases of alcohol from other countries is reduced if these bottles are not allowed to be resold on the market (p. 5).

The piece also points out that the EC does not have a common alcohol policy, but that all EC member states have agreed to the WHO goal of lower consumptn by 25%.

[20] This was also a concern for Norway and Finland, where special excise taxes and alcohol are also used as a means of regulating alcohol consumption.

minimum tax levels and goals for alcohol drinks (COM (89) 527 final). This resulted in some shifts in Sweden, whereby the progressive system was replaced by taxes related to volume percent of alcohol on spirits, a flat tax rate on all categories of wines, and tax classes related to beer classes (based on volume percent of alcohol (SOU 1994:24: p. 46).[21]

Although Sweden was granted a right to maintain high price levels, the Commission warned that practical, rather than legal, barriers to this practice might arise in the future with open borders:

> Sweden would be able to maintain this level of taxation after accession , but would have to consider the consequences of the abolition of restrictions on private individuals' purchases in other Member States (pp. 14–15).

Also of interest is that this statement links taxation measures to travelers' quotas, which were also considered problematic within the EU framework. One of the "four freedoms" of the union is the free movement of goods across borders. For Sweden, where travelers' quotas on alcoholic beverages had been highly restricted, this posed a problem, as shall be further discussed below. On this point, Sweden as well as Finland, were able to negotiate an exception to the free movement of goods. Travelers' quotas were increased from previous levels, but remained more restricted than otherwise would have been the case (Ugland 1996: p. 69; SOU 1994:24: p. 42).[22]

Tax levels and travelers quotas were not the only issues of concern to the EC. At the time of Sweden's negotiations with the EC, Sweden maintained monopolies on the production, export, import, distribution and whole and retail sale of alcohol through its two state companies: *Vin och Sprit* and *Systembolag*. This monopoly structure came into question during the negotiation process. In a 1992 Bulletin of the European Communities it was noted that several state monopolies would need to be deregulated and that the alcohol monopoly, "seems to be the most worrying" (p. 25). The report further noted that:

> In general, the granting of exclusive rights concessions must respect the basic principle of equal opportunity for all economic operators, whether domestic or from other Member States (ibid.)

Domestic monopolies were largely regarded as instruments of projectionist policies, and hence a threat to equal opportunity within the community. From a legal standpoint, Sweden's alcohol monopolies were seen as demonstrating a

[21] As a result of this new policy, a number of formerly expensive and exclusive wines become much cheaper. Ironically, the price of wine is often much cheaper (before taxes are applied) in Sweden than in other European countries. This is because the *Systembolag*, as the sole retail operator, makes large purchases at a discounted rate. Even with the taxes applied, prices can be lower than on the continent.

[22] Sweden received an exemption from travellers quotas on alcohol until the year 1997, when this would be reviewed. Travellers from other EU countries were allowed to bring the following amounts into Sweden for private consumption: 1 liter spirits, or 3 liters strong wine; 5 liters wine; and 15 liters beer. This was a substantial increase over previous limits.

breech of Article 37 of the Treaty of Rome[23], which assured free competition. The burden of demonstrating that this was not the case for alcohol products fell upon the Swedish government (see below).

Although the Swedish delegation argued that the monopolies were strictly a response to a public health necessity, the letters exchanged between Sweden and the Commission indicate that the inevitable link between alcohol as a public health threat and the monopolies as the 'only' correct solution was not immediately clear. Or, as Ugland (1996) has pointed out, "... alcohol policy rhetoric and argumentation can be interpreted from other viewpoints and interests" (p. 65). With respect to the monopolies, the EU was unconvinced that this policy goal could not be met by other means "less obstructive of competition".[24]

> The Court in its judgment of 12 March 1987 on case 178/84 considered that the protection of public health should entail the erection of barriers to free trade only if absolutely necessary. The Commission is of the opinion that the health objective of the alcohol monopoly could be achieved by means which are less obstructive of competition (SOU 1994:25, Appendix 10: p. 306).[25]

Despite European skepticism, the Swedish government argued that in addition to being a response to a public health problem, the monopolies did not discriminate in favor of domestic products. The anti-discrimination claim was repeated in all documents from the government. As I shall discuss in the final section, Swedish negotiators managed to salvage the state retail monopoly for alcohol sales, *Systembolag*. However, state monopolies for import, export, production and distribution of alcohol were sacrificed for membership, after being deemed incompatible with the Maastricht Treaty .[26]

---

[23] Article 37 reads as follows:

Member states shall progressively adjust any State monopolies of a commercial character so as to ensure that when the transitional period has ended no discrimination regarding the conditions under which goods are procured and marketed exists between the nationals of Member States.

The provisions of this Ariticle shall apply to any body through which a Member State, in law or in fat, either directly or indirectly supervises, determines or appreciably influences imports or exports between Member States. These provisions shall likewise apply to monopolies delegated by the State to the others.

[24] The Commission's rhetoric here implicitly refers to the principle of proportionality, whereby discrimination or practices that hinder the free market under Article 37, must be in proportion to the aims of the practice to protect public health.

[25] Similar statements were made by the EC-Commission in response to Finland's application for membership. In one letter the Commission expressed:

Broadly speaking the Finnish government defends these exclusive rights on the grounds of public health as a means of combatting alcoholism. The Commission takes the view that health-objectives sought by the alcohol monopoly could be achieved by other means less obstructive to competition (SOU 1994: 25, Appendix 10: p. 307).

[26] Ugland's (1996) work shows that the Swedish delegation expressed a willingness to harmonize the monopolies with EU practices, but also expressed a willingness to maintain these.

Defending Swedish Solutions Outside Sweden

During negotiations with the EC/EU, Sweden (and Finland) argued that the retail monopoly was the most important of the state monopolies in relation to protecting health and fulfilling social and health policy goals (Ugland 1996: p. 66). This argument was presented as a legal issue; and negotiators sought a legal foundation for operating the monopoly. Swedish strategies were defined in relation to the legal framework established by the EU. Article 36, of the Treaty of Rome, provided for the operation of some state monopolies in unique instances where the aims of the monopoly were to protect the health of the people. In an analysis of the EES agreement, the alcohol commission saw this as an opportunity to defend Swedish practices before the Commission:

> Article 36 provides for exceptional practices that hinder the free movement of goods under the condition that these are motivated with respect to "public morality, public policy, or public security; the protection of health and life of humans, animals or plants" (SOU 1994:25, Appendix 10; p. 319).

For Swedish defenders, the 'fact' that the monopolies were a response to public *health* needs, placed it under the provisions of this article. A letter to the EU in 1993 from the Swedish government sought to clarify this by stating:

> The Swedish alcohol monopoly structure is based on important health and social policy considerations and not on commercial grounds. It constitutes a strategic part of a comprehensive policy aiming at the reduction of the total consumption of alcohol and thus minimizing the damage caused by consumption of alcohol in accordance with the European Alcohol Action Plan adopted by the European Region of the World Health Organization (SOU 1994:25, Appendix 10: p. 305).

This construction of the situation transformed the Swedish monopoly from a strange anomaly to something already 'known' and 'recognized' by the Commission. In addition, it shifted the framework for interpreting the situation from an economic sphere, where the Swedish case was weak to the social political sphere where Swedish claims were more resonant. The government pointed out that commitments had already been made to support such a structure, and hence their claims fit well within the EU framework. From the quote above, it is also interesting that in seeking justification for the claims, Swedish supporters referred to the WHO 25% goal for the year 2000. This also suggested that Europe had already recognized the Swedish approach as legitimate. In one letter to the EC-Commission the Swedish government argued for instance that:

> It constitutes a strategic part of a comprehensive policy aiming at the reduction of the total consumption of alcohol and minimizing the damage caused by consumption of alcohol in accordance with the European Alcohol Action Plan adopted by the European Region of the World Health Organization (SOU 1994:25, Appendix 10: p. 305).

Eventually, the Swedish membership negotiations resulted in the maintenance of the retail monopoly in addition to the aforementioned exemption from practicing common travelers' quotas. However, the government also agreed to deregulate the import, export, distribution and production monopolies. These were replaced by an "Alcohol Board" under the jurisdiction of the Department of Social Affairs, which was introduced as an authority for overseeing and regulating the 'new' alcohol market (Prop. 1993/94:136, Ds 1994:92).

Swedish Alcohol Discourse in Motion: Challenges and Confrontations

Defending the Swedish Solution Inside Sweden

Above I cited some statements made by the Swedish government and Swedish representatives in order to defend the Swedish response to alcohol issues before the EU Commission. Similar statements also emerged inside Sweden in order to defend the system there and in some cases to reassure citizens that the government sought to maintain a restrictive alcohol policy. In defending the Swedish response to alcohol issues inside Sweden, public officials were also joined by a number of other individuals and collectives. Among others, this collection of voices included several medical doctors, especially from the field of Social Medicine, temperance movement organizations, and other traditional defenders of a restrictive policy approach.

In the official discourse, the protection of the Swedish system was said to be limited by factors outside the state's power of influence. This discourse can be contrasted with the Swedish position in negotiations with the EU. Ugland (1995) has noted that the Swedish government expressed a willingness to both maintain the basic elements of its system, but also expressed a willingness to adjust these in order to comply with EU laws. Inside Sweden, the adjustments were presented as inevitable and impossible to prevent, although the government and negotiators wished to maintain the traditional policy as much as possible:

> Over consumption of alcohol brings with it extensive social, medical and socioeconomic problems. For this reason, Sweden has long maintained a restrictive alcohol policy.
>
> At the same time, tremendous changes are taking place in the world that affect the heretofore alcohol policy. ... The basis for using a price instrument as an alcohol policy tool will shift. The basis of policy must following this, with information, opinion-building and other alcohol preventive measures having a greater importance in attempting to realize different drinking habits in our country (Prop. 1994/95:89: p. 46).
>
> In the long-run, however, it is likely that the process of European integration will have an impact even in this area. This is particularly the case with price policies (Dir. 1991:124: p. 3).

Discussions of EU membership in relation to alcohol policy became more distinct after the government instated a public commission in 1991. Then Minister of Social Affairs, Bengt Westerberg, appointed a public commission to "investigate current alcohol policy and develop future strategies – not least importantly, in consideration of an EU perspective" (Dir 1991:124). The commission was also directed to "map the familial-social consequences of alcohol abuse and provide an overview of treatment for alcohol abusers" (Dir. 1991:124). The goal of Swedish policy was largely maintained as it had previously been formulated, a line that was followed in subsequent propositions introduced in parliament :

> The Swedish alcohol policy goal to reduce alcohol consumption and alcohol harm remains intact. The means of achieving this goal, even in the future, must be in part a combination of measures to improve awareness of alcohol use and influence attitudes, and in part to limit the availability of alcohol (Dir. 1991: 124, p. 4).

Also in line with the former goals of policy, the commission was asked to develop policy that aimed to affect the demand for alcohol and thereby lower consumption (p. 4).

With respect to EU integration, it was speculated that the major difficulties in the future would be Sweden's price policy. It was feared that the EU would insist upon a harmonization of tax levels, and more importantly of travelers' quotas on alcohol (p. 3). A price policy would not be deemed viable if consumers could cross the border to nearby Denmark and purchase an unlimited number of bottles that could be brought back to Sweden. At the time, a closer examination of Swedish alcohol laws had not been carried out, and this was also seen as an important part of the commission's work.

In total, the Alcohol Policy Commission presented six reports. The first report was made public during the spring of 1993 and addressed questions related to the distribution of alcoholic beverages to restaurants and pubs (SOU 1993:50); as well as providing some documentation for the deregulation of the monopolies in later propositions (Prop. 1993/94:136, Prop. 1994/95:89). The commission also proposed a number of changes in practice in order to avoid discrimination of European operators and products. For example, one of the more controversial proposals by the working group was that foreign distributors should be free to sell directly to establishments rather than using *Systembolag* as their distributor, as was the case at the time. The balance of the reports was not presented until March of 1994, coinciding with the conclusion of formal EU negotiations between the Swedish team and EU Commission.

It is possible to detect the public health formation in the emerging official discourse. For example, the commission's directive was clearly based upon the public health concept and the total consumption model, and the research findings included in the final reports included explorations of the model's applicability and suggestions for how increased availability, fewer restrictions, and/or lower prices would affect alcohol consumption levels and therewith rates of harm. However, numerous shifts can also be detected, which are legitimized in discourse through reference to 'harmonization with EU laws'.

Previously, and during negotiations and debates leading up to Swedish membership in the European Union, the monopoly system in combination with border controls and high taxes were described as *the* solution or means of dealing with the public health threat posed by alcohol consumption. However, when changes in legislation became necessary, what was emphasized was that the goals of policy remained intact, but the means would be somewhat different. The 'problem' was still formulated as one of public health, but the means of protecting this had shifted.

> The Swedish alcohol policy goal of reducing total consumption in order to counteract medical and social damage caused by alcohol was not questioned by the EC-court. It is the discriminatory effects of measures taken to meet this goal that are not allowed. The EC-court legal praxis indicates that import monopolies are forbidden, independent of whether they are exercised in a discriminatory way or not (Prop. 1994/95:89; p. 47).

In addition, scientific evidence and models have remained very important. While the government acted to define alcohol issues for both the international EU community as well as Swedish society, medical and social science experts offered analyses of the situation based on established definitions of these issues, which could in turn, be cited and used by the government and temperance organizations, for example. Their studies emphasized the need to support and maintain the status quo approach to resolving alcohol issues. One means of illustrating this point was the presentation of frightening scenarios of Swedish membership in the EU if control measures were not protected.

> If Sweden were to harmonize alcohol prices with those of the EC average, prices would drop by half. This would lead to at least 3000 more alcohol-related deaths per year—in other words: the EC would harvest ten dead Swedes per day! (Andréasson, DN 1992a: p. 61)
>
> The turbulance would be visible in increased drinking to intoxication, and above all, in an increase in alcohol-related illnesses and death (Kühlhorn 1990: p. 150).
>
> In all liklihood, the transition to a more continental alcohol policy would be accompanied by a tremendous increase of alcohol harm and therewith a greater challenge for the treatment system (Andreasson 1992b: p. 1854).

Temperance organizations actively spread these messages, as did key people in the official discourse as exemplified in the two excerpts below:

> We can calculate almost exactly how many more persons will die of alcohol-related illnesses, how many additional cases of spousal abuse, cases of children born with alcohol-related defects, domestic violence and generally ruined childhoods there will be, when alcohol consumption increases as a result of lower prices (Johansson DN 10/11/91).
>
> With the minimal increase... the number of early deaths increase by 3000 persons per year in Sweden. This is a completely unacceptable effect of closer cooperation with Europe (Ranebäck DN 6/8/93).

Members of the scientific community measured the alcohol problem and estimated changes with reference to the basic assumptions of the total consumption formation. It was argued that if Swedish alcohol policy was not maintained, EU membership would translate to greater availability of alcoholic beverages and therewith increases in death, destruction, and violence. The relevance and usefulness of the total consumption model was also supported through research commissioned in relation the public inquiry into alcohol policy (Hibell 1994, Kühlhorn 1994, Norström 1994 Olsson 1994).

The quantitative approach to operationalizing the alcohol problem and the success or failure of control systems was encoded in discussions of the proposed effects of integration. These were related to the degree to which the system Sweden eventually constructed would deviate from the current organization of alcohol solutions. The discourse presented current solutions as the apex of alcohol control restrictions; it was the best alternative.

> How great this increase in harm will be, is dependent upon how radically policy is restructured (Andréasson 1992: p. 63).
>
> Unfortunately the truth is that Sweden has already applied those instruments that are generally recommended as an alternative to the price instrument and a alcohol monopoly. Information, quite simply, cannot compensate for the tremendous increase in alcohol consumption and alcohol harm that will arise if we are forced to sank prices and abolish the monopoly (Romanus 21/10/93, DN).
>
> Assume that alcohol prices are stabile until the year 1994 and that inflation is 7 percent per year. Assume also that the price elasticity of alcohol consumption is minus 0.75, with an income elasticity of .085, which is suggested by Anti Somervuori from Sweden's state monopoly ALKO, economic research institute. With these figures... alcohol consumption, after EC integration in 1994, will have increased by over 20 percent. Alcohol harm would unfortunately have increased even more (Romelsjö 1991: p. 1351–1352).

According to this scenario, the current system was regarded in the discourse as a key to protecting public interests and protecting society, that must be guarded.

> Different defense mechanisms have been constructed against alcohol-related phenomena that pose a threat to vital functions in our society. It is important to become familiar with this defense system, and above all, to identify the vulnerable points in the system of measures against alcohol harm (Kühlhorn 1990: p. 152).
>
> Some of the most important tasks of the alcohol commission will therefore be to maintain the basic traits of current alcohol policy while an alternative is being built up... Initiatives must be taken to develop primary preventive strategies in order to successfully make the transition from a 'dry' to a 'wet' alcohol policy; therewith, secondary prevention strategies must be developed to reduce the majority of the alcohol-related problems that are found among people with moderately increased consumption habits (Andréasson 1992: p. 64).

Evidence of the 'self-evident' success of the Swedish solution was provided through comparisons with other EU countries, where monopolistic practices did not exist, and the rates of consumption and harm that could be calculated for them.[27]

> Economic interests, together with consumer opinion, prevent a policy in the EC that aims to limit demand in the way in which we in the Nordic countries have followed with the help of taxes and a state monopoly. Each and every EC-country therefore has a higher alcohol consumption than Finland, Norway and Sweden. The social side of the alcohol question is denied or defined as a problem only at the level of the individual (Nycander DN 25/3/90).
>
> Tell people what the Swedish restrictive policy means for alcohol consumption, abuse and harm, and they will understand that it is this policy that has made our alcohol problem as limited as it is, at least in comparison to other countries (Olsson & Romanus DN 10/10/91).
>
> From the debate, one can get the impression that in other countries, where alcohol is readily available in food stores, that there are not big problems with alcohol. But this is not true. France's problem with alcohol-related liver damage is, for example, much greater than ours. And this is why the World Health Organization's (WHO) goal to reduce alcohol consumption by a fourth by the year 2000, calculated from 1980 levels, has had such support (Westerholm DN 18/1/92).
>
> There are countries where alcohol sales are two to three times as much as they are in Sweden. But then these countries also have many more inhabitants who are harmed by alcohol. This shows that the total consumption model, when it comes to alcohol, is correct. (Systembolag brochure, "Systemet, vad är det bra för?": p. 24)

These excerpts point to "an even worse situation" in Europe. Or in the best case, that Europeans were simply naive or misguided. Moreover, this argument was also transformed to a means of justifying future action on Sweden's behalf in order to 'educate' the EU and Europeans.

> When one sees who belongs to the influential network in EC-questions and who has a monopoly on insight into the negotiations, one gets anxious. In these industry and trade corridors, the majority are senselessly unconscious of the social dimension of the alcohol question. (Nycander DN 25/3/90).
>
> But the social committee in the EC will guard health questions, and alcohol consumption is foremost a threat to the health of individuals and the nation—socially and medically (Westerberg 1992: p. 69).
>
> That high levels of alcohol consumption have a proven correlation with illnesses and early death is an only and uncontroversial truth. This truth seems to have slipped past the Danish attorney general, who has posited that a bottle of wine per day is nothing but healthy (Ridderspore, Uppdraget 1997: p. 11).

Reactions of supporters were not only directed at sources outside Sweden, but also to emerging liberal claims *inside* Sweden. For example, in many of the cases above, supporters were arguing against the claim that, "In all other countries beer, wine and spirits are sold freely. And this works just fine. So why

[27] Elsewhere I have pointed out that Denmark and France are particularly selected as comparisons. France represents the culture that 'can handle its liquor', but really cannot; and Denmark symbolizes a 'fallen' Nordic country (Sutton 1996: pp. 66–67).

should the state have a monopoly for alcohol sales in Sweden?" (e.g. Systembolag brochure, "Systemet, vad är det bra till?" p. 29), or that "there is no alcohol problem in Europe, and there are no restrictions there".[28] Supporters also reacted to the fact that grocers were seeking to sell alcohol. Such strategies were regarded as attempts to profit through others' misfortunes. Moreover, these attempts provided 'evidence' that the state approach of limiting private profit interest was correct.

> If we leave the lion's share of the alcohol trade to commercial interests, we create new forces for increased sales and the further spread of alcohol habits. At the same time, we create a political lobby that aggressively fights attempts to regulate alcohol sales and likewise attempts to increase people's awareness of alcohol as a primary causal factor in social isolation, violence, accidents and poor health; alcohol capital is a fog-creating apparatus (Nycander DN 11/1/92).
>
> Above all, when it comes to the retail monopoly, it is easy to see that the commercial alternative would fuel sales and therewith consumption. If 8000 retailers could earn money on every bottle they sold, sales will be more active. It is really quite obvious. Competition and private profit interest are the dynamic drivers of the market economy. They should be kept out of a sector that one does not want to grow. This has been a basic principle of Swedish alcohol policy throughout the entire twentieth century (Romanus DN 21/19/93).
>
> One [grocery chain] even wants to begin now, in order to get the Swedish people used to the freedom to booze it up, by complimenting the regular assortment of alcohol (Strömstedt 1992).
>
> Studies from other countries have shown that privatization and increased locations for sales increase alcohol consumption and problems. It would be very unwise to lower prices and at the same time double many times over the number of locations for sales, letting loose commercial forces (Systembolag brochure, "Varför ska vi behöva lida" Fråga 4).
>
> Common sense tells us that alcohol consumption increases dramatically if one allows nearly 8000 shops sell alcohol (compared to Systembolaget's approximately 360). Increased availability leads to increased sales... Higher alcohol consumption leads to alcohol-related problems in the form of violence, illness and social isolation. A majority of the world's alcohol researchers are in agreement on this. (Systembolag Brochure, "Varför ska vi behöva lida...", Fråga fem).
>
> There is no private retail chain or businessman who does not seek to sell more. And alcohol researchers around the world have determined that the easier it is to attain alcohol, the more people drink. And the more alcohol harm among the population increases. In the scientific terms, this is called the "total consumption model" (Systembolag brochure, "Systemet, vad är det bra för?": p. 22).

---

[28] For example, a commission report from 1994 (SOU 1994:25) dedicated an entire chapter to the state of alcohol policy and alcohol harm in nine other countries. This is presented against a backdrop where:

A major misunderstanding behind these opinions regards the alcohol situation in, e.g. France and Italy. One seems to think that in these countries, although one knows that they often drink substantially more than in Sweden, there is no sign of damage such as ours. But one cannot judge their alcohol culture and alcohol damages after a tourist's visit to the Eiffel Tower in Paris, or the Seven Coins Fountain in Rome. Today, there is a great deal of knowledge on alcohol's harmful effects even in these countries. So, in France, for example, there is a mortality rate for liver cirrhosis, among other things, that is substantially higher among the population than in Sweden (p. 73).

Challenges to the Solution Inside Sweden

As the Swedish debate on EU got underway during the late 1980s and early 1990s, an increasingly 'liberal' group of voices found a space to express their claims and demands on legitimate grounds. Some of the more visible groups to join in debating the solution to the alcohol problem were protest parties, grocers' associations, and various politicians whose views had previously been excluded from 'legitimate' discourse. Common to these groups was a challenge to a major assumption of Swedish discourse; they emphasized private responsibility rather than state responsibility for alcohol consumption. Moreover, they linked their claims to the challenges the EU had already made to the Swedish solution, and in so doing, engaged an alternative source of facts and concepts.

Following the EU discourse, free-trade became a central concept within the alternative discourse. Opposition to monopolies of any nature, and hence *Systembolag,* became a matter of principle. Free competition was argued to be a major goal of the union, and one that was widely accepted 'even in Sweden'. While medical professionals and others referred to 'what everyone knows about alcohol problems', opponents referred to alternative collective knowledge that was based on 'what everyone knows about the market'. As the chairman of one grocers' association stated:

> Increased competition is currently an accepted goal of economic policy. There is broad political concensus that compeititon stimulates better use of ecnomic resources, strengthens trade and, which is important not least from the point of view of the consumer, competition puts pressure on prices and broadens variety. In other words, monopolies are against the interests of the consumer (Näslund DN 10/8/92).

The condition of free competition was presented as something positive for grocers, but more importantly as a public good that everyone was in agreement over. In identifying 'consumer interests', the issue was constructed as a public problem, just as alcohol had been defined in the past. However, attention was drawn to the economic 'threats' associated with a monopoly structure, rather than the health 'benefits' of a monopoly or the 'health threat' of alcohol.

Following from the interests constructed, hinders to competition were extended to two types of 'problems' related to alcohol: competition from across the border and unfair competition within Sweden. Opponents argued that the Swedish people were rational actors who were looking to maximize their purchasing power. Similar to the assumptions of the dominant discourse on alcohol, it was viewed that if people can buy, they will. At the same time the threat was redefined, the subject (the alcohol consumer/drinker) was also transformed. This is revealed in the arguments below, which point out that the consumer is a rational actor who will purchase alcohol where it is the least expensive, and most available. Since free trade is regarded as a public good, the subject that is constructed through this discourse is not a potential patient or risk-taker, but a consumer with interests in free trade. Hence, the lower prices across the border, as well as better availability, would be damaging for Sweden:

> The Swedish people will be able to purchase cheaper alcohol freely within the framework of the EC as soon as we are members. The most relevant question is where they will make their purchases. If we maintain our system of monopolies and the world's highest tax levels, these purchases will take place abroad. One can finance a car trip between Stockholm and Helsingör, for instance, by purchasing a bottle of whiskey if the price differences are maintained between Sweden and Denmark tomorrow (Näslund DN 16/4/92).
>
> [R]elaxed border controls and a free flow of goods will have a detrimental effect on trade in Southern Sweden, under the condition that Denmark has harmonized its prices and ours are maintained at the high level, with respect to both the sales tax and alcohol tax (Nils Eric Näsland, DN 26/4/92).

As is evidenced in the quote above, levels of taxation became an important question for opponents of the system. In contrast to supporters who linked high prices to public health protection, opponents transformed taxation levels within the alternative framework as a matter of unfair competition.

Free competition was a question not only between nations of the EU, but also within Sweden. National balances would be disturbed, since grocers in the North would maintain their customers, while those in the south would lose them. Grocers associations demanded that the government:

> ensure that companies have reasonable opportunities to compete in a fair way, regardless of whether their store is in Värmland or Skåne (Näslund DN 16/4/92).

The arguments that were made by opponents, illustrate that within the economic framework, the problem was not public health, but the monopoly system itself. This system was defined in the latter example above as a threat to equality within Sweden. It was also constructed as a threat to economic prosperity in Sweden, according to the former arguments presented above.

Interestingly, there were limits to the demand for free trade. The notion that alcohol was a public health problem was not directly challenged. In fact, participants in the media debate pointed out at times that it was precisely this. One debate article in the media even ran under the heading, "Släpp inte alkoholen fri" (Don't Sell Alcohol Freely). No group actually argued in favor of 'free alcohol'.

> For example, few would dare to want to lower the minimum age limit or make strong spirits more available, but many certainly want to abolish Systembolag's retail monopoly on strong beer and wine (Fällman DN 10/8/92).
>
> Of course, [a grocery story] will submit itself to the restrictions concerning forms for sales of alcohol drinks that state representatives establish. It goes without saying, and should not be a problem. In all due respect for Systembolag's personnel, the staff of Konsum can certainly—after appropriate training—manage sales of strong beer and wine in their shops (Fällman DN 10/8/92).

> Those of us in the trade generally feel that beer and wine can be sold in our stores, but spirits, even in the future, should be limited to Systembolag. We also recognize that restrictions are necessary if stores sell alcohol. Anything else would be unrealistic given the long history we have had in Sweden with an alcohol monopoly (Fahlin DN 19/12//93).

Grocers and others argued that what they challenged was the solution to this problem. While it was up to the government to legislate solutions, practices related to regulating alcohol consumption did not have to be carried out by the state as well. For the grocers and many others, the point of shifting policy was primarily aimed at the monopoly, and they argued their own capabilities in relation to the state's. In short, they questioned the distribution of authority with respect to applying solutions. What is also interesting is that they maintained, or revived, some old divisions within the discourse, namely, they distinguished beer and wine, from other spirits.[29] As I shall note below, this is consistent with a shift towards an interpretation of alcohol issues based upon behavior and 'cultural competence', rather than on universal health concerns.

Thus far I have primarily dealt with the claims and constructions of grocers. Dissenting claims from the former discursive formation can also be detected among government officials and political representatives. One of the most radical suggestions for a new social order for alcohol came from a protest party that gained seats in the 1991 parliamentary election, NyDemokrati (New Democracy).[30] This was the first parliamentary party to openly argue for a liberal approach to alcohol. In line with its broader ideology that criticized the "power elite" for treating citizens as incapable, this party called for a complete deregulation of all alcohol-related monopolies including the *Systembolag* and to replace these with information campaigns (Piaszczyk 1996). The high taxes on alcohol were seen as a mechanism that encouraged citizens to turn to moonshine. It was argued that taxes on alcohol in restaurants should be lowered since "it is more pleasant to have a drink at a bar than to booze it up on a park bench" (Piaszczyk 1996, p. 17, see also Karlsson & Wachtmeister, Expressen 22/12/90). Blame was shifted to the practices that have been constructed in the name of 'protecting people'. Moreover, cultural competence (Sulkunen 1992) as a concept and means of evaluating alcohol issues also emerged.

Although not quite as extreme, similar approaches were also suggested by

---

[29] One of the aims of policy during the 1970s, with the introduction of prop. 1976/77:108, was to shift alcohol consumption from stronger spirits to "weaker beverages" of beer and wine. Although the current official discourse does not focus on the construction of 'good alcohol habits', there are some subtle remnants of this earlier approach in disourse. For example, Gabriel Romanus, director of the Systembolag, stated in an interview that he "(is) a moderate drinker. Who appreciates a good wine or cool beer at the appropriate time" (Systembolag brochure, "Systemet vad är det bra för?" p. 20). Hence, although the dominant discourse maintains that there is not a strong division between moderate consumption and heavy consumers, there are notions of 'good' drinking and 'bad' drinking that emerge.

[30] This was the first time a protest party was elected to the national parliament, and since the three-year term beginning in 1991, no other protest party has gained enough seats. NyDemokrati has since shifted its party structure and leadership.

the Moderate party, which formed a government between 1993 and 1996. In its program from 1993, the party argued that alcohol policy should focus on public opinion building and measures to reduce alcohol abuse among target groups, particularly young people and those already abusing alcohol. In addition, the party argued that lower prices on alcohol in restaurants would support the development of a 'better' drinking culture (Piaszczyk 1996). Similar claims were also made by other politicians, including Kjell Olof Feldt, former finance minister and then Director of the state monopoly *Vin och Sprit* (e.g. Feldt, DN 4/11/93) and the chairman of the parliamentary EC delegation (Cars, DN 22/9/93).

In addition to the breaks in the official discourse, alternative views were also expressed within the medical community. The normative message contained in the arguments of the politicians above aligned them with one medical doctor and professor, Sune Rosell. In a series of articles in *Svenska Dagbladet*, one of two major morning papers in the Swedish capital, Rosell argued for a shift in alcohol culture, as a new strategy.

> A new policy must include powerful measures that aim to change our alcohol culture, among other things to teach young people how to handle alcohol (Rosell, SvD 21/9/92).

In arguing for a new alcohol culture, Rosell shifted the locus of the problem from health concerns to the behavior of drinkers. His argument is reminiscent of those presented by Bratt and others during the first decades of this century (see *Chapter* 2). Again, a key shift in this definition of the problem is a transformation of the drinker. The drinker is seen as possessing a capacity for drinking appropriately. At the same time, the drinker is held accountable for her behavior. This construction of the subject compliments the consumer definition presented by the grocers.

With a shift in the problem, it is possible to detect a shift in the scientific basis for discussing alcohol problems. Rosell, like the politicians noted previously, argued that the total consumption model had seen its "better days".

> The total consumption model, as a basis for an active alcohol policy, has seen its better days. In my opinion, we should replace this goal with a goal of building up an alcohol culture, in other words a socially acceptable relationship to alcohol's two faces, both it's brighter and darker sides... (Rosell SvD 3/12/9).

The total consumption model was furthermore regarded as a hinder to the development of meaningful policy in the future since:

> A more serious problem is that the total consumption model has become a dogma that politicians who wish to be 'politically-correct' cannot question. (Rosell SvD 21/9/92)
>
> Today this is impossible since the total consumption dogma states that young people shall abstain from alcohol. Alcohol use is so taboo in Sweden that many parents likely avoid teaching young people how to handle alcohol (Rosell SvD 21/9/92).

The dominant discourse was viewed as drawing attention away from "the real problems" related to alcohol:

> Why should we maintain an alcohol policy that does not direct our attention to the large alcohol problems in our society, but rather to the, for the individual, uninteresting goal of decreasing total alcohol consumption? To maintain current alcohol policy is to sweep the problem under the rug (Rosell SvD 21/9/92).

According to this alternative discourse, the scientific foundations of policy were transformed to a scapegoat that allowed politicians and others to ignore the 'real' issues and problems. Blame was assigned to current policy and practices.

Hence, what took place within this alternative discourse is not only a shift in the solution, but also a shift in the 'facts' and bases of legitimacy for building arguments for such solutions. As indicated in the first part of this section, the 'necessity' and 'obvious' agreement over the importance of free competition form a basis for developing discourse. In line with this, a different field of 'facts' are pointed to in support. For many, a 1993 report sponsored by the Brewers Association provided a different platform of 'facts' (Philipson et al. 1993). According to the report, unregistered consumption of alcohol—in the form of illegal travelers' imports, moonshining, and consumption outside Sweden, was as great as 40% of the registered level of consumption. This figure was presented as evidence that undermined the 'truth' behind the total consumption model. If it could be shown that the many studies that linked alcohol consumption to various medical and social issues were based on inaccurate data, this would undermine the basis for restricting availability.

A second 'fact' that was also 'discovered' during this period was that 'alcohol is good for one's health'. The release of reports and coverage of them in the media, on the effects of red wine led to discussion among medical researchers in particular. Although such studies are not new, this particular study had been conducted in Sweden, and hence gave greater weight to the question than others studies. Emerging debates involved many who argued that these were 'quasi-scientific results', as well as those who used them to support their demands for rethinking alcohol policy (e.g. Rosell).

Epilogue Swedish Alcohol Policy in the European Union

Following Sweden's entrance in the EES on 1 January 1994, *Systembolag* was challenged by a Swedish citizen who openly acted against Swedish laws by selling wine in a grocery store. This led to a case before the Court of Justice (Case C-189/95), when the Swedish court system requested guidance in applying national laws under the EU. The interpretive framework of the EU, whereby economic interests are placed above health interests, becomes particularly clear in the public defender's advisory opinion on the case (Elmér 4

March 1997). Elmér presented four arguments to justify his opinion that the state retail monopoly contradicted the aims and intentions of the Maastricht Treaty, and should therefore be abolished:

- that it aims to limit sales and therewith consumption of such products, and in fact must be assumed to have this affect, and
- that the law gives the state-owned enterprise the sole rights to retail sales of alcoholic beverages, which take place at a limited number of shops, etc., and
- that the retail monopoly in question is placed is positioned after the import position, but is the only legal purchaser of alcohol drinks on the commercial market in the member-state in question and therefore in practice determines which products shall be imported to this market from other member-states, and
- that producers and others who are legally recognized and run businesses in other member-states may not sell such drinks on the market in the member-state in question if the sale in question does not take place through a middleman who has a trade license, or if the producer and others themselves hold a commercial license issued by the authorities in the member-state in question and pay fees which are forbidden herewith.

The first two arguments are particularly interesting as they are precisely the same arguments the Swedish government presented in order to justify the necessity of *Systembolag* as an effective means of regulating public health (see below). Elmér argued that indeed people drink less, and have fewer places to go in order to purchase their alcohol. However, the public defender interpreted this in a very different way. For him, these 'facts' constituted 'evidence' that the Swedish system "obstructed" the free trade of alcohol in the union since it aimed to limit the purchase of alcohol. That is, they constituted evidence for a very different problem and threat. According to Elmér, the restriction of alcohol sales was defined as an obstruction of trade between member-states of the union.

The Swedish official discourse on alcohol, as I argued in *Chapter 4,* has pointed to the use of a state retail monopoly as a means of limiting availability. As a further step in this direction the Swedish government has also limited business hours, and the number of sales outlets. The prosecutor found this latter practice particularly damaging since:

> This limiting of the number of shops, etc. makes it more difficult to attain alcohol drinks (I-27, Paragraph 80).
>
> ... it must be determined whether the limiting of the number of sales outlets makes it so difficult to attain alcohol drinks, that this limitation in itself constitutes a... quantitative import restriction *jf. artikel 30.*

The limiting of sales outlets was likened to quantitative restrictions, which are forbidden according to Article 30.

The juxtaposition of the public defender's discussion of the Swedish system with the Swedish government's defense of these very same practices illustrates an important point. Namely, a 'fact' is not self-evident or objective, but must be interpreted within a discourse where it takes on meaning. Hence, the "success" of restricting sales outlets as a means of decreasing consumption constitutes 'evidence' of the problem and viability of the solution for the Swedish discourse, but from within the EU discourse the effects of these practices can be viewed as 'evidence' of unfair competition. This shifted issues into another arena—with new divisions and classifications, etc.

The attorney did not accept the public health argument presented by Swedish officials. He argued instead that less 'harmful' means could be utilized to combat alcohol problems:

> Such a coordinated system cannot be motivated by reference to an interest in protecting people's lives and health, compare article 36 in the treaty, since this concern can be met through measures that do not limit the free movement of goods to a lesser extent.

During the final stages of completing this dissertation, the European Court of Justice heard and considered the case involving Harry Franzén and the constitutional status of the *Systembolag* (Case C-189/95). A judgment was presented on 23 October 1997. At the heart of the case was whether the Swedish Law on Alcohol (1994:1738) is or is not compatible with EU law. In particular, the Swedish national court sought guidance in response to the question: "whether Articles 30 and 37 of the Treaty preclude national provisions governing a domestic monopoly on the retail of alcoholic beverages". The Court argued that:

> ... Article 37 does not require national monopolies having a commercial character to be abolished but requires them to be adjusted in such a way as to ensure that no discrimination regarding the conditions under which goods are procured and marketed exists between nationals of Member States.

Unlike the public defender, the Court accepted the public health argument the Swedish government provided for *Systembolag*, and its appeal to Article 37 therewith.

> In the present case, it is not contested that, in aiming to protect public health against the harm caused by alcohol, a domestic monopoly on the retail of alcoholic beverages, such as that conferred on *Systembolaget,* pursues a public interest aim.

Since the monopoly could be defined in this way, the court was able to appeal to Article 36 which provides for state monopolies which aim to protect public health, if it can be shown that discrimination between products of member-states does not occur, and that these measures are relevant to the public health aim described. The linchpin of the court's argument was not the public health concern, however. Rather, the key point was that *Systembolaget* was not regarded as leading to discrimination, or pursuing a monopoly in order to achieve protection for domestic products. This becomes clear in the second point. The Court did not find the public health argument convincing with respect to the organization of the private import market introduced in Sweden in 1995.

> The licensing system constitutes an obstacle to the importation of alcoholic beverages from other Member States in that it imposes additional costs on such beverages, such as intermediary costs, payment of charges and fees for the grant of a license, and costs arising from the obligation to maintain storage capacity in Sweden.

With respect to these practices, the Swedish government was not successful in convincing the court that the resulting discrimination was reasonable. Moreover, the facts provided by the state revealed that this market was dominated by Swedish operators. This was interpreted by the Court as evidence of discrimination.

This most recent chapter in Sweden's alcohol discourse points up that how issues are framed and defined has relevance for what practices and policies will be deemed relevant and acceptable. Where legal frameworks, and documents such as the Treaty of Rome, and later the Maastricht Treaty, have precedence over other interpretive schemes, rhetoric becomes a very important tool for the preservation and transformation of practices and policies. This would seem to indicate that discourse and claims-making are important objects of investigation for understanding future policy directions. Hence, as researchers and policy-makers argue for a common alcohol policy in the EU, it will be important to take into consideration the local discourses of the different countries and how alcohol issues are defined in order to locate common ground. This issue forms a point of discussion in the following chapter.

CHAPTER 6

Current Challenges and Future Directions

In the foregoing chapters I have investigated variations in the conceptualization of alcohol as a social problem in Sweden through three studies in the alcohol discourse. In this chapter, I identify some of the more salient points that have been raised in the dissertation, and iterate some of the current challenges for research as well as offer some suggestions for future applications.

Taking Stock

In the dissertation my own empirical work has primarily been concerned with three discursive formations (see Table 8). In addition, these were complimented with two formations by way of background information provided in *Chapter 2*. In chronological order, the first formation can be referred to as the early discourse, and can roughly be located in time from about 1900 to the late 1940s or early 1950s. This was followed by the second formation, which was one of two formations in medical discourse, and occupied the late 1940s through the 1950s. The third formation concerned the official discourses, and it overlapped the medical discourse, falling approximately between the mid 1950s to mid 1970s. Formation 4 was detected in both the official and the medical discourse, and emerged during the late 1970s and continues to resonate in contemporary discourse. Finally, the EU integration formation emerged around 1990, and appeared together with the late total consumption /public health formation.

Keeping in mind the conceptual framework for deconstructing definitions of alcohol issues, a number of observations can be made beginning with the causal story. The causal story associated with alcohol issues has undergone several transformations. The location of a causal mechanism has moved from the moral orientation of individuals, to an undefined and uncontrollable bio-chemical reaction in the body, to the social structure, to the substance itself, and in the final formation to government responsibility as the entire problem shifted. Recalling that blame and accountability are linked to causal stories, one can detect important conceptual shifts here as well. In Formation 1, individuals were responsible for their problems, while in Formation 2 they were transformed to victims who were free from responsibility. Indeed, responsibility for illness shifted largely to the medical community, which was expected to find a cure. Later in the context of Formation 3, there was a combination of blame. On the one hand, individuals were regarded as risk-takers, who were therefore subjects in their own health and ill-health. At the same time, the ultimate causal mechanism was located in the beverage, and specified 'risk groups' could be particularly vulnerable against their own will. This meant that consumers were both victims and adversaries in their own poor health. With the introduction of the EU discourse, there appeared to be some evidence of shifting responsibility for incompetent drinking practices back onto individuals, in addition to practices of public health that placed expectations upon individuals to be informed and regulate their levels of health.

Interesting shifts are also detectable in relation to the threat associated with alcohol issues. These shifts reveal a transference of the 'social' impact of the problem. For example, in the context of Formation 1, dangerous individuals posed a threat to society at large. It was in society's collective interest to control these individuals. In the context of Formation 2, this collective threat was overshadowed by the threat posed by an unknown medical mystery to individuals. Yet, the social consequences of this illness provided a basis for defining the problem as a collective concern. In Formation 3, the social aspect of the phenomenon was located in the cause rather than the harm done. It was argued that the problem could only be overcome through solidarity against social structures that threatened individuals. According to Formation 4, the collective interest in alcohol was located in several points. Individuals contributed to a collective level of alcohol consumption that led to greater or lower consumption levels of alcohol in society in general and this was correlated with the number of persons harmed by alcohol. At the same time, alcohol was described as posing a threat to all citizens, and there was therefore a collective interest in maintaining regulation. In Formation 5, the threat defined in Formation 4 was pitted against the threat to state regulation of the alcohol market by the principle of free and open competition.

The dispersion of the problem has also been reconfigured over time. During Formation 1, this dispersion was based on types of 'drinkers', while in Formation 2, important divisions were made between stages of illness, symptoms found at each of these stages, and types of alcoholics. In the context of Formation 3, treatment considerations were separated from considerations of the causes for alcohol abuse; and in the official discourse, the dispersion of the problem concerned the locations of causal mechanisms behind abuse. Formation 4 reveals an additional logic for organizing the problem. Drinking habits and forms of harm as well as a scale of health, provided important divisions around which aspects of the problem were constructed, and specialty areas in science were organized. In Formation 5 a very different division emerged. Here, the

Table 8. *Definitions of the alcohol problem in Sweden*

Definitional Component	Formation 1 Early Discourse Chapter 2	Formation 2 Alcoholism, Medicine 1 Chapter 3	Formation 3 Chapter 2	Formation 4 TC/PH, Medicine 2 Chapters 3 & 4	Formation 5 EU Integration Chapter 5
Causal Story	Poor behavior and low morals	Bio-chemical or environmental causes of disease make 'alcoholics' to drink against their will.	Social structure leads to poor social integration, causing persons to drink against their will.	Individual consumers take risks that can lead to harm. Individuals contribute to a total aggregate consumption that is correlated with number of heavy consumers.	Same as Formation 4 + 'Unnatural' state intervention leads to unfair competition.
Threat	'Dangerous' individuals threaten society.	Unknown mechanism threatens individuals.	Social/ economic structure threatens individuals.	Individuals as collective contribute to aggregate health Alcohol is a causal agent.	Same as Formation 4 + Improper market mechanisms create unfair competition.
Dispersion of Problem	1) Dangerous and less dangerous 'drinkers 2) Volunteer and non -volunteer patients	1) Stages of illness 2) Symptoms at different stages 3) Types of alcoholics (personalities)	1) Alcohol configuration (person, environment, substance) 2) Alcohol abuse related to other forms of abuse, and other forms of social problems requiring social assistance	1) Drinking habits (level of consumption, rate of consumption occasions) 2) Forms of harm, as related to direct and indirect result of drinking 3) Scale of health	Same as Formation 4 + According to relation to legal constitution in EU
Distribution of Authority	Medical professionals and clergy act as gatekeepers to treatment; lay people provide local knowledge of treatment and known alcoholics; police exercise surveillance; treatment by temperance societies and others.	Same as Formation 1 + Medical professionals provide knowledge and acute care; Psychotherapists help patients to understand their illness.	Social workers, sociologists provide knowledge; social workers provide therapy.	Shared authority for providing knowledge among most social and medical scientists.	Same as Formation 4 + Legal and economic authority above other forms of expert authority.
Solution Complex	Monopoly, registration and rationing system aimed to discipline individuals.	Cure—through psychotherapy, medical treatment, and some forms of longer term care.	Provide social networks, shift consumption to weaker beverages.	Prevention at different levels of risk.	Same as Formation 4 + Surveillance of regulation system to ensure protection of market principles in EU.

divisions were not centered on the problem or the cause, but on the solution. Discourse was organized around legal and economic principles contained in the paragraphs of the Treaty of Rome and Maastricht Treaty.

Finally, my work has confirmed the findings of other researches of the social history of alcohol in Sweden, by pointing out that the response to alcohol issues has varied over time in important ways. What my work contributes to this field, is a context for these solutions that emerges out of the discourse itself. For example, the dispersion of the problem has had important consequences for how solutions have been conceptualized. Therefore, the state monopolies were defined as a means to regulate individual drinkers in the context of Formation 1, while in the context of Formation 5, the monopolies were presented as an important instrument of primary prevention of poor health.

In sum, my work detected major shifts in the basic ontological frame for legislating and studying the alcohol problem, as well as equally important shifts in epistemology, the distribution of authority, the causal explanations awarded, the dispersion of the problem (i.e. the series to which the problem is linked, the divisions made, etc.), and the solution(s) proposed to resolve it. Taken together, these findings problematize the generally assumed 'objective' nature of the phenomenon and hence its stability over time and space. Following from this, my work suggests that neither science nor state intervention are neutral activities; they are active agents in constructing the objects about which they speak.

The More Things Change, the More They Stay the Same

Above, I discussed the discontinuous attributes of the problem definitions studied. However, during my investigation of Swedish discourse on alcohol I also located a number of continuities that deserve attention. These have little to do with the problem itself, however. They have more to do with deeper cultural perceptions of how social problems in general shall be viewed and dealt with. At least three such deep assumptions can be identified.

First, throughout this decade, the discourse reveals the basic assumption that state intervention is necessary and useful in order to resolve alcohol issues. The form this takes may be questioned and transformed, but the basic parameters for devising solutions has remained intact. This was particularly evident in *Chapter 3*, which considered medical discourse on the alcohol problem. Although researchers in other countries have noted a 'medicalization' of alcohol problems, medical discourse in Sweden pointed to the need for state intervention and the assistance of other groups and non-medical institutions in society in order to successfully counteract the problem. This was true even at the high point of the 'alcoholism formation', which in other countries has been associated with medical autonomy and control. This implies that in Sweden, the alcohol problem as a social problem is both a legislative concern and a professional or scientific concern. Alcohol issues cannot be handled strictly within a professional arena, but must be coordinated and steered first through collective arenas, i.e. legislation and state apparatuses. An explanation for this can be linked to the fact that the alcohol problem has not been strictly defined as one of alcoholism, as in many other countries. Drinking as such has been problematized and linked to alcohol abuse in various ways throughout the century. The steering and regulation of an entire population, as opposed to a limited and deviant group, requires greater resources and forms of intervention that are not available to a single professional group such as medicine. This characteristic is particularly clear, and perhaps most developed, in the context of the total consumption/public health formation. However, even in the context of the Bratt system, which was seen as imposing individually-centered restrictions (Bruun 1985), individuals (i.e. problem drinkers) were reached and identified through an elaborate system to which all drinkers were initially subjected.

Second, although the state is regarded as an important coordinating body, the alcohol discourse displays a reliance upon *expert knowledge*, particularly scientific expertise with respect to generating 'facts' about the problem. In the dissertation I have specifically investigated the discourse of medical professionals, who have played a substantial role in providing models and concepts to official discourse. However, I also pointed out that other types of professional groups and experts have been involved in the problem. During the 1970s, sociologists and social workers gained a greater influence over shaping legislation. In *Chapter 4*, I noted that the public health/total consumption formation also supported a distribution of authority that included medical and many other types of researchers. This indicates that although the expert group upon which official discourse relies, may be replaced, the underlying assumption that the problem can be objectively studied and 'known' through scientific method has remained intact.

Finally, and related to the points above, there may be some patterns in how the alcohol problem has been characterized as a social problem. The total consumption/public health formation revealed that the 'social-ness' of the alcohol problem was located in two major characteristics. The first is a construction of the problem whereby society is not only collectively viewed as being threatened by the problem, but also, in which individuals together are seen as contributing to the problem. In this way, the universalism of the problem is constructed on both sides of the threat equation. Second, there is a form of consensus that emerges through the alcohol discourse that has yet to be taken up in similar research. While these observations are based primarily on the one formation, further research might look more closely at earlier formations to test this proposition. The notion that Swedish legislative practices reflect consensus-seeking is not new. As I have already pointed out, both Rothstein (1992) and Johansson (1995 1997) have illustrated how this process takes place in Sweden in the field of alcohol. What my work adds to their discussions, is a consideration of precisely what it is that constitutes the eventual compromise, as well as how this provides the basis for future cooperation and discourse. Outcomes are not simply a resolution, but also give rise to continued cooperation, consensus and discourse.

Discursive Transformation Today

An important contribution of my dissertation is its presentation of current changes in conceptualizations of alcohol issues against a backdrop of previous shifts in not only perceptions of appropriate alternatives, but also shifts in notions of the essential nature of the problem. There is, however, an important difference with respect to the changes currently taking place, which, I believe, offers an exciting context for future sociological studies. This concerns the context for the production of discourse, which I would characterize as an ontological confrontation. This condition, and responses to it, are aptly described by Berger and Luckmann (1966):

> A major occasion for the development of universe-maintaining conceptualization arises when a society is confronted with another society having a greatly different history. The problem posed by such a confrontation is typically sharper than that posed by intra-societal heresies because here there is an alternative symbolic universe with an 'official' tradition whose taken-for-granted objectivity is equal to one's own (p. 125).

In other words, one means of describing the discursive context of EU integration is to say that the Swedish discourse on alcohol has confronted a European discourse on free trade. This context has structured the terrain upon which discourse must be generated in an important way. The EU discourse has an 'official' tradition that has been recognized in Sweden and as such, its ontological status is at least equal to that of the Swedish alcohol discourse. This has the effect of questioning the unity and self-evidence of the Swedish belief systems, since in questioning it, "it loses its self-evidence; it indicates itself, constructs itself, only on the basis of a complex field of discourse" (Foucault 1972: p. 23). In the case of Sweden and the EU, it became explicitly clear that alcohol and problems could be conceptualized in very different ways.

This context appears to have opened up the space of discourse to two different momentums. First, the presence of an alternative ontology, with a legitimate status, provided opponents of the Swedish monopoly system (within Sweden) a unique opportunity. Such groups were no longer confined to the former parameters of discourse, but could choose to link their claims to a new set of 'experts', institutions, narratives and 'facts'(or interpretation of facts). From within this alternative set of parameters, the Swedish system and in particular, solutions, could be openly questioned and challenged.

Second, as Berger and Luckmann suggest, this situation provided a "major occasion for the development of universe-maintaining conceptualization". Through investigating the statements of those participants who supported the heretofore Swedish organization of alcohol problems, the definition of alcohol as a public health problem became very clear. Very little was 'new' in the statements formed by defenders of the system. To the contrary, these parties interpreted potential integration, and a potential future, from within the parameters of the former discursive regime. Established theories, narratives, 'facts' and bases for legitimacy were drawn upon in order to construct normative statements concerning policy within the EU and its effects upon Sweden.

In light of the discussion above concerning the social consensus surrounding the alcohol problem in Sweden, this situation is interesting since it raises questions about what kind of model will allow such competing interests to cooperate in the future. Already there have been indications that the official discourse has been more open to such entities as the Brewers Association, which has begun cooperating with the Public Health Institute on a new project. Throughout the twentieth century the field of professionals, interest groups and experts has expanded around alcohol, and in turn models have had to include these. It will be interesting to see to what extent this will hold true in the future.

Finally, given that conceptualizations of alcohol issues have been transformed over time within Sweden, it would be naive to assume as a point of departure that there is one 'correct' and 'truthful' way to conceptualize alcohol as a social problem. Just as there were differences between my own homestate and Sweden, there will be incongruencies between members-states of the EU. This provides challenges, of course, but the current context also provides an exciting field against which the particularities and cultural characteristics of Swedish belief systems become more visible, and thus more readily accessible to the scientific gaze. In the following section, I want to review some of these.

Future Investigations and Applications

In *Chapter 1* I indicated that one of the purposes of the dissertation was to create an intellectual space within which new questions could be posed and addressed. Some of these questions have been dealt with in the context of the dissertation, but far more have fallen outside its parameters. Let me pick up some of the strands of thought and questions that my work points to, and begin to systematize the type of research program they contribute to. This discussion is organized around three themes: 1) future sociological studies of alcohol in Sweden; 2) future sociological studies of alcohol in Europe from a Swedish perspective; and 3) more general applications of discourse analysis for policy studies from a sociological perspective.

Future Sociological Studies of Alcohol in Sweden

Future studies of alcohol in Sweden should begin with ourselves; that is, with the expert discourse on alcohol issues. In this dissertation I investigated only one of several potential expert discourses—the medical community. Medical discourse, I believe, offered a good starting point since medical professionals, as a group, have been a consistent participant in the alcohol arena, and provided 'facts' for the official discourse. Further investigation into the alcohol discourse should, however, more fully examine the contributions of other expert and scientific participants. It would be very interesting, for example, to further explore how the emergence of social science, and social work, in particular, shaped the context for debating alcohol during the 1960s to mid 1970s. As I argued in *Chapter 4*, medical expertise was challenged during this period by social workers and sociologists. There are many questions around this: What has been the relationship of social work to the official and medical discourses? What methods, theories, and concepts has social work offered to the alcohol discourse? To what extent and how are these reflected in the official discourse?

It is not only expert discourses that warrant attention. The most recent discursive formation reveals a number of new discursive participants who are entering the alcohol arena for the first time, or making a return. The discourses of these groups, with their own concepts, theories, methods, etc. will likely contribute to shaping the 'nature' of the alcohol problem in the future in important ways. Studies similar to those conducted here could be produced using data from these groups. For example, the Swedish Brewers Association, while once an active participant in public discourse on alcohol has been largely excluded over the last 40 years. However, the EU discourse has allowed this group to contribute 'facts' and theories. In a similar vein to the discussion above, we can ask: What has been the relation between the discourse(s) of the alcohol industry and the official discourse? How has the alcohol problem been conceptualized and described in these discourses? What kinds of models can we expect in the future? This type of investigation would also allow the analyst to also investigate excluded discourses and to identify under what conditions they are allowed access to official arenas.

A great deal of emphasis has been placed on the discontinuity of the definitions. However, continuities I identified raise questions concerning the broader discourse on social problems in Sweden. A reliance upon expert knowledge and heavy control and intervention by the state, even in the face of EU integration, *was maintained as important and necessary* even if additional discourses were also recognized. Such cultural patterns cannot be explained solely from within the alcohol arena, but must be sought out through comparative studies between different types of social issues in Sweden. By investigating discourses on other objects of social policy, can we locate any patterns in the ontological and epistemological underpinnings of these? In the shifts that take place in these? Do we find similar distributions of authority? etc.

Building on the foregoing suggestion, it is also of interest to further investigate the broader dispersion of social problems, through the divisions, categories and similarities that are constructed between them. The alcohol discourse has defined the problem in part by identifying what other phenomena it is similar and different from. Hence, alcohol had much in common with poverty during the 1910s, while according to current logic alcohol has much in common with sexually transmitted diseases, as evident in the construction of a public health institute that deals with these two 'health risks' as well as narcotics, etc. These categorizations, or divisions, hint that the alcohol discourse is, at any time, linked to broader meta-discourses. These provide a basic terrain upon which alcohol discourse is constructed, as well as providing grounds for what become 'related' discourses. Investigation into what groupings alcohol has been associated with over time, may provide some interesting insight into deep cultural conceptualizations.

Alcohol in a Future Europe

A number of investigations are also worthwhile with respect to the possible future of alcohol policy and the conceptualization of alcohol issues in Europe. Many concerns have been raised throughout the Nordic countries regarding the possibilities for protecting alcohol policy traditions at home, and for a common alcohol policy in Europe. An important task for the research community today is to map out the terrain upon which discourse can be constructed, both in Sweden (and her Nordic neighbors), in other member-states (and regions), and on an EU level.

Between member-states, we will need to identify both the more stable characteristics and deeper levels of change, as I have begun to do in the Swedish case, as well as those more discontinuous points of transformation. There will likely be variations in these patterns. For example, one would expect tremendous differences in the relationship between experts and the state in Sweden as compared to Italy. These variations will have consequences for how and to what extent expert models developed in Sweden and other northern countries can be transported to other areas of Europe, or as the basis for developing common European practices.

As my work indicates, professional and expert discourse is also important. With the general rise in world-wide discourse on the 'new' public health, the development of social medicine, and EU-sponsored programs in this direction, the currency of concepts such as 'risk' and 'prevention' are becoming universal. At the same time, the inter-disciplinary field of epidemiology is also growing. The combination of these two factors, perhaps more than any other factor, may provide some insight into how alcohol issues will be defined in a future Europe. In *Chapter 5* I indicated that the World Health Organization, through the European Regional Office, has been a primary source of expert discourse in Europe. Texts published by this entity offer a point of departure for the type of analysis I am proposing. Even here, shifts can be detected in how alcohol issues are defined. These shifts should be mapped and contextualized as well as explained. What experts, in which countries, have shown an interest in alcohol issues? What models, concepts, and explanations have they devised? In what ways have they cooperated with experts across nations?

Increased awareness of alcohol harm in Europe has been accompanied by an ironic counter-trend in Sweden. The growth of epidemiological models for explaining health and illness have generated a heightened interest in alcohol harm in Europe. Through international cooperation, 'experts' from other European countries have gained access to the established models (e.g. the Total Consumption Model), and tested approaches of the Nordic discourses. This might result in a more Nordic approach to alcohol in Europe of the future. However, it has been argued that the Nordic mentality is shifting away from the previous ideals of 'solidarity', the 'public good', and universal policy, in favor of more consumer-oriented and individualistic notions of the public good (Sulkunen 1991). Hence, while European discourse is now open to discussions of public health, shifts in discourse within the Nordic countries themselves seem to indicate that public health will be shaped in Sweden in a much different manner than has heretofore been the case.

Implications for Policy Analysis in General

the type of discourse analysis that I have applied in the foregoing work, offers an approach to studying policy arenas, and in particular, for investigating and mapping out the transformation of such fields. Although social constructionists studying social problems have expanded their repertoire to investigating policy outcomes, the process of defining reality in relation to a policy arena has been studied as a bounded process with a point of initiation and a point resolution. Policy can be viewed as a "process of argumentation in which a particular version of reality is promoted deliberately and aggressively." (Hastings 1996: p. 1). Scientific investigation of a particular process generally ends with the adoption of a piece of legislation, or with the production of it. This point of departure was found to be less appropriate in the Swedish case where social policy arenas become institutionalized. Within the welfare state the definition of social reality is an *ongoing phenomenon* that is not bounded in linear time. Studying policy and expert knowledge as discourse, rather than as a bounded process, allows one to investigate policy transformation that might not emerge as a 'deliberate' and 'aggressive' argumentation; but rather, as subtle and consensus. We can imagine any number of policy arenas within Sweden and the context of the welfare state where transformations have occurred in less dramatic fashions, or around subjects where there is a great deal of consensus. One such arena is labor market policy. Here too, the policy arena was dominated for a long period of time by a single model of social reality that integrated different 'interest groups' in a single project.

In particular, my work pointed to the social form that consensus took in the Swedish case of alcohol. This involved the construction of an issue as having potential consequences for all individuals. Additionally, the social-ness of the social problem was located in the distribution of authority between many different types of experts and professionals who were united around a common model and conception of the problem. There are certainly other examples of this in Swedish social policy, as suggested above. Such models might provide an interesting basis for comparison with the case of alcohol, in a further effort to explore the 'social' aspects of Swedish social problems.

References

Abrahamson, M. (1989) "Synen på missbruk—80 år av diagnostisk rundgång" in *Nordisk Sosialt Arbeid*, Vol. 9, No. 2, pp. 38–49.

Alkoholen och Samhället (1912). Svenska läkaresällskapets kommitterade. Stockholm.

Allardt, E. , S. Lysgaard & A-B. Sørensen (Eds.) (1987) *Sociologin i Sverige*. HSFR, UHÄ, Uppsala: Ord & Form AB.

Allebeck, P. & S. Andréasson (1991) "Nyttan med alkoholrestriktioner vetenskapligt väl dokumenterad" in *Läkartidningen,* Vol. 88, No. 10, pp. 831–832.

Almersjö, O. (1989) "Kulturchock återvända till fyllans Sverige efter ett år i arabvärlden" in *Läkartidningen,* Vol. 86, No. 1–2, pp. 26–31.

Alsén, M., T. S:son Frey (1959) "Om behandling av alkoholpsykoser med Truxal" in *Svenska Läkartidningen,* Vol. 56, No. 48, pp. 3344–3351.

Alström, C. H. (1965) "Alkoholproblemet och samhället" in *20 års medicinsk forskning 1945–1965*. Stockholm: Norstedts.

Ambjörnsson, R. (1991)*Den skötsamme arbetaren.* Malmö: Carlssons.

Åmark, C. (1951) *A Study in Alcoholism, Clincial, Social-Psychiatric and Genetic Investigations.* PhD dissertation, Acta Psychiat. et Neurol. Scand. Suppl. 70.

Åmark, C. (1955) "Alkoholismens orsaker" in *Svenska Läkartidningen*, Vol. 52, pp. 2297–2314.

Andréasson, S. (1992a) "EG-anslutning kostar minst tio svenskar livet om dagen" in *Livstil och livskvalitet i det nya Europa,* A. Winderdal (Ed.), Malmö: Sober.

Andréasson, S. (1992b) "En 'våt' alkoholpolitik ökar skadorna" in *Läkartidningen,* Vol. 89, No. 21, pp. 1854–1855.

Andréasson, S. (1992c) "EG alkoholpriser kommer att skörda tio nya svenska liv varje dag" in *livstil och livsqvalitet i det nya Europa*: Winberg, A. (Ed.). Malmö: Sober.

Appleton, L.M. (1996) "Rethinkning Medicalization: Alcoholism and Anomolies" in *Images of Issues*, J. Best (Ed.). Hawthorne: Aldine de Gruyter.

Ask-Upmark, E. (1956) "Förslag till åtgärder mot alkoholkonsumtion" in *Svenska Läkartidningen*, Vol. 53, pp. 3206–3207.

Barrows, S. & R. Room (Eds.) (1991) *Drinking, Behavior and Belief in Modern History.* Oxford: University of California Press.

Baumohl, J. & R. Room (1987) "Inebriety, Doctors, and the State. Alcoholism Treatment Institutions before 1940" in *Recent Developments in Alcoholism,* M.Galanter (Ed.). New York: Plenum.

Beck, U. (1992) *Risk Society.* London: Sage publications.

Becker, H.S. (1963) *Outsiders: Studies in the Sociology of Deviance.* Glencoe:The Free Press of Glencoe.

Becker, H.S. (1966) "Introduction" in *Social Problems: A Modern Approach,* H.S. Becker (Ed.), London: John Wiley & Sons, Inc.

Berger, P. & T. Luckmann (1966) *The Social Construction of Reality*. London: Penguin Books.

Bergmark, A. & L. Oscarsson (1990) "Den svenska alkoholdiskursens retorik: Den politiska och administrativa nivån" in *Alkoholpolitik- Tidskrift för nordisk alkoholforskning*, Vol.7, pp. 213–218.

Bergmark, A. & L. Oscarsson (1994) "Swedish alcohol treatment in transition" in *Nordisk Alkoholtidskrift,* Vol. 11, English Supplement, pp. 43–54.

Bergsman, A. (1969) *Alkoholism*. Södertälje: Astra, Informationsavdelningen.

Berridge, V and B. Thom (1996) "Research and Policy: What Determines the Relationship?" in *Policy Studies*, Vol. 17, No.1, pp. 23–34

Berridge, V. (1996) "Drug policy: should the law take a back seat?" in *The Lancet*, Vol. 347, February 3, 1996, pp. 301–305.

Best, J.(Ed.) (1995) *Images of Issues*. New York: Aldine de Gruyter.

Best, J. (1987) "Rhetoric in Claims-making: Constructing the Missing Child Problem" in *Social Problems,* Vol. 34, pp. 101–121.

Best, S. & D. Kellner (1991) *Postmodern Theory*. New York: the Guilford Press.

Björ, J. (1988a) "Några tankar kring Magnus Huss" *in Alkoholpolitik—Tidskrift för nordisk alkoholforskning,* Vol. 5, pp. 160–167.

Björ, J. (1988b) "När fylleriet skulle botas" in *Alkohol och narkotika,* Vol. 3–4, pp. 52–58.

Bloomfield, K. (1997) "A Comparison of Western and Eastern drinking patterns in reunited Germany", paper presented in the 22nd Annual Alcohol Epidemiology Symposium of the Kettil Bruun Society for Social and Epidemiological Research on Alcohol, Edinburgh, 3–7 June 1996.

Blumer, H. (1971) "Social Problems as Collective Behavior" in *Social Problems,* Vol. 18, pp. 19–52.

Boström, G. (1956) "Några synpunkter på alkoholistvård i brytningstid" in *Svenska Läkartidningen,* Vol. 2, pp. 2961–2965.

Boström, G. & Allebeck, P. (1989) "Alkoholen som folkhälsoproblem—hur gå vidare?" in *Läkartidningen,* Vol. 86, No. 40, pp. 3388–3389.

Bourdieu, P. (1990) *In Other Words*. Cambridge: Polity Press.

Bromme, R. (1996) *Fransmannen Sully Ledermanns banbrytande upptäckt.* Malmö: Sober.

Brown, R.H. (1990) "Rhetoric, Textuality, and the Postmodern Turn in Sociological Theory" in *Sociological Theory*, Vol. 8, No.2, Fall 1990.

Brulle, R. J. (1994) "Power, Discourse and Social Problems: Social Problems From a Rhetorical Perspective" in *Perspectives on Social Problems*, Vol. 5, pp. 95–121.

Bruun, K. (1968) "Alkoholism och narkomani" in *Sociala avvikelser och social kontroll,* Stockholm: Almquist & Wiksell.

Bruun, K. (1971) "Finland: The Non-Medical Approach", paper presented at teh 29th International Congress on Alcoholism and Drug Dependence, Melbourne Sessions, 545–555, Australia.

Bruun, K. (1975) "Bakgrund och åtgärder. Kommentarer till alkoholpolitiska utredningens slutbetänkande" in *Alkohol och Narkotika*, Vol. 69, No.1; pp. 8–14.

Bruun, K. (1983) "Vidga perspektivet!" in *Sociolgisk forskning,* No. 1, pp. 3–9.

Bruun, K. (1985) Maktens Centrum: centraladministration" in *Den Svenska Supen:* Bruun, K. and P. Frånberg (Eds.).

Bruun, K, G. Edwards, M. Lumio, K. Mäkelä, L. Pan, R.E. Popham, R. Room, W. Schmidt, O-J Skog, P. Sulkunen, E. Österberg (1975) *Alcohol control policies in public health perspective.* Helsinki: The Finnish Foundation for Alcohol Studies.

Bruun, K. and P.Frånberg (Eds.) (1985) *Den svenksa supen.* Stockholm: Prisma.

Bulletin of the European Communities (1992) Luxembourg.

Burns, T. & C. Sutton (1995) "Words, Deeds, and Social Orders: Discourses, Institutions, and Human Agency in Stabilityand Change." Paper presented at Workshop, "Discourse and Rhetoric: Social Science Perspectives", Uppsala, 29–30 May, 1995.

Cars, H. (1993) "Reformera Systembolaget!", *Dagens Nyheter,* Debatt, 22/9/93.

Clarke, M (1975) "Social problem ideologies" in *The Brittish Journal of Sociology,* Vol. XXVI, No.4, December, pp. 406–416.

Cohen, J.L. & A. Arato (1992) *Civil Society and Political Theory.* London: MIT Press.

COM (87) 328 (1987) EC Proposals for Council Directives on VAT & Excise Tax.

COM (94) 202 final 1 (1994) A Programme of Community Action on Health Promotion, June 1994.

COM (95) 356 final (1995): Europe Against Cancer, Report 1994.

Conrad, P. & J.W. Schneider (1980) *Deviance and Medicalization.* London: C.V. Mosby Company.

Cronholm, B. (1984) "Sammanfattning av forskarsynpunkterna" in *Alkohol och forskningen,* Arvidsson, O (Ed.).

Dahlgren, L., Gustavsson, R., Holmberg, B., Johansson, B., Löfgren, B., Rydberg, U. (1991) *Vid dina sinnens fulla bruk.* Stockholm: Systembolaget.

Danielsson, H. (1954) "Några synpunkter efter 5 års samarbete med en nykterhetsnämnd jämte resultat av 5 års disulfiramterapi" in *Svenska Läkartidningen,* Vol. 1, No. 10, pp. 565–570.

Davies, P. & Walsh D. (1983) *Alcohol problems and alcohol control in Europe.* London: Croom Helm.

Dean, M. (1994) *Critical and Effective Histories.* London: Routledge.

Dimberg, R. (1949) "Några erfarenheter av antabusbehandling" in *Svenska Läkartidningen,* Vol. 46, Nr. 14, pp. 756–768.

Dimberg, R. (1960) "Hydroxidionbehandling av akuta alkoholpsykoser" in *Svenska Läkartidningen,* Vol. 57, No. 15, pp. 1112–1144.

Dimberg, R. & I. Salum (1955) "Medicinsk behandling av alkoholism" in *Svenska Läkartidningen,* Vol. 52, pp. 581–596.

DsS 1977:1 Beredningsgruppen för frågor avseende alkoholpolitiken

DsS 1980:10 Om alkoholpolitiken. Förslag från Samordningsorganet för alkoholfrågor (SAMO)

DsS 1981:23 Alkoholpolitiska restriktioner

DsS 1981:25 Om alkoholpolitiken II. Förslag från Samordningsorganet för alkoholfrågor (SAMO).

DsS 1994:92 En ny alkoholpolitisk tillsyns- och tillstånds myndighet samt förslag till ny alkohollag.

Edelman, M. (1988) *Constructing the Political Spectacle.* Chicago: University of Chicago Press.

Edwards, G, P Anderson, T. F. Babor, S. Casswell, R. Ferrence, N. Giesbrecht, C. Godfrey, H.D. Holder, P. Lemmens, K. Mäkelä, L.T. Midanik, T. Norström, E. Österberg, A. Romelsjö, R. Room, J. Simpura, O-J Skog. (1994) *Alcohol Policy and the Public Good.* Oxford Medical Publications. Oxford: Oxford University Press.

Elmér, Å. (1983) *CAN 1961–1981.* Stockholm: Norstedts Tryckeri.

Elmér, Å. (1993a) *Svensk Socialpolitik.* Stockholm: Liber.

Elmér, Å. (1993b) "Vad nytt under solen? Om missbrukarvården i ett historiskt perspektiv" in *Socialt Perspektiv,* Jan., pp. 4–13.

Esping-Andersen (1990) *Three Worlds of Welfare Capitalism.* London: Princeton University Press.

European Commission (1993) Commission communication on the framework for action in the field of public health. COM (93) 559, final.

European Commission (1977) "Alcohol & Spirits", Panorama of EU Industry. DG III, Luxembourg. Eurostat.

Fahlin, R. (1993) "Släpp inte alkoholen fri!", *Dagens Nyheter,* Debatt, 19/12/93.

Fahrenkrug, H. (1992) "Alcohol and the State in Nazi Germany, 1933–1945" in *Drinking*, S. Barrows, R. Room (Eds.).

Fahrenkrug, H. (1993) "Alkoholpolitik i EG:s medlemsstater" in *EG, alkohol och Norden,* C. Tigerstedt (Ed.), NAD Publication No. 19.

Fällman, U. (1992) "Starköl och vin på Konsum", *Dagens Nyheter,* Debatt 10/8/92.

Feldt, K-O (1993) "Alkoholen släpps fri", *Dagens Nyheter,* Debatt, 4/11/93.

Fine, G. A. (1995) "Public Narration and Group Culture: Discerning Discourse in Social Movements" in *Social Movements and Culture,* H. Johnston & B. Klandermans (Eds.), Minneapolis: University of Minnesota Press.

Fingarette, H. (1988) *Heavy Drinking. The Myth of Alcoholism as Disease.* Berkeley: University of California Press.

Folkhälsoinstitut, Centralförbundet för Alkohol- och Narkotikaupplysning. 1996. *Rapport 96. Alkohol- och narkotika utvecklingen i Sverige.* Stockholm: Folkhälsoinstitut, CAN.

Folkhälsoinstitut, CAN, Systembolaget, Socialstyrelsen (1993) *Bakgrunden.* Stockholm.

Forssman, H. (1950) "Erfarenheter med abstinyl i psykiatrisk poliklinisk verksamhet" in *Svenska Läkartidningen,* Vol. 47, pp. 2817–2824.

Foucault, M. (1972) "Orders of Discourse" in *Social Science Information,* Vol. 2, No. 10, pp. 7–30.

Foucault, M. (1977) *Power/Knowledge.* New York: Pantheon Books.

Foucault, M. (1978) *Discipline and Punish.* London: Penguin Books.

Foucault, M. (1992) *The Archaeology of Knowledge.* Bristol: Routledge.

Fridjonsdottir, K. (1991) "Social Science and the 'Swedish Model' : Sociology at the Service of theWelfare State" *in Discourses on Society.* Wagner, P., B. Wittrock, and R. Whitley (Eds.). London: Kluwer AcademicPublishers.

Frånberg, P. (1983) *Umeåsystemet en studie i alternativ nykterhetspolitik.* PhD dissertation, Umeå University.

Frånberg, P. & I. Koskikallio (1985) "Regionala och lokala varianter" in *Den Svenska Supen,* K. Bruun & P. Frånberg (Eds.).

Fuller, R.C. and R. Myers (1941) "Some Aspects of a Theory of Social Problems" in *American Sociological Review,* Vol. 6, pp. 24–32.

Gabe, J. (1995) *Medicine, Health and Risk.* Oxford: Blackwell.

Godfrey & Powell (1989). "Nationalekonomi, hälsa och alkohol i västeuropa" in *EG, Alkohol och Norden*, C. Tigerstedt (Ed.). NAD publication 19, Helsinki.

Gould, A. (1988) *Conflict and Control in Welfare Policy: The Swedish Experience.* London and New York: Longman.

Grönberg, A. (1956) "Alkoholisten och internisten" in *Svenska Läkartidningen,* Vol. 53, pp. 2668–2673.

Gusfield, J.R. (1967) *Symbolic Crusade: Status Politics and the American Temperance Movement.* Urbana: Universityof Illinois Press.

Gusfield, J.R. (1981) The Culture of Public Problems. Drinking-driving and the Symbolic Order. Chicago:The University of Chicago Press.

Gusfield, J.R. (1989) "Constructing the Ownership of Social Problems: Fun and Profit in the Welfare State" in *Social Problems,* Vol. 36, No. 5, pp. 431–441.

Gusfield, J.R. (1996) *Contested Meanings. The Construction of Alcohol Problems.* Madison: The University of Wisconsin Press.

Gustavsson, A. (Ed.) (1991) *Alkoholister och nykterister.* Uppsala.

Hamberg, O. (1984) *Svensk bryggeriindustri, 1885–1985.* Stockholm: Norstedt.

Hastings, A. (1996) "An exploration of the politics of urban regeneration policy through the close analysis of the language of policy documents", paper presented at the European Network for Housing Research Conference, Helsinki, August 1996.

Hauge, R. (1991) "Alkohol og folkhelse" in *Nordisk Alkoholtidskrift*, Vol. 8, No. 1, pp. 40–41.

Hein, R. (1996) "Nordic Alcohol Statistics 1991–1995" in *Nordic Alcohol Studies*, English Supplement, Vol. 13, pp. 82–85.

Helling, S. (1987) *Från mjöd till martini: alkoholens historia i Sverige*. Stockholm: Norstedt.

Helmersson Bergmark, K. (1995) *Anonyma Alkoholister i Sverige* (Alcoholics Anonymous in Sweden). Acta Universitatis Stockholmiensis. Stockholm: Almqvist & Wiksell International.

Hibell, B. (1994) "Oregistrerad alkoholkonsumtion" in SOU:1994:25, Appendix 7, pp. 253–264.

Hibell, B. , Romelsjö, A., Rydberg, U. (1989) "Utvecklingen av alkoholkonsumtionen och alkoholskadorna i Sverige" in *Läkartidningen,* Vol. 86, No. 1–2, pp. 17–26.

Holder, H.D. & G. Edwards (Eds.) (1995) *Alcohol and Public Policy: Evidence and Issues.* Oxford: Oxford University Press.

Hort, S. (1998) "The Lost World of Scandinavian Sobriety", session at SNAPS conference, "Alcohol Policy and the Welfare State in Consumer Society", Lillehammer, Norway, 14–18 January 1998.

Hugemark, A. (1994) *Den fängslande marknaden. Ekonomiska experter om välfärdsstaten.* Lund: Arkiv.

Isaksson, T. (1982) "Läkarförbundets alkoholpolitiska program" in *Läkartidningen,* Vol. 79, Nr. 30–31, pp. 2519–2520.

Ja till Europa. *Frågor och svar om EG,* 14 december 1992.

Jagger, E. (1997) "The Production of Official Discourse on 'Glue Sniffing' in *Journal of Social Policy,* Vol. 26, pp. 445–465.

Johannisson, K. (1993) "Att bygga ett folk" in *Socialmedicinsk tidskrift,* No.2–3, pp. 64–72.

Johannisson, K. (1997) *Kroppens tunna skal.* Stockholm: Norstedt.

Johansson, L. (1997) "Svenskarna och alkoholmonopolet—ett historiskt perspektiv" in *Nordisk alkohol-narkotikatidskrift,* Vol. 14, pp. 137–153.

Johansson, L. (1995) *Systemet Lagom.* Lund: Lund University Press.

Johansson, S. (1972) "Om levnadsundersökningen: utkast till kapitel 1 och 2 i betänkande (om svenska folkets levnadsförhållande) att angivas av Låginkomstutredningen.". Stockholm.

Johansson, S. (1991) "Ödesidigert EG-medlemskap", *Dagens Nyheter,* Debatt, 10/11/91.

Johnson A. (1983) *50 miljarder kostar supen.* Göteborg: Sober.

Johnson A. (1983) *100 miljarder kostar supen.* Göteborg: Sober.

Johnston, H. (1995) "A Methodology for Frame Analysis: From Discourse to Cognitive Schemata" in *Social Movements and Culture,* H. Johnston & B. Klandermans (Eds.), Minneapolis: University of Minnesota Press.

Jonsson, J. & M. Tåhlin (1987) "Omorientering i svensk sociologi: en studie av artiklar i Sociologisk Forksning 1975–1986" in *Sociolgin i Sverige,* Allardt, E. , S. Lysgaard, & A.B. Sørensen (Eds.).

Jonsson, R. (1972) *Missbruk och Återfall.* PhD dissertation, Department of Sociology, Uppsala University, 1972.

Kaprio, L. (1975) "Foreword" in *Alcohol Control Policies,* Bruun et al.

Karlsson, B. & I. Wachtmeister (1990) "Stoppa alkoholbluffen", *Dagens Nyheter,* Debatt. 22/12/90.

Karlsson, T. (1997) *Alkoholfrågan på Åland. ur ett konstruktionistiskt perspektiv i jämförelse med övriga Finland och Sverige.* Socialpolitiska institutionen, Ser. A:472. Åbo.

Kindstrand, W. (1956) "Alkoholistvård i tjugonde seklet" in *Svenska Läkartidningen,* Vol. 2, pp. 2275–2285.

Kitsuse, J. & A. Cicourel (1964) "A note on the uses of official statistics" in *Social Problems,* vol. 11, pp. 1331–139.

Knöös, H. & G. Johnson (1954) "Nya medel i behandlingen av alkoholsjuka" in *Svenska Läkartidningen,* Vol. 1, No. 20, pp. 1337–1343.

Kortteinen, X (1990) "Alkohol och Jordbruk" in *EG, alkohol och Norden,* C. Tigerstedt (Ed.).

Kreitman, N. (1986) "Alcohol consumption and the preventive paradox" in *British Journal of Addiction,* Vol. 82, pp.1279–1288.

Kristenson, H. (1993) "Alkoholism—sjukdom eller last?, konsumtionsminskning ett måste" in *Läkartidningen,* Vol. 90, No. 47, pp. 4197–4203.

Kritiska Europa Fakta. EES special, Nej till EG: 1993.

Kühlhorn, E. (1994) "Totalkonsumtionsmodellen i perspektivet av 17 svenska undersökningar på alkoholområdet" in SOU 1994:25, Appendix 4, pp. 191–221.

Laclou, E. & C. Mouffe (1994) *Hegemony & Socialist Strategy.* London: Verso.

Lakoff, G. & M. Johnson (1980) *Metaphors We Live By.* Chicago: University of Chicago Press.

Leifman, H. (1996) *Perspectives on Alcohol Prevention.* PhD dissertation, Acta Universitatis Stockholmiensis, Stockholm University.

Lemert, E. M. (1951) *Social Pathology.* McGraw-Hill Inc.

Lenke, L. (1975) "Alkohol och våldsbrottslighet" in *Alkohol och Narkotika,* pp. 8–14.

Lenke, L. (1983) "Totalkonsumtionens betydelse för alkoholskadeutvecklingen i Sverige" in *Sociologisk forskning,* No. 1, pp. 45–57.

Lenke, L. (1989) *Alcohol and criminal violence: Time series analyses in a comparative perspective.* PhD dissertation. Lund: Institutionen för socialt-arbete.

Levine, H.G. (1978) "The Discovery of Addiction" in *Journal of Studies on Alcohol,* Vol. 39, No.1, pp. 143–173.

Levine, H. G. (1984a) "The Alcohol Problem in America: From Temperance to Alcoholism" in *British Journal of Addiction,* Vol. 79, pp. 109–119.

Levine, H.G. (1984b) "What is an alcohol-related problem? (or, what are people talking abut when they refer to alcohol problems?) in *Journal of Drug Issues,* Vol. 14, No.1, pp. 45–60.

Lindblad, H. & S. Lundkvist (1996) *Tusen Nyktra.* Malmö: Sober.

de Lint, J. (1978) Alcohol consumption and liver cirrhosis mortality. The Netherlands, 1950–78. *Journal of Studies on Alcohol*, Vol. 42, No.1, pp. 48–56.

Lublin, H. (1957) "Personligt om dagens alkoholproblem" in *Svenska Läkartidningen,* Vol. 54, No. 11, pp. 820–829.

MacAndrew, Edgerton (1969) *Drunken Comportment.* Chicago: Aldine.

Magnusson, N. (1990) "Ny raseras alkoholpolitiken", *Dagens Nyheter,* Debatt, 16/01/90.

Manning, N. (1985) *Social Problems and Welfare Ideology.* London: Gower.

Mårtens, S. (1955) "Psykoterapi i poliklinisk alkoholistvård" in *Svenska Läkartidningen,* Vol. 1, No. 21, pp. 1349–1365.

Morgan, P. (1980) "The state as mediator: alcohol problem management in the postwar world" in *Contemporary Drug Problems,* Vol. 9, pp. 107–136.

Moser, J. (1992) *Alcohol problems, policies and programmes in Europe.* Copenhagen: Regional Office for Europe, WHO.

Myhrman, G. (1955) "Behandling av alkoholism som en uppgift för lasarettens medicinska avdelningar" in *Läkartidningen,* Vol. 1, pp. 1520–1524.

Mäkelä, K. (1983) "Alkoholkonsumtionens vågrörelser" in *Sociologisk Forskning,* No.1, Vol. 20, pp. 11–19.

Mäkelä, K., Room, R., Single, E., Sulkunen, P., & Walsh, B. with Bunce, R. , Cahannes, M., Cameron, T., Gisbreth, N., de Lint, J., Makinen, H., Morgan, P., Mosher, J., Moskalewicz, J., Müller, R., Österberg, E., Wald, I., & Walsh, D, (1981) *Alcohol, Society, and the State I: A Comparative Study of Alcohol Control.* Toronto: Addiction Research Foundation.

Mäkelä, K. & C. Tigerstedt (1992) "Changing Responsibilities of Nordic Monopolies", paper presented at the Symposium on Alcohol Monopolies and Social and Health Issues, October 27–30, 1992.
Näslund, N-E. (1992) "Låt matbutiker sälja vin", *Dagens Nyheter,* Debatt, 26/4/92.
Norell, H. (1949) "Om behandlingen av för fylleri anhållna" in *Svenska Läkartidningen,* Vol. 1, No. 13, pp. 722–726.
Norström, T. (1994) "Projectioner av alkoholskadeutvecklingen i Sverige", in SOU 1994:25, Svensk Alkoholpolitik, Appendix 6, pp. 240–252.
Nycander, S. (1990) "Tid för en folkkampanj mot EG:s alkoholpolitik", *Dagens Nyheter,* 25/03/90.
Nycander, S. (1967/1996) *Svenskarna och spriten.* Stockholm: Prisma.
Olsson, B. (1990) "Alkoholpolitik och alkoholens fenomenologi. Uppfattningar som artikulerats i pressen" in *Alkoholpolitik-Tidskrift för nordisk alkoholforskning,* Vol. 7, pp.184–194.
Olsson, B. (1994) *Narkotikaproblemets bakgrund.* Stockholm: Centralförbundet för alkohol- och narkotikaupplysning.
Olsson, O. (1991) *Prisets och inkomstens betydelse för alkoholkonsumtion, missbruk och skador. En forskningsöversikt* (Price and income effects on alcohol consumption, abuse and damage. A review of research). Stockholm: Centralförbundet för Alkohol- och Narkotikaupplysning.
Olsson, O. (1994) "Metoder för bedömning av missbrukets omfattning" in SOU 1994:25, Appendix 9, pp. 293–301.
Olsson, S. (1990) *Social Policy and Welfare State in Sweden.* Lund: Arkiv.
Olsson, S. & G. Therborn (Eds.) (1991) *Vision möter verklighet.* Stockholm: Allmänna förlaget.
Petersen, A. & D. Lupton (1996) *The New Public Health.* London: Sage.
Petrén, A. (1948) "Har sinnessjukvården resurser för övervakning av från sinnessjukhusen utskrivna alkoholister?" in *Svenska Läkartidningen, Vol.* 2, Nr. 48, pp. 2311–2315.
Petrén, A. (1950a) "Om behandlingen av paranoiska alkoholmissbrukare" in *Svenska Läkartidningen,* Vol. 2, pp. 2354–2358.
Petrén, A. (1950b) "Problemet sinnessjukvård eller alkoholist vård ifråga om psykiskt abnorma alkoholister" in *Svenska Läkartidningen,* Vol. 2, pp. 2709–2716.
Petrén, A. (1952) "Om trängande behov av vård å sinnessjukhus vid alkoholdepression" in *Svenska Läkartidningen,* Vol. 2, No. 52, pp. 3182–3186.
Petrén, A. (1953) "Om f.d. alkoholbrottslingars behov av läkarhjälp till förekommande av ny brottslig handling" in *Svenska Läkartidningen,* Vol. 1, No. 14, pp. 775–778.
Petrén, A. (1956) "Redogörelse för av riksdagen avslagna motioner med nykterhetsfrämjande syfte" in *Svenska Läkartidningen,* Vol. 2, pp. 3503–3506.
Philipson, C., T. Kolk, L. Lindström (1993) "Hembränning – En empirisk studie och beräkning av dess utbredning och omfattning i Sverige", Stockholm, 23 March 1993.
Piaszczyk, A. (1996) "Medborgare Franzén". C-uppsats, Stockholm University, Dept. of Sociology.
Pogacar, I. (1994) *I vått och torrt.* C/D uppsats in Media and Communications, Dept. of Sociology, Uppsala University.
Proposition 1984/85 Om utvecklingslinjer för hälso- och sjukvården.
Proposition 1990/91 Om vissa folkhälsofrågor.
Proposition 1991/92:170, Bilaga A.
Proposition 1993/94:136 Riktlinjer för ett nytt tillståndssystem för import, export, tillverkning och partihandel med alkoholdrycker.
Proposition 1994/95:89. Förslag till alkohollag.
Ragnarsson, L. (1993) *Från motbok till snabbköp.* Stockholm: Systembolaget AB.

Randall, E. (1997) "Health Policy & the European Union" in *The Future of Europe,* V. Symes, C. Levy, J. Littlewood (Eds.).
Ranebäck, O. (1993) "För högt pris för EG", *Dagens Nyheter,* Debatt, 6/8/93.
Reinerman, C. (1988) "The Social construction of an alcohol problem. The Case of Mothers Against Drunk Drivers and social control in the 1980s" in *Theory and Society,* Nr.17, pp. 91–120.
Reinerman, C. (1993) "The Social Construction of Drug Scares" in P. Adler and P.Adler (Eds.) *Constructions of Deviance.* Belmont: Wadsworth Publishing Company.
Reuter, S. & C. Tigerstedt (1992) "Alkoholpolitiken i Norden sedan 1980" in *Nordisk Alkoholtidskrift,* Vol. 9, No.2, pp. 9–27.
Riddarspore, K. (1997) "Danmark dålig förebild" in *Uppdraget,* No. 3, p. 13.
Romelsjö, A. (1982) "Alkoholfrågan—läkarskandal på väg?" in *Läkartidningen,* Vol. 79, No.8, p 592.
Romelsjö, A. (1991) "Klart samband mellan alkoholkonsumtion och skador" in *Läkartidningen,* Vol. 88, No. 15, pp. 1351–1352.
Romanus, G. (1989) "Bli själv en riktig nolla" in *Uppdraget,* No. 3, p. 4.
Romanus, G. (1991) "Ingen frivillig prissänkning", Debatt in *Dagens Nyheter,* 25/10/91.
Romanus, G. (199a3) "Introduction to the Swedish Alcohol Retailing Monopoly during the visit of the EC-Sweden Joint Parliamentary Committee", 22 February 1993, Stockholm.
Romanus, G. (1993b) "För eller emot alkoholskador?", *Dagens Nyheter,* Debatt, 21/10/93.
Romanus, G. & O. Olsson (1991) "Ingen frivillig prissänkning", *Dagens Nyheter,* Debatt, 25/10/91.
Room, R. (1978) *Governing Images of Alcohol and Drug Problems.* PhD dissertation, University of California, Berkeley, 1978.
Room, R. (1984) "Alcohol Problems and the Sociological Constructivist Approach: Quagmire or Path Forward", paper presented at the Alcohol Epidemiology Section Meetings of the International Council on Alcohol and Addictions; 4–8 June 1984, Edinburgh, Scotland.
Room, R. (1991) "En omöjlig dröm? Hur minska alkoholproblemen i en nykterhetskultur?" (An impossible dream? How can the alcohol problem be reduced in a temperance culture?) in *Nordisk Alkoholtidskrift.* vol. 8: pp. 195–207.
Rose, G. (1992) *The Strategy of Preventive Medicine.* Oxford: Oxford University Press.
Rose, N. (1996) "Governing 'advanced' liberal democracies" in *Foucault and Political Reason,* Barry, A. , T. Osborne, & N. Rose (Eds.), London: UCL Press Limited.
Rosell, S. (1992) "Vi behöver en ny vetenskaplig alkoholpolitik", *Svenska Dagbladet,* Debatt, 21/09/92.
Rosell, S. (1992) "Avmonopolisera vin- och sprithandeln", *Svenska Dagbladet,* Debatt, 03/12/92.
Rosenqvist, P. (1985) "Nykterhetsnämnderna" in *Den Svenska Supen,* K. Bruun & P. Frånberg (Eds.).
Rosenqvist, P. (1987) "The physicians and the Swedish alcohol question in the early twentieth century" in *Contemporary Drug Problems,* Fall 1986, pp. 503–525.
Rosenqvist, P. & N. Kurube (1992) "Dissolving the Swedish Alcohol Treatment System" in *Cure, Care, or Control. Alcoholism Treatment in Sixteen Countries*; H. Klingemann, J-P Takala, G. Hunt (Eds.). New York: State University Press.
Rothstein, B. (1992) *Den korporativa staten.* Stockholm: CE Fritzes.
Rouse, T. P. & N. P. Unnithan (1993) "Comparative Ideologies and Alcoholism: The Protestant and Proletarian Ethics" in *Social Problems,* Vol. 40, No.2, pp. 213–227.
Rydbeck, K. (1995) Nykter Läsning. PhD dissertation, Institute for the Sociology of Literature at the Dept. of Literature, Uppsala University.

Rydberg, U. (1982) "Normalkonsumtionens risker" in *Risken att bli alkoholist*, O. Arvidsson (Ed.), Riksbankens Jubileumsfond, 1982:1.
Rydberg, U. (1986) "Begrepp och terminologi" in *Problemet Alkohol,* Svenska Läkarsällskapets handlinger, Band 95, Häfte 4, pp. 7–18.
Scherstén, B. (1954) "Fyra års terapeutiska erfarenheter av antabus" in *Svenska Läkartidningen*, Vol. 1, No. 7, pp. 341–356.
Schneider, J. (1978) "Deviant Drinking as Disease: Alcoholism as a social accomplishment" in *Social Problems*, Vol. 25, No. 4, pp. 361–372.
Skog, J-O (1979) *En kritisk gjennomgåelse av Ledermanns teori om alkoholkonsumets fordelning i befolkningen* (A critical analysis of Ledermann's theory of the distribution of alcohol consumption in populations). Oslo: Statens institutt for alkoholforskning.
Skog, J-O (1980) "Is alcohol consumption lognormally distributed?" *in British Journal of Addiction*, Vol. 75, Nr. 2, pp. 169–173.
Skog, J-O (1985) The collectivity of drinking cultures: A theory of the distribution of alcohol consumption. *British Journal of Addiction,* Vol. 81, No. 3, pp. 83–99.
Simpura, J. (1987) "Sociala problem och hur de definieras i samhälleliga informationssystem" in *Alkoholbruk och dess konsekvenser.* NAD publication, No.15, Helsinki.
Simpura, J. & C. Tigerstedt (1992) *Social Problems Around the Baltic Sea.* NAD publication No.21, Helsinki.
Snow, D.A. & R.D. Benford (1992) "Master Frames and Cycles of Protest" in *Frontiers in Social Movement Theory,* A.D. Morris & C. McClurg Mueller (Eds.) London: Yale Univesity Press.
Socialstyrelsen & Systembolaget (1988) *Bakgrunden.* Stockholm.
Socialstyrlesen 1987:5 Alkohol och Sjukvård, Socialstyrelsen redovisar.
Socialstyrelsen 1987:15, Folkhälsorapport, Socialstyrelsen redovisar.
Söderquist, J. (1980) "Hälsopersonal bör samlas och kräva motboken åter!" in *Läkartidningen,* Vol. 77, No. 25, p. 2307.
SOS rapport 1991:11 Folkhälsorapport 1991.
SOU 1974:90 APU Del 1 Bakgrund.
SOU 1974:91 APU Del 2.
SOU 1974: APU Del.
SOU 1981:1 Hälsorisker.
SOU 1993: 50 Serveringsbestämmelser.
SOU 1994:24 Svensk Alkoholpolitik—en strategi för framtiden.
SOU 1994:25 Svensk Alkoholpolitik—bakgrund och nuläge.
SOU 1994:26 Att förebygga alkoholproblem.
SOU 1994:27 Vård av alkoholmissbrukare.
SOU 1994:28 Kvinnor och alkohol.
SOU 1994: 29 Barn Föräldrar Alkohol.
Sournia, J.C (1990) *A History of Addiction.* Cambridge: Basil Blackwell.
Spector & Kitsuse (1973) "Social Problems: A Reformulation" in *Social Problems,* vol. 21, no. 2, pp. 145–159.
pode, H. (1993) *Die Macht der Trunkenheit,* Pladen, 1993.
Spode, H. (1997) "From the 'Brandy Plague' to the 'Alcohol question'", paper presented at the NAD European Summer School, 31 Aug – 7 Sept. 1997, Trouville Training Center, Hornbaeck, Denmark.
SStenius, K. (1996) "From Co-operation to Competition" in *Nordisk Alkoholtidskrift,* Vol. 13, English Supplement, pp. 4-21.
Stone, D. (1989) "Causal stories and the Formation of Policy Agendas" in Political Science Quarterly, vol. 104, No.2, pp. 281–300.
Strömbeck, J-E. (1979) *Frihet, Jämlikhet, Dryckenskap*. Stockholm: Ordfront.
Strömstedt, X. (1992) "Behåll Systembolaget" in *Uppdraget*, No. 3, pp. 32–33.

Sulkunen, P. (1977) "Åtkomlighet och alkoholpolitik i EEC-länderna II" in *Alkoholpolitik,* Vol. 40, pp. 19–27.
Sulkunen, P. (1991) "De stora projektens död" in *Nordisk Alkoholtidksrift,* Vol. 8, pp. 208–220.
Sulkunen, P. (1992) *The European New Middle Class.* Aldershot: Avebury.
Sulkunen, P. (1994) "The New Conservative Mind. Why does the New Middle Class Hate Alcohol Control?" in *Addiction Research,* Vol.1, No.4, pp. 295-308.
Sulkunen, P., Alasuutari, P., Nätkin, R., Kinnunen, M. (1997) *The Urban Pub.* Helsinki: STAKES.
Sutton, C. (1993) *The European Community and Sweden: A new definition of a 'social problem'?* Diploma paper, International Graduate School, Stockholm University.
Sutton, C. (1995) "A Discourse on Death. The Discursive Accomplishment of Medical Practice: The Case of "Brain Dead" Donors in Sweden." OTS Project Report. Dept. of Sociology. Uppsala, 1995.
Sutton, C. (1996) *The Swedish Alcohol Discourse.* International Graduate School, Stockholm International Studies 1996:2.
Sutton, C. & S. Sutton Hort (1996) "Integrating an Alcohol Problem", paper presented at the Second European Conference on Social Movements, 3–6 October 1996, Vitoria-Gasteiz, Spain.
Svenska Läkaresällskapet (1986) *Problemet Alkohol.* Svenska Läkaresällskapets handlingar, Band 95, Häfte 4.
Svenska läkarnas nykterhetsförening (1949) "Yttrande över 1946 års alkoholistvårdutrednings förslag till lag om nykterhetsvård" in *Svenska Läkartidningen,* Vol. 46, No. 7, pp. 397–399.
Svensson, A. (1973) *Svensk alkoholpolitik.* Malmö: Sober.
Sveriges Läkarförbund (1982) *Läkare om alkohol.* Stockholm.
Systembolaget. unknown year. *Kvinnor och alkohol.* Stockholm.
Systembolaget. unknown year. *Det svenska systemet.* Stockholm.
Systembolaget. unknown year. *Vad gör alkoholen i ditt barn?* Stockholm.
Systembolaget. unknown year. *Hemligheterna avslöjad.* Stockholm.
Systembolaget. unknown year. *Varför ska vi behöva lida för några få alkoholisters skull? och sjutton andra frågor.* Stockholm.
S:son Frey, T. (1957) "Om 'lögner och sanningar om alkoholismen'" *in Svenska Läkartidningen,* Vol.54, No. 11, pp. 814–820.
Takala, J-P & J. Lehto (1992) "Finland: The Non-Medical Model Reconsidered" in *Cure, Care or Control,* H. Klingemann, J-P Takala & G. Hunt (Eds.) New York: State University of New York Press.
Therborn, G. (1973) "De sociologiska verksamheterna", in *Sociologisk Forskning,* No. 53, pp. 21–26.
Thullberg, B. (1956) "Lögner och sanningar om alkoholismen" in Läkartidningen, Vol. 2, pp. 2956–2961.
Tigerstedt, C. (Ed.) (1990) *EG, alkohol och Norden.* NAD publication, No.19, Helsinki.
Tilley, R. (1992) "Michel Foucault: Towards an Archaalogy of Archaelogy" *in Reading Material Culture,* C. Tilley (Ed.), Cambridge: Basil Blackwell Ltd.
Tillgren, J. (1959) "Antabusmedikation och patientens medverkan" in *Svenska Läkartidningen,* Vol. 2, No. 41, pp. 2791–2795.
Turner, B. (1987) *Medical Power and Social Knowledge.* London: Sage.
Ugland, T (1996) *EÖS, EU og alkoholmonopolene: En komparativ studie av de nordiske lands respons og stregivalg.* SIFA rapport, Nr. 4/96. National Institute for Alcohol and Drug Research.
Uusitalo, I. (1998) "The Temperance Movement and Alcohol Policy in Västerbotten 1955–1995", paper presented at SNAPS conference "Alcohol Policy and the Welfare State in Consumer Society", Lillehammer, Norway, 14–18 January 1998.

Verhey, J. (1991) "Sources for the Social History of Alcohol" in S.Barrows & R. Room (Eds.) *Drinking.*

Weiss, J. (1989) "The powers of problem definition: The case of government paperwork" in *Policy Sciences,* vol. 22, pp. 97–121.

Westerholm, B. (1992) "Moderaterna driver med väljerna", *Dagens Nyheter,* Debatt, 18/01/92.

WHO (1995) European Charter on Alcohol.

Wiener, C. (1981) *The Politics of Alcoholism. Building an Arena Around a Social Problem.* New Brunswick: Transaction Books.

Appendices

APPENDIX I

Data Sources

Propositions:

(Kungl. Maj:ts Nådiga) Proposition Nr 193 1913
(Kungl. Maj:ts) Proposition nr 164 1931
(Kungl. Maj:ts) Proposition 1954:151 Riktlinjer för den framtida nykterhetspolitiken m m.
(Kungl. Maj:ts) Proposition 1954:158 Vissa anslag till nykterhetsvård, m.m.
(Kungl. Maj:ts) Proposition 1954:159 med förslag till lag om nykterhetsvård, m.m.
Proposition 1975/76:113 Ändring i brottssbalken, m.m.
Proposition 1976/77:108 Om alkoholpolitik
Proposition 1977/78:178 Förslag till lagstiftning om marknadsföring av alkoholdrycker och tobaksvaror
Proposition 1981/82:143 Om åtgärder mot alkohol- och narkotikamissbruket
Proposition 1984/85 Om utvecklingslinjer för hälso- och sjukvården
Proposition 1990/91 Om vissa folkhälsofrågor
Proposition 1991/92:170, Bilaga 4
Proposition 1993/94:136 Riktlinjer för ett nytt tillståndssystem för import, export, tillverkning och partihandel med alkoholdrycker
Proposition 1994/95:89 Förslag till alkohollag

Official Reports:

SOU 1934:39 1928 års rusdryckslagstiftningsrevision. Betänkande med förslag.
SOU 1948:23 Betänkande med förslag till lag om nykterhetsvård m.m. avgivet av 1946 års alkoholistvårdsutredning
SOU 1952:53 Principbetänkande, 1944 års nykterhetskommitté 5.
SOU 1974:90 APU Del 1 Bakgrund
SOU 1974:91 APU Del 2
SOU 1974: APU Del
SOU 1981:1 Hälsorisker
SOU 1993:50 Serveringsbetämmelser. Förslag till ändringar i lagen (1977:293) om handel med drycker (LHD).
SOU 1994:24 Svensk Alkoholpolitik – en strategi för framtiden
SOU 1994:25 Svensk Alkoholpolitik – bakgrund och nuläge
SOU 1994:26 Att förebygga alkoholproblem
SOU 1994:27 Vård av alkoholmissbrukare

SOU 1994:28 Kvinnor och alkohol
SOU 1994:29 Barn Föräldrar Alkohol
DsS 1977:1 Beredningsgruppen för frågor avseende alkoholpolitiken
DsS 1980:10 Om alkoholpolitiken. Förslag från Samordningsorganet för alkoholfrågor (SAMO)
DsS 1981:23 Alkoholpolitiska restriktioner
DsS 1981:25 Om alkoholpolitiken II. Förslag från Samordningsorganet för alkoholfrågor (SAMO).
DsS 1994:92 En ny alkoholpolitisk tillsyns- och tillstånds myndighet samt förslag till ny alkohollag.

Socialstyrelsen Bestämmelser rörande handel med drycker per den 1 juli 1990
Socialstyrelsen 1987:15, Socialstyrelsen redovisar, Folkhälsorapport
SOS rapport 1991:11 Folkhälsorapport 1991.

Directives:

Directive 1980:47
Directive 1981:23
Directive 1991:124

Informational Materials:

Folkhälsoinstitut, Socialstryelsen & Systembolaget. *Bakgrunden* 1993.
Socialstyrelsen, Systembolaget. *Bakgrunden.* 1988.
Systembolaget. *Vid dina sinnens fulla bruk*
Systembolaget. *Systemet, vad är det bra för?*
Systembolaget. *Vad gör alkoholen i ditt barn? Kloka ord om tonåringar, alkohol och droger.*
Systembolaget. *Kvinnor och alkohol*
Systembolaget. *Hemligheterna avslöjade*
Systembolaget. *Varför behöver vi lida för några få alkoholisters skull och sjutton andra frågor.*
Systembolaget. *Det svenska systemet.*

Journals and Other Media:

Uppdraget, 1989–1996
Dagens Nyheter, Debatt, 1989–1995
Läkartidningen 1948–1962; 1980–1995; with follow-up 1963–1979

Additional Data for European Discourse:

Michael B. Elmér Case C-189/95 ; Public Prosecutor vs. Harry Franzén
Judgement of the Court; Case C-189/95,

COM (87) 328 EC Proposals for Council Directives on VAT & Excise Tax.
COM (93) 559 Final Commission Communication on the framework for action in the field of public health.

COM (94) 202 final 1 (1994) A Programme of Community Action on Health Promotion, June 1994.
COM (95) final (1995) Europe Against Cancer, Report 1994.

European Charter on Alcohol; WHO 1992

Additional Data for Medical Discourse:

Alström, Carl Henry (1965) "Alkoholproblemet och samhället" in *20 års medicinsk forskning. Statens Medicinska Forksningsråd 1945–1965.* P.A. Norstedt & Sönders Förlag: Stockholm.
Arvidsson, Ola (1984) Alkoholpolitiken och forskningen. Rapport från ett symposium om forskning och alkoholpolitik den 10 mars 1983. Riksbankens Jubileumsfond 1984:1.
Arvidsson, Ola (1982) Risken att bli alkoholist. Rapport från ett symposium om uppkomst av alkoholmissbruk. RJ 1982:1.
Bergsman, Arne (1969) *Alkoholism. Några synpunkter på klinik och behandling.*
Svenska Läkarsällskapet: *Alkoholpolitiskt Program 1985*
Svenska Läkarsällskapet (1986) *Problemet Alkohol*, Svenska Läkaresällskapets handlingar; Band 95. Häfte 4, 1986.
Sverigers Läkarförbund (1982) *Läkare om Alkohol- Forskningsresultat och förslag till åtgärder*

Other scientific texts cited as data:

Additional scientific reports and works have been used as data for the study and are cited. These are included in the reference list.

Other works used for background, but not used as data:

To familarize myself with the field and the discourse, I also examined other literature that has not been used as data in the study. These included:

Riksdagsregister 1900–1995
Alkohol och Narkotika, English Summaries, 1975–1991
Review of dissertation titles from approximately 1950
Review of news clippings at CAN library for alcohol-related articles 1989–1993,
Review of news clippings at CAN library for EU-related articles 1994–1995.

APPENDIX II

Working with Texts

Selecting Data

To conduct a discourse analysis as I have proposed here, it is highly unlikely that one will locate all potential texts that could be included and which constitute a discursive formation. Moreover, the population from which one is selecting texts is often not known. Therefore, the aim in selecting texts is to locate statements and texts that provide insight into the various parameters of the discourse, and later, those texts that touch upon the key components: causal story, story of threat, dispersion of the problem, the distribution of authority and the solution complex suggested. This means that one is interested in variety, as well as similarities and repetition among this variety. Moreover, one aims to work in an iterative process between known texts and potential data, as well as the growing selection of texts for analysis.. Because the number of potential texts is so great, one also tries to work strategically. In my case, I was particularly interested in selecting texts that provided argumentation for lines of action, etc. These types of texts implicitly, and sometimes explicitly, assumed conceptualizations of alcohol issues, and hence provided a more direct approach to my object of analysis (how problems are conceptualized) than might have been the case with other texts.

Data for studying the official discourse was selected in this manner. I chose to investigate propositions for laws (rather than the actual laws themselves, which do not provide argumentation), and commission reports. A second principle for selecting data was that texts should deal with what is regarded as a public issue, a problem for all of society, rather than aspects of alcohol issues that are regarded as something problematic for a small group. This meant that a number of propositions that were related to alcohol were excluded from the main analysis, although they did provide a backdrop. In order to identify the potential texts for this analysis, I went through the parliamentary registers from 1900 to 1995, looking for any motions, propositions, and other actions related to alcohol during this time frame. This endeavour provided mixed results. It provided a basis for locating data, but did not provide much insight into how the alcohol problem was specifically conceptualized over time, and which of the actions was related to the public issue of alcohol issues. The register contains quick summaries of each action, but these are written in a legal language that notes the action taken, but does not present ‘why’ this was taken.

I also attempted to look for institutionalized locations for discourse on alcohol by different groups. In this respect I discussed my interests with various persons who were knowledgeable about journals and information production in the area. In the social scientific community, there has not been a single journal or outlet for ventiliating discussions on alcohol. Alcohol studies is an international field and contributions are found among a range of journals. However, a librarian at CAN (Swedish Council for Information on Alcohol and other Drugs) suggested that CAN's journal *Alkohol och Narkotika* might provide a window into the discourse over time. Each issue, from 1975–1990, contained an English summary for each article it contained, and this provided access to a broad field of materials. For each issue, I identified key concepts, objects, subjects, etc. found in each article, and looked for similarities and repetition. At one point I also used a loose coding of m-medical, s-social science, b-bureacratic, a-administrative to denote which source of discourse the author belonged to. These journal articles were eventually excluded from analysis due to the short period of time, and because they were primarily written by social scientists or bureacrats and administrators—two discourses that were excluded from the study at this time. However, the discursive regularities that I had begun to detect in these summaries provided me with better knowledge of the field than I had previously had. For example, the notion of 'problem' shifted from the 1970s to the 1980s, as did the implications of other concepts.

I also used this technique for locating materials for the medical discourse. I spoke with several researchers and medical representatives who acted as informants on the discourse. Initially I worked with a librarian from the medical library at Uppsala University Hospital. I then learned that the medical association established a working committee on alcohol questions, and I contacted the current secretary of the committee. Three journals were considered as potential sources of data for the study: *Opuscula Medica*, *Social medicinska tidskriften*, *Nykterhetsnämndenstidskrift* and *Läkartidningen.* The first first journal was excluded from the study since it contained strictly scientific findings and was considered less accessible to me as a sociologist. Moreover, I was also interested in potential medical reflections over alcohol-related policy. *Social medicinska tidskriften* concerned primarily one field within medicine and it was thought that this might not provide the collective statements of the medical profession at large. *Nykterhetsnämndenstidskrift* was also excluded since it was related to a specific political institution to which some physicians were attached, but not all. Moreover, the temperance boards were abolished during the 1970s and the journal therefore did not cover the second formation of alcohol discourse. Eventually, *Läkartidningen,* was selected as a primary source of data since it was, and is, the professional journal for the Swedish medical association. It contained reviews of medical findings, debate pieces concerning social and political issues, as well as general issues facing the medical profession. As discussed in *Chapter 1*, the study included articles from 1948 to 1962, and 1980 to 1995.

The data was later complimented with a review of *Läkartidningen* articles from 1963 to 1979. This turned out to be an enormous task. During the 1970s, particularly following the presentation of commission reports in 1974, the number of alcohol-related articles increased dramatically. In 1974 alone, I located over 50 entries in the index, and in 1980 there were over 70. In order to manage this volume of discourse, I selected every third article listed under alcohol-related headings in the index of the journal. In addition, I also selected articles that appeared to 'belong' to the public health formation or the alcoholism formation, as well as any entries that specifically noted opinions on alcohol policy in the titles. Book reviews as well as letters to the editor were omitted. Some debate pieces were included, and all editorial pieces that dealt with alcohol were included.

The purpose of this additional review was to ensure that the time frames selected for the studies were indeed the most appropriate and reliable for investigating the formations I was interested in. The extra review showed that there were certainly traces of the alcoholism as disease formation during the 1960s and 1970s. However, there were also other shifts taking place, probably due to the fact that the medical profession was no longer the primary professional group in the field. Within medicine, an increasing complexity of alcohol could be detected, whereby an increasing number of specialty areas became involved, and the range of topics related to alcohol was expanded. Hence it was felt that the 1950s, which were covered in the study, were the years in which a medicalized definition was most evident. This was also true for the 1980s and the public health formation. Although there were some articles which provided traces of public health 'ways of thinking', it was not until the position piece in 1982 that the total consumption model, and related strategies of public health, as outlined in Bruun et al. (1975), became explictly a point of departure for knowledge-building. Indeed, it is not until the latter part of the 1980s that this was very clear. One shift that appeared in the index itself concerns the subjects listed. Before 1970, "Alcoholic Treatment" and "Alcohol legislation" was listed under Social medicine, "Medical Policy, and Professional Policy". After 1970, the major headings were "Alcoholism" and "Ethyl Alcohol", "Alcohol Poisoning", and "Alcoholic Beverages", and towards the latter half of the 1970s, "Alcohol Habits". After 1985 a new subject heading, "Alcohol consumption" was listed, and the number of articles attributed to it grew throughout the 1980s.

Limitations related to data

One limitation of the data is that I investigated discourse on the public issue of alcohol issues. That is, those aspects of alcohol issues that were presented as concerns for *all of society,* not just a few people or for a few adminstrative or care facilities. As mentioned in the dissertation, sometimes the public problem has been that some people drink more than they should—alcoholism, alcohol abuse, drinkers, etc. At other times, this is problematic, but it is only considered an issue for those persons who drink too much and those facilities and entities that will rehabilitate, help, or control those persons. When overindulgence is pushed to the sidelines in this way, other aspects of alcohol issues have been raised as public issues. As this shift in discourse took place, my own interest then shifted from examining overindulgence as a public problem to alcohol as a public problem. I was aware of this general shift when searching for data, and I therefore excluded some propositions that related to care and treatment (e.g. during the 1970s) as well as some research reports, etc. One of the difficulties associated with this limitation was that some of the pieces on alcohol abuse, alcoholism etc. that I eliminated from the data, may in fact provide statements on the more general problem. This is likely to be a particular problem at the boundaries of discursive formations where there is a transformation from overindulgence to general consumption. For example, a text came to my attention during the final stages of preparing my dissertation, that I had originally excluded, but which an expert in the field , who had participated in the discourse, felt was a key text from the time.

A second characteristic of my work that poses a limitation at first sight, is the use of a single journal for the medical discourse. For example, although it was known that a more medically-inspired model was adopted in official discourse in 1948, indicating that the medical community itself was interested in the alcohol problem, this line of thinking did not appear in my data until 1950. Moreover, Dr. Ivan Bratt, considered the founder of the alcohol control system, did not submit any articles. This would seem to suggest that the medical views may have been contained in other sources of medical discourse. Although future studies should investigate additional sources, I judged this to be a relatively minor problem at this time, since my interest was not to focus on identifying the roots or moment in time when the concept of disease emerged. I was interested in the concept as such, which was well-represented in the material I selected. With respect to Bratt's lack of contributions, this can probably be explained by the fact that Bratt did not practice medicine after 1913 (Bruun 1985: p. 59).

Working with Texts

In a very general sense, the method deployed in the studies is a form of text analysis. However, I want to reiterate that I have not engaged in a content analysis, which was deemed inappropriate. Rather, the text analysis involved a process of confronting the texts based on what I had thus far detected in the discourse. Based on this, I posed questions, sought out dissimilarities with other texts (particularly in the synchronic analysis), and thereby reformulated my questions so that an additional set of texts, or the same set, could be confronted. During the process, I kept what can be likened to field notes. These included my reactions to the texts, including such things as what the works emphasized, concepts that were used, things I did not understand but which the text seemed to take for granted, statistics that were repeated (often without citing sources for them), what images I was left with, etc. Texts were read and re-read numerous times, and on numerous occassions.

The earliest round of questions began with some very broad questions, that were increasingly honed as more specific accomplishments of the discourse were 'discovered'. My earliest analysis was guided by the assumption that there are conditions that are regarded as problems, i.e. something is bad, deplorable, etc. and that these problems are often linked to solutions, i.e. something will fix the problem. Consequently, texts were scrutinized for what they could tell me about these two concepts. One observation during this round of questioning was that the problem was often assigned a location. It could be in the substance (or the bottle), in the person or his or her character, or mind, it could be in the social structure, or it could be a mystical force (such as "evil" or the devil). This brought about a new round of questioning that was pursued in additional texts as well, based on: Where is the problem located? Eventually this led to a more specific version of this question, namely: What is the perceived cause or causes of the problem?

The search for solutions revealed a similar process of questioning. In searching for the presentation of solutions, I discovered that solutions were often assigned to different institutions, professional groups, or individuals. These were then deemed responsible for resolving them. This led to a search for the identification of different groups, etc. in the texts. In addition to discovering links between institutions, etc. and proposed solutions, another discovery was that institutions, individuals, etc. could be awarded blame for the problem. This initiated a new round of questioning that focused on looking for the assignment of blame, and later the boundaries of this blame. Questions around this issue, included: Who is regarded as knowledgeable about this problem? In what capacity? Where are the limits to this authority? Is this group or person's authority on the question taken-for-granted or is it argued for in the text?

It was based on the continuing results and 'discoveries' of these rounds of questioning that the analytic framework for analysis of the results was developed. Through the process of questioning, it was noted that the questions could be related to different components, or cues, that indicated in what way alcohol was regarded as a social problem. Moreover, they pointed out that the problem had been broken down in different ways.

Sorting Texts and Identifying Formations

In the process of my text analysis, I identified assumptions, concepts, constructions, understandings, etc. that appeared repeatedly. In an iterative process of working with the data and identifying patterns or components in my data, I developed a model of the components of a problem definition, as discussed above. As I read texts, I looked for these components, and based upon what I found I sorted texts into three discursive formations that I constructed. Of course, some texts, as I point out below, could be placed in more than one of these formations.

My approach to texts means that time and space are treated somewhat differently. The texts that comprise a discourse are nodes in a web of texts that refer to one another. Since disocourses construct a history as well, they identify texts that are not necessarily contemporary, but which come to have an important meaning within the current context. Moreover, discourses point to texts that are not necessarily local. So, although I want to understand the Swedish alcohol discourse, this discourse sites texts from the WHO, the United States, etc. which then become a part of the discourse (though not necessarily on their own terms). In short, discourses wander without respect to conventional notions of time and space.

For example, one discursive formation I identify, is what I call the 'public health formation', this followed a discursive formation within which alcohol issues were seen as 'symptoms of other social and political practices'. The central texts in the public health formation referred to a piece of legislation in 1977 as the 'root' of policy, etc. in a new era (of which I see these texts belonging to). Yet, in analyzing this text I found that it was on the edge of two formations. It included formulations of the problem, concepts, models that were central to the public health formation, yet in 1977 public health as an alcohol project was not fully articulated. This meant that within current discourse this text takes on different implications than at the time it was first written. A second text from 1955 also falls into this category and is discussed in *Chapter 4*.

Research as a Personal Experience

A final point related to method, which should not be overlooked, is that my confrontation with the texts was also influenced by my experience as a foreign researcher in Sweden, with an American background. Clearly, my interest in the topic was the result of a personal curiosity in something that was very different from my own cultural knowledge. But this influened my work in other ways as well. Most importantly, while I was attempting to examine the scientific discourse, I was also a student of it; I was both an observer and a participant. For example, I attended two conferences, several working meetings for a Nordic project on alcohol, and participated in two courses on alcohol studies during the research period. I also followed the media discourse on alcohol. And, though I began my work, knowing very little about alcohol in Sweden, I found myself representing Swedish research on alcohol during the final months of my graduate work.

My experience as a participant-observer can be broken down into two phases. During the early phase of my work, I did not know the discourse. There were a number of propositions, assumptions and statements that were made, but which did not make sense to me since I was not 'fluent' in the field of knowledge. To some extent this position was to my advantage. These were 'learning opportunities', but I later found that the notes I took, turned out to be field observations. My earliest notes from these occasions are filled with questions around what seemed to be taken for granted that I as yet did not understand. During this early phase it was easy to see the that the discourse was constructed, and to see the contours of it. I did not take it for granted.

Over the four-year research period, my 'outsider' status dulled, along with my lens. And, during the second phase, I experienced a certain tension in my work. Where the assumptions of the discourse were once sharply defined and stood out against my own cultural background, I too began to take these for granted. Although I had the advantage of greater knowledge of the Swedish alcohol discourse, it began to make "too much" sense to me. Most recently, I found myself struggling to gain some distance to the Swedish discourse in order to maintain the critical perspective that was once so easy to hold.

APPENDIX III

Time Line of Events in the Official History of Alcohol

This timeline of events is based on SOU 1993:50, pp. 49–60 and Systembolaget, *Svensk Alkoholhistoria,* unknown year, p. 18.

1901 First motion referring to individual restrictions based on the rationing of spirits was presented in the Swedish parliament.

1905 A spirits ordinance (Brännvinsförordning) introduced restrictions upon the sale of spirits in conjunction with various types of public performances (e.g. theater performances, dressage, etc.).

Parliament voted that all sales of spirits were take place at appointed shops, under some form of state control.

1909 A prohibition on spirits was introduced during a major strike. At the same time, the temperance movement organized an unofficial public referendum; 56% of the adult population voted for a permanent prohibition.

Doctor Ivan Bratt, published his proposed program for temperance policy in a major newspaper in the capital city, Stockholm. Bratt's position challenged the temperance movement, and sought to avoid a complete prohibition.

1911 A temperance committee was commissioned to "as quickly as possible work through and propose necessary measures for successfully bringing forth a local veto for the sale and distribution of spirits, wine and beer; and to furthermore, after an appropriate investigation, map out proposals for other well thought out and useful ordinances for limiting the spirit trade's harmful effects, among other things a reform of the so-called Göteborg system, as well as bring about a thorough investigation of a general prohibition."

Bratt presented an additional series of articles in the news media calling for a compromize between absolutists and moderate reformers.

1912 The Göteborg system (Andréesystemet) introduced purchase controls, without a maximum purchase limit. Purchase controls, included an application to the local stores.

1913 The parliament adopted the first "Alcoholics law" (alkoholistlagen). Legislation adopted also called for the introduction of local temperance boards.

1914 The temperance committee, commissioned in 1911, presented its report, which largely followed Bratt's proposals for a compromize. Sales in Stockholm were assumed by one of Bratt's companies, and shortly thereafter a "pass book" and purchase limit of 16 liters per quarter, were introduced.

"Liter boozing" became more widespread, and surpassed drinking in pubs. Drinking took place at home, in the workplace, and outdoors.

The Stockholm System began introducing a "pass book" and individual rationing.

1915 The parliament sanctioned purchase controls and the "pass book" at all Systembolag stores. A five-day rule (femstämpling) was introduced, which stated that there was to be at least five days between each purchase of one liter of spirits. Restrictions were also introduced for sales on the premises. Spirits were to be served only with meals, and a minimum price level for such meals (30 öre) was also introduced.

The Alcoholics Law came into force, and gave public authorities the right to intern alcoholics.

With Ivan Bratt in the lead, a program was introduced to monopolize the alcohol trade. Through his company in Stockholm, Bratt purchased nearly all wine and spirits trade companies. AB Vin- & Spritcentralen was also created, with Ivan Bratt as its director, to handle wholesale trade.

1917 An Ordinance concerning the sale of spirits (Rusdrycksförsäljningsförordningen) was adopted by the Parliament. It included:

- regulations that stated that a "pass book" would be introduced nationally, with a maximum purchase limit of 4 liters of spirits per month.
- Detailed "centiliter restrictions" were introduced at restaurants serving spirits, as well as meal requirements.
- Spirits were not to be sold at public dances; although in some rare cases exceptions could be made.

1920 The temperance commission from 1911 presented its main report, which included a proposal for the introduction of a total prohibition.

The first regulations concerning traffic and temperance were introduced.

The "pass book" was introduced across the country. Initially, purchases could only be made by persons over 25 years of age, and for a maximum of 4 liters per month. These rules were adjusted several times thereafter.

1922 A public referendum on prohibition took place on August 22. Opponents of the prohibition won with a marginal victory of 28.3% of the votes against 27.2%.

1923 A prohibition on strong beer was introduced.

Vin & Spritcentralen was granted official rights to operate as a monopoly; it had operated as such in practice since 1917.

Taxes were introduced as a means to restrict consumption; the higher the amount of alcohol, the greater the tax.

1928 A group was appointed to review and revize the Spirits Law (Rusdryckslagstiftningsrevision).

1934 Revisions were presented; these were regarded as the high point of public opinion in favor of Bratt's reforms.

A law was passed and came into force to allow blood tests of alcohol level on suspicion of drinking-driving.

1937 A revised law on the sale of spirits was adopted (rysdrycksförsäljningsförordning). The municipal veto on retail is abolished. The Systembolag was granted an autonomous right to run so-called 'people's restaurants' (folkrestauranger). The aim of this policy was to discourage private profit motives in alcohol service. Prices for spirits consumed on the premises were set much higher than those on retail sales. Quantitative restrictions were also introduced in restaurants.

1938 The number of Systembolag stores was decreased from 121 to 41 in accordance with a new ordinance.

1940s The Bratt System came under heavy criticism. The "pass book" was viewed by temperance supporters as 'suggesting' the consumption of spirits. 'Taking one's full ration' was also likened to carrying out one's civic duty. Regulations concerning the sale of food with spirits led to strange practices, such as carrying the same "restriction food" in and out of the kitchen over and over again to different guests.

1941 The maximum ration was lowered from 4 to 3 liters per month per person/family.

1944 A temperance commission was appointed, which eventually proposed the abolishment of the pass book system in 1953.

1954 The pass book met with serious criticism in the parliamentary debate. It was argued that the only successful means of combatting the alcohol problem was through long-term socializing (uppfostring) of the population.

1955 The pass book system was abolished on 1 October, in what is today known as the "October Revolution". All retail stores were organized under a single state-owned monopoly. Food prepared in bars, no longer needed to be cooked; sandwiches could be ordered, and a so-called "ölgåsen" was born.

The ban on strong beer was also lifted.

1956 Alcohol consumption increased dramatically after 1 October, and a tax was introduced on the sale of spirits in order to counteract this.

1957 The parliament voted in favor of the introduction of 'black lists' at the Systembolag, which included the names of persons who were banned from purchasing alcohol. At this time, identification controls were also introduced.

1958 Alcohol consumption returned to a more "normal" level following the price increases of 1956.

1962 Despite price levels, alcohol consumption (calculated according to 100% alcohol) was 5.14 liters per person per year; which was considered much greater than during the years of the pass book.

1963 Practices for restricting individuals from purchasing alcohol and identification controls were sharpened.

1965 A medium strength beer was introduced and sold at grocery stores.

An alcohol policy commission (APU) was appointed.

1969 Age limit for purchasing alcohol was dropped to 20 years of age.

1974 APU provided its final report, which was an object for extensive review by many organizations and interest groups. Among some of the suggestions for change, was that the "restriction meals" should be replaced by a general food service that was to constitute an important part of a given establishment's business.

1977 The parliament voted on alcohol policy reforms based on recommendations from the APU. Regulations concerning retail and wholesale trade of alcohol were coordinated in a single law on the drinks trade (LHD).

Medium beer was abolished.

'Black lists' at the Systembolag were abolished.

Public drunkenness was decriminalized.

1978 A hotel and restaurant commission presented a report, focused primarily on economic corruption within the branches.

1979 More restrictive controls of marketing alcohol were introduced, including a ban on advertising in all forums except trade magazines.

1981 The Care of Alcoholics and Drug Users Act, LVM, was passed, and came into effect in 1982.

A new law on boot-legging and sale of alcohol to minors was introduced.

1982 The Parliament voted to close the Systembolag on Saturdays from 1 July.

The Parliament voted on changes in LHD. Conscientious finances were necessary (ekonomisk skötsamhet) to receive a license to sell alcohol for consumption on premise; likewise the license could be revoked if irresponsible economic activity is discovered.

1984 Minister of Social Affairs, Gertrud Sigurdsen appointed a commissioner to investigate and summarize regulations within alcohol policy. The alcohol trade commission proposed that several regulations concerning retail sales should be abolished; in particular time limitations on the sale of class II beer, which was sold in grocery stores. The proposals did not lead to any legislative propositions.

1985 Time limitations for class II beer were abolished.

1986 Longer store hours, one day per week were introduced at several Systembolag stores.

1988 The LVM law was revised.

1991 Minister of Social Affairs, Bengt Westerberg, following a government directive, appointed an alcohol policy commission to evaluate alcohol policy to date, and present proposals for the future. Among other things, the commission was to consider the impact of closer cooperation with Europe.

30 June 1991, Prime Minister Ingvar Carlsson submitted an application for Sweden's membership in the European Community.

1992 A new tax category for beer was introduced.

Medium beer was reintroduced, but was allowed to be sold at restaurants and at the Systembolag only.

1993 LHD/LVM commission presented its report. The commission proposed that applications for licenses to sell for consumption on premises should be transferred from the county councils to the municipalities.

The alcohol policy commission, presented its first report concerning regulations surrounding the alcohol industry, with proposals for changes in the alcohol trade law.

1994 The alcohol policy commission presented its final reports.

1995 1 January, Sweden became a member of the European Union.